D0684606

# Minerals
## and Gemstones

# Minerals
## and Gemstones
### 300 of the Earth's Natural Treasures

Dr. David C. Cook & Dr. Wendy L. Kirk

amber
BOOKS

Revised edition published in 2015

Copyright © 2015 by Amber Books Ltd.

First published in 2007

Reprinted in 2016

All pictures © DeAgostini Picture Library

Published by
Amber Books Ltd
74–77 White Lion Street
London
N1 9PF
United Kingdom
www.amberbooks.co.uk
Appstore: itunes.com/apps/amberbooksltd
Facebook: www.facebook.com/amberbooks
Twitter: @amberbooks

ISBN: 978-1-78274-259-3

Project Editor: Sarah Uttridge
Design: Joe Conneally

Printed in China

# CONTENTS

# Introduction

**M**inerals are mostly naturally occurring, inorganic, crystalline solids found in varying quantities in the Earth and beyond. Gems are usually minerals that are prized for beauty and strength; they have an eye catching colour, lustre or clarity coupled with a durability to make them items of lasting value. These definitions can be somewhat blurred at the edges; this has been reflected in our choice of some of the entries. To help identify minerals we list their properties after each entry.

## COLOUR

The most immediately noticeable property, colour is only occasionally useful if the mineral has a distinctive, inherent colour such as yellow sulphur or blue azurite. For minerals whose colour varies with impurity content, it is much less useful. For example pure quartz is colourless, but may be of almost any hue through to black.

*Lazurite has a distinct blue colour and sky-blue streak which is helpful in identification.*

## STREAK

Streak is the colour of a mineral in a finely powdered form. This is usually demonstrated by scratching across unglazed porcelain, crushing a sample or scratching the surface with a knife. The streak tends to remain the same for minerals which appear to be coloured differently in larger masses. It is therefore a more consistent indicator of a mineral. Streak is not useful for most silicate minerals as they are usually white and often too hard to powder easily.

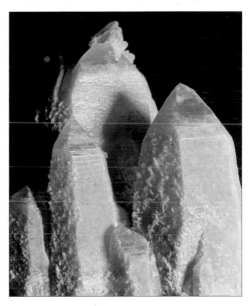

*Quartz has a typical crystal form of six-sided prismatic crystals with pointed terminations (as seen in the picture here).*

## LUSTRE

Lustre describes the nature of light from the surface of a mineral. A *metallic* lustre is shown by opaque minerals such as metals and many sulphides; if imperfect, it is called *submetallic*. A *non-metallic* lustre is a catch-all term for all the rest and is shown by transparent and translucent minerals. It includes:

**Adamantine** highly reflective like diamond
**Vitreous** glassy, as in quartz
**Resinous** like resin, as in amber and opal
**Pearly** like a pearl, due to alignment of platy minerals under the surface, as in talc and mother-of-pearl
**Silky** like silk, due to an underlying fibrous structure, as in satin spar, a variety of gypsum
**Greasy** produced by an irregular surface
**Earthy** or **dull** matt surface shown by minerals having no lustre

*A diamond has few weaknesses and many strengths: it is the hardest
mineral known and is the highest on Moh's scale of hardness.*

## OPACITY OR TRANSPARENCY

It is usual to indicate if a mineral is transparent, translucent or opaque, although
this is not a diagnostic property. A mineral may be inherently opaque or be so
because it contains many small fragments; translucency (partial transparency)
may be a function of the specimen thickness or the number of internal flaws.

## HARDNESS

The hardness of a mineral has been defined as its resistance to abrasion or
scratching. A practical system for measurement was devised by the Austrian
mineralogist Friedrich Mohs in 1812. A set of ten common minerals was chosen
of different hardnesses such that each one will scratch the surface of all softer
minerals. These were then given the number 1 to 10 in increasing order of
hardness. Most literature gives hardness to the nearest half unit, for example as
3.5, as a working approximation.

## Mohs' scale of hardness

Tests may be roughly carried out using a fingernail (hardness 2-2.5), a
copper coin (hardness 3) or a steel knife (hardness 5.5-6.5); minerals of
hardness over 6 will scratch glass.

| Number | Mineral | Number | Mineral |
|--------|---------|--------|---------|
| 1 | Talc | 6 | Orthoclase |
| 2 | Gypsum | 7 | Quartz |
| 3 | Calcite | 8 | Topaz |
| 4 | Fluorite | 9 | Corundum |
| 5 | Apatite | 10 | Diamond |

### SPECIFIC GRAVITY

This is the weight of a mineral compared to an equal volume of water and can be
taken as equivalent to density. Thus the density of water is taken as 1 g/cm$^3$ (i.e.
one cubic centimetre weighs one gram, or one litre weighs one kilogram), and its
specific gravity is *defined* as 1 (note: it has no units).

*In contrast to the diamond, Talc is the softest mineral, it is the lowest on
Moh's scale of hardness.*

## HABIT AND FORM

The form of the mineral is given first in the properties box and describes the shape adopted by crystals. Some shapes may be well-defined closed geometric forms such as a cube, octahedron or dodecahedron, or describe an open form such as a prism. Some terms are used to describe the appearance of aggregates of crystals. Common terms used to describe single crystals or aggregates include:

**Acicular** needle-shaped
**Bladed** flattened like a knife blade
**Botryoidal** like a bunch of grapes
**Dendritic** branching like a tree or moss
**Fibrous** fine strands
**Lamellar** forming distinctly flat sheets
**Mammilated** round, mutually interfering masses
**Massive** crystalline aggregates with no distinct form
**Radiating** radial arrangement of needles or fibres
**Reniform** kidney-shaped
**Tabular** showing broad, flat surfaces

*An aggregate of natrolite crystals display an attractive radiating, acicular habit.*

*An aggregate of small cubic crystals of sal ammoniac, which is not often in a visually appealing habit.*

## CRYSTAL SYSTEM

Crystals are made up of atoms or molecules arranged in a regular three-dimensional repeated pattern. Each unit which can be seen to repeat in order to build this structure is called a *unit cell*. Crystallography is governed by geometric possibilities (for example a cube can be repeated but a sphere or dodecahedron cannot), rather like the equivalent two-dimensional property of tessellation. Only seven possible patterns are recognised in unit cells. These are referred to as the *crystal system* adopted by that particular mineral. Each crystal system constrains the shape that crystals can adopt. Some crystal shapes can be characteristic of a crystal system such as the cube and the octahedron in the cubic system, but many require specialised knowledge and measurement to be diagnostic. Crystal systems are summarised below.

| Crystal System | Unit cell shape |
|---|---|
| Cubic | all three sides equal in length; all angles 90° |
| Tetragonal | two sides equal in length; all angles 90° |
| Orthorhombic | all sides different lengths; all angles 90° |
| Monoclinic | two angles 90° |
| Triclinic | no angles at 90° |
| Hexagonal | prism of regular hexagonal cross-section |
| Trigonal | prism of regular triangular cross-section |

*Pseudohexagonal muscovite crystals apparently made up of stacked thin sheets – illustrating the mineral's perfect cleavage in one direction.*

## CLASSIFICATION

The minerals in this book are divided into groups following a conventional system based on their chemical composition. Classification is firstly on minerals in the same chemical grouping or those having similar properties. The silicates, being the largest group are further subdivided according to structure. All silicates are based on the 'silicate tetrahedron' – a silicon atom bonded to four oxygen atoms which are arranged as if at the corners of a tetrahedron. They are then classified according to how these tetrahedra are joined and arranged.

## Classification

| | |
|---|---|
| 1 | **Native elements** comprise single elements which occur uncombined in nature. |
| 2 | **Sulphides** contain the $S^{2-}$ group and are classed with arsenides, antimonides and tellurides. |
| 3 | **Oxides** contain the $O^{2-}$ group. |
| 4 | **Carbonates, nitrates and borates** |
| 5 | **Sulphates** |
| 6 | **Phosphates** |
| 7 | **Nesosilicates** contain isolated $SiO^{4-}$ tetrahedra. |
| 8 | **Sorosilicates** have two tetrahedra joined as $Si_2O_7^{6-}$ groups. |
| 9 | **Cyclosilicates** contain three, four or six tetrahedra joined as a ring. |
| 10 | **Inosilicates** have the tetrahedra joined into indefinite chains, usually as single or double chains. |
| 11 | **Phyllosilcates** comprise indefinite two-dimensional arrays of tetradedra joined at three corners in hexagonal arrangements. |
| 12 | **Tectosilicates** are joined at all four corners into indefinite three dimensional frameworks containing voids or 'cages' |

*Transparent crystals of hyalophane showing some brown iron oxide staining.*

# Copper

Copper has a characteristic reddish colour darkened by a coating of black copper oxide. Further weathering produces a covering of green copper carbonate. Native copper is quite rare, but the metal is easily obtained from ores. Copper was one of the earliest metals known, and bronze, a hard alloy of copper and tin, has been used since *c.* 3000 BC. Native copper is found in altered copper deposits, cracks in basaltic lavas, and cemented sandstones and conglomerates. The southern shore of Lake Superior (USA) is the best location to find copper, allegedly the source of a piece weighing 381 tonnes (420 tons); others localities include Mansfeld (Germany), Bisbee (Arizona), Tsumeb (Namibia) and Burra Burra (Australia).

## Cu

| | |
|---|---|
| Colour: | light rose-red on fresh surface |
| Lustre; opacity: | metallic; opaque, translucent green when very thin |
| Streak: | copper-red |
| Hardness: | 2.5–3 |
| Specific gravity: | 8.93 |
| Cleavage; fracture: | absent; hackly, conchoidal |
| Habit: | rarely hexahedral, tetrahedral, dodecahedral crystals; wiry, arborescent, massive |
| Crystal system: | cubic |

# Silver

Silver has been prized, like gold, as one of the 'noble' metals. Jewellery has been made of silver for millennia (c. 4000 BC, the ancient Egyptians were using silver beads). Sterling silver is the term for metal containing at least 92.5 per cent silver. Its high reflectivity makes silver plating an excellent coating for mirrors, utensils and ornaments. Silver's exceptionally high electrical conductivity is utilized in high-quality electronics. Silver occurs in the oxidized zone of hydrothermal sulphide veins associated with other silver-bearing minerals. Good localities to find native silver include Kongsberg (Norway), Freiberg (Germany), Jáchymov (Czech Republic), the Comstock Lode (Nevada, USA) and Cobalt (Canada).

## Ag

| | |
|---|---|
| Colour: | silver-white |
| Lustre; opacity: | metallic; opaque, highly reflective (95 per cent) |
| Streak: | silver–white |
| Hardness: | 2.5–3 |
| Specific gravity: | 10.5 |
| Cleavage; fracture: | none |
| Habit: | crystals very rare; wiry or scaly |
| Crystal system: | cubic |

# Gold

Gold was the first metal known to humans, and has long been highly valued. It is chemically very unreactive and one of the 'noble' metals, used in coinage and jewellery for thousands of years. Gold is graded according to its purity, from pure 24 carat to 9 carat, which contains 37.5 per cent gold. Gold can be made harder and paler by alloying with silver, platinum, zinc or nickel. The largest nuggets include one of 153kg (337lb), found in Chile, and one of 93kg (205lb), found in Hill End (Australia). Gold is found in igneous rocks, often associated with quartz veins, and as placer deposits. The main mining areas are in Wittwatersrand (South Africa), California and Alaska (USA), Australia, South America and Siberia.

## Au

| | |
|---|---|
| **Colour:** | characteristic yellow |
| **Lustre; opacity:** | metallic; opaque |
| **Streak:** | yellow |
| **Hardness:** | 2.5–3 |
| **Specific gravity:** | 19.3 |
| **Cleavage; fracture:** | none; hackly, malleable |
| **Habit:** | crystals octahedral, dodecahedral, hexahedral; grains, nuggets, compact, dendritic |
| **Crystal system:** | cubic |

# Mercury

Mercury, also known as quicksilver, is the only metal that is liquid at room temperature, having a freezing point of –39°C (–38°F). Such mobility is the reason it was named after the mythical messenger of the gods. Mercury occurs as small droplets in cinnabar deposits and in some volcanic rocks. It has a high coefficient of thermal expansion, which makes it useful in thermometers. Mercury forms amalgams with other metals, and these are used in gold extraction, tooth fillings and chemical processes. Locations where mercury is found include Almaden (Spain), Monte Amiata (Italy), Idrija (Slovenia), Moschellandsberg (Germany) and Juan Cavelica (Peru). Almaden is the oldest and largest mercury mine in the world.

## Hg

| | |
|---|---|
| Colour: | tin-white |
| Lustre; opacity: | metallic; opaque |
| Streak: | not applicable at room temperature |
| Hardness: | liquid at room temperature |
| Specific gravity: | 13.6 |
| Cleavage; fracture: | not applicable at room temperature |
| Habit: | droplets; rhombohedra (at -39°C/-38°F) |
| Crystal system: | trigonal (at -39°C/-38°F) |

# Nickel-Iron

Nickel-iron is a term for native iron, as there is invariably some nickel content. Terrestrial nickel-iron is formed in basalts in contact with carbonate rocks. Iron of low nickel content (2–3 per cent), in masses up to 23 tonnes (25 tons), is mined at Ovifak and Disko Island (Greenland). Nickel-iron in the form of meteorites is rare, but of great interest. Characteristic of these meteorites is the 'Widmanstätten pattern' of intergrowths of two different phases, brought out by chemical etching: a dark, low-nickel phase (kamacite) and a lighter one of high nickel content (taenite). The most famous meteorite, with pieces found at Canyon Diablo (Arizona, USA), fell *c.* 20,000–40,000 years ago, creating a crater 1.6km (1 mile) wide.

## Ni–Fe

| | |
|---|---|
| Colour: | grey to black |
| Lustre; opacity: | metallic; opaque |
| Streak: | grey |
| Hardness: | 4–5 |
| Specific gravity: | 7.0–7.8 |
| Cleavage; fracture: | perfect in rare iron crystals; hackly |
| Habit: | never distinct crystals; massive or disseminated grains |
| Crystal system: | isometric |

# Platinum

Platinum is a rare and valuable metal, used in laboratory equipment, electrical couplings and jewellery. It is invariably mixed with impurities such as iron, iridium, palladium, rhodium, nickel and/or osmium. Platinum and the related metal palladium are used in chemistry as powerful and versatile catalysts. It was discovered by the Spanish during their conquest of South America in the sixteenth century. Named *platina del Pinto* (Pinto silver) after the Rio Pinto in Colombia, it is also found at Nizhni Tagil and Norilsk (Russia), Ontario (Canada) and Bushveld (South Africa). It occurs in igneous rocks, associated with ilmenite, magnetite and chromite, and as a placer deposit. Like gold, it does not dissolve in any acids except aqua regia.

## Pt

| | |
|---|---|
| Colour: | steel-grey, silvery–white |
| Lustre; opacity: | metallic; opaque |
| Streak: | steel-grey, silvery–white |
| Hardness: | 4–4.5 |
| Specific gravity: | 14–19 (21.5 when pure) |
| Cleavage; fracture: | absent; hackly |
| Habit: | rarely crystals; grains, nuggets, irregular lumps |
| Crystal system: | cubic |
| Other: | ductile, malleable |

# Arsenic

A rsenic is rare as a native element and obtained commercially as a by-product from the smelting of sulphide ores. It is well known as a poison, a property put to positive use in pesticides, preservatives and pharmaceuticals for treating parasitic illnesses. Arsenic has been added to copper to strengthen it since *c.* 2000 BC. The name is derived from the Greek *arsenikos*, for 'masculine' or 'brave'. Native arsenic is found in hydrothermal veins associated with silver, cobalt and nickel ores and in some igneous and metamorphic rocks. It is found in Erzgebirge and the Harz Mountains (Germany), Gikos (Russia), Sterling Hill (New Jersey, USA), Jáchymov and Pribram (Czech Republic) and St Marie-aux-Mines (France).

## As

| | |
|---|---|
| **Colour:** | light grey tarnishing quickly to dark grey |
| **Lustre; opacity:** | metallic; opaque |
| **Streak:** | light grey |
| **Hardness:** | 3.5 |
| **Specific gravity:** | 5.7 |
| **Cleavage; fracture:** | perfect; uneven, brittle |
| **Habit:** | crystals rare, pseudo-cubic; granular, massive, concentrically layered nodules or stalactites |
| **Crystal system:** | trigonal |

# Antimony

A ntimony is a metalloid related to arsenic, with some metallic and non-metallic characters. Of its three various forms, the metallic one is more stable and is bright, silvery and hard. It is used in alloys to increase hardness and lower the melting point. Antimony compounds are toxic and have been used as antiparasitic agents in medicine. The word *antimony* is its old Greek name. Native antimony is formed by the alteration of sulphides, such as stibnite, in hydrothermal veins often accompanying silver and arsenic. It is found at St Andreasberg (Germany), Sala (Sweden), Coimbra (Portugal), Pribram (Czech Republic), New Brunswick (Canada), Kern County (California, USA), Sardinia (Italy) and Sarawak (Borneo).

## Sb

| | |
|---|---|
| Colour: | light grey |
| Lustre; opacity: | metallic; opaque |
| Streak: | greys |
| Hardness: | 3–3.5 |
| Specific gravity: | 6.6–6.7 |
| Cleavage; fracture: | perfect; uneven, very brittle |
| Habit: | rare crystals as rhombohedra or coarse plates; usually massive and reniform |
| Crystal system: | trigonal |

# Bismuth

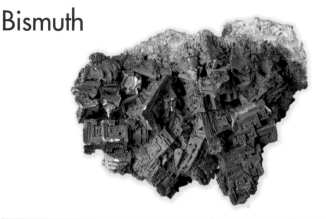

Native bismuth is rare and is found in hydrothermal veins associated with gold, silver, cobalt, tin, nickel and lead. Bismuth is related to arsenic and antimony. It has a low melting point (271°C/520°F) and is used in low-melting alloys for electrical fuses and fire protection devices. Native bismuth is an ore, although the metal is mostly obtained as a by-product from the smelting of bismuth-rich ores. Many specimens of bismuth on sale are crystallized masses, artificially produced but nevertheless in impressive geometrical squared patterns with an attractive iridescence. Bismuth is found at Kongsberg (Norway), Erzgebirge (Germany), Cornwall (England), Ontario (Canada) and Oruro and Tasna (Bolivia).

## Bi

| | |
|---|---|
| Colour: | lead-grey, pink tarnish |
| Lustre; opacity: | metallic; opaque |
| Streak: | silver-white, shiny |
| Hardness: | 2–2.5 |
| Specific gravity: | 9.7–9.8 |
| Cleavage; fracture: | perfect; uneven, sectile |
| Habit: | rare crystals; massive, granular, branching forms |
| Crystal system: | trigonal |

# Graphite

G raphite is a form of carbon made of stacked sheets of hexagonally arranged
atoms that can quite easily slide past each other, whereas diamond (another
carbon form) has a rigid three-dimensional lattice structure. Buckminsterfullerene
($C_{60}$), a third form, is a recently synthesized molecule found in nature in minute
traces. Graphite is used as a lubricant, in crucibles, as a moderator in nuclear
reactors and in pencils (as pencil 'lead'). It has a greasy feel and, unusually for a
non-metal, conducts electricity. Graphite is found in metamorphosed sediments,
basic igneous rocks, pegmatites and quartz veins. Graphite deposits are in Sri
Lanka, Madagascar, Russia, South Korea, Mexico, the Czech Republic and Italy.

## C

| | |
|---|---|
| Colour: | black |
| Lustre; opacity: | dull metallic; opaque |
| Streak: | black, shiny |
| Hardness: | 1–2 |
| Specific gravity: | 2.1–2.2 |
| Cleavage; fracture: | perfect, producing thin flexible sheets |
| Habit: | rare six-sided flat crystals; scales, foliated or earthy masses, compact lumps |
| Crystal system: | hexagonal |

# Diamond

**D**iamond is the most famous gemstone and the hardest mineral on Earth. Low-quality diamonds are used in industry for cutting and drilling equipment. Bort is a variety of diamond that has a rounded, fibrous, radiate structure, and carbonado is black and microcrystalline. A diamond is formed at very high temperatures and pressures deep within the Earth's mantle (c. 80 km/50 miles), and is then brought to the surface through kimberlite pipes. Diamonds are found in ultramafic rocks, especially kimberlite breccias, and as placer deposits. The main mining areas include the Argyle pipe (Western Australia), Kimberley (South Africa), Golconda (India), Diamontina (Minas Gerais, Brazil) and Yakutia (Russia).

## C

| | |
|---|---|
| **Colour:** | colourless, yellowish to yellow, brown, black, blue, green or red, pink, champagne-tan, cognac-brown |
| **Lustre; opacity:** | adamantine, greasy; transparent to opaque |
| **Streak:** | none, too hard to abrade |
| **Hardness:** | 10 |
| **Specific gravity:** | 3.52 |
| **Cleavage; fracture:** | perfect; conchoidal; uneven |
| **Habit:** | octahedral, dodecahedral, cubic crystals |
| **Crystal system:** | cubic |

# Diamond: Gem Varieties

Diamond's unequalled hardness, brilliant lustre and considerable 'fire' make it the most highly prized of gems. Jewellers usually favour the 'brilliant' cut, which gives maximum internal reflection of light and thus minimum loss through the back of the stone, enhancing the natural fire. Diamonds are measured in carats, derived from the weight of a carob seed pod, which is now a standard 0.2g. The Cullinan diamond, originally from South Africa, was of 3106 carats and cut into 104 gemstones, the largest of which was of 531 carats. The Koh-i-Noor diamond (109 carats) is set in the crown of British Queens. The largest deep blue diamond, and some would say the most beautiful, is the Hope diamond (44.5 carats).

## C

| | |
|---|---|
| Colour: | colourless, yellowish to yellow, brown, black, blue, green or red, pink, champagne-tan, cognac-brown |
| Lustre; opacity: | adamantine, greasy; transparent to opaque |
| Streak: | none, too hard to abrade |
| Hardness: | 10 |
| Specific gravity: | 3.52 |
| Cleavage; fracture: | perfect; conchoidal; uneven |
| Habit: | octahedral, dodecahedral, cubic crystals |
| Crystal system: | cubic |

# Sulphur

Sulphur has a characteristic yellow colour, is very brittle and will often crumble if roughly handled. Also called brimstone, it usually forms in volcanoes as a sublimate around vents and fumaroles. Sulphur can also be found precipitated in hot springs, in shales associated with gypsum and bitumen, and in the cap rock of salt domes. Sulphur is used in gunpowder, matches, sulphuric acid production and is extremely important as the vulcanizing agent for rubber. It has a low melting point (113°C/235°F) and burns to give sulphur dioxide. Sulphur is mined in Louisiana and Texas (USA), Sicily, Japan, Indonesia and the South American Andes. The best examples of crystalline sulphur come from Sicily and the Romagna (Italy).

## S

| | |
|---|---|
| Colour: | yellow, brownish or greenish yellow, orange, white |
| Lustre; opacity: | resinous, greasy; transparent to translucent |
| Streak: | none |
| Hardness: | 1.5–2.5 |
| Specific gravity : | 2.05–2.08 |
| Cleavage; fracture: | imperfect, fair; irregular, uneven, conchoidal |
| Habit: | massive, encrusting, powdery and stalactitic |
| Crystal system: | orthorhombic |

# Chalcocite

Chalcocite occurs in two distinct forms, forming orthorhombic crystals below 103°C (217°F) and hexagonal crystals above this. Chalcocite is also called chalcosine or copper glance. It is found in hydrothermal veins and in the reduced zones of copper deposits. It is an important copper ore, often produced by the alteration of chalcopyrite, with which it is often associated, and which, in turn, may be altered to malachite, azurite and covellite. Good examples of pseudohexagonal crystals come from the Transvaal (South Africa), Bristol (Connecticut, USA) and Redruth (Cornwall, England). Large deposits are mined in Butte (Montana, USA), Bisbee (Arizona, USA), Chuquicamata (Chile), Tsumeb (Namibia), Peru and Russia.

## $Cu_2S$

| | |
|---|---|
| Colour: | black or lead grey, often with greenish or bluish tarnish |
| Lustre; opacity: | metallic; opaque |
| Streak: | greyish black, sometimes shiny |
| Hardness: | 2.5–3 |
| Specific gravity: | 5.5–5.8 |
| Cleavage; fracture: | indistinct; conchoidal, uneven |
| Habit: | rarely as tabular, pseudohexagonal, striated crystals; mostly dull grey, granular aggregates |
| Crystal system: | orthorhombic, hexagonal above 103°C (217°F) |

# Bornite

Bornite, named after the Austrian mineralogist Ignatius von Born (1742–1791), is known as peacock ore because of the beautiful iridescent tarnish shown by many specimens. Too much weathering, however, produces an unattractive black tarnish. Bornite is a dense mineral that settles in magmas and so is found concentrated in igneous rocks, especially mafic rocks. It also occurs in pegmatites, hydrothermal veins and as a secondary mineral in copper deposits. A well-known deposit is found in the copper shales of Mansfeld (Germany). Good crystals come from Cornwall (England), Tsumeb (Namibia) and Butte (Montana, USA). Large quantities are mined in the USA, Mexico, Peru, Chile, Australia and Zambia.

## $Cu_5FeS_4$

| | |
|---|---|
| Colour: | copper-red or bronze when fresh, tarnishes to an iridescent blue, red and/or purplish surface film |
| Lustre; opacity: | metallic; opaque |
| Streak: | grey-black |
| Hardness: | 3 |
| Specific gravity: | 5.1 |
| Cleavage; fracture: | poor/indistinct; conchoidal, indistinct |
| Habit: | crystalline as cubes, dodecahedra or octahedra; commonly as compact granular masses |
| Crystal system: | orthorhombic |

# Acanthite-Argentite

A canthite occurs in the monoclinic system below 179°C (354°F); above this, cubic argentite is the stable form. As it is usually deposited at high temperatures, acanthite often occurs as cubic pseudomorphs after argentite. Acanthite's metallic lustre quickly blackens and is best seen on a freshly exposed surface. It is named from the Greek for 'arrow'; argentite is named from the Latin *argentum*, meaning 'silver'. It is found in hydrothermal veins with other silver minerals or disseminated in galena deposits. It can also occur in cemented parts of lead and zinc deposits. Acanthite is the main ore for silver and is mined extensively in Mexico, Peru and Honduras. Good crystals come from Kongsberg (Norway) and Freiberg (Germany).

## $Ag_2S$

| | |
|---|---|
| Colour: | shiny lead grey, black on surface |
| Lustre; opacity: | metallic; opaque |
| Streak: | black |
| Hardness: | 2–2.5 |
| Specific gravity: | 7.2–7.4 |
| Cleavage; fracture: | poor; conchoidal, uneven |
| Habit: | distorted, pseudo-cubic crystals in groups; dendritic aggregates, masses and encrustations |
| Crystal system: | monoclinic (acanthite) – cubic (argentite) |

# Sphalerite

Sphalerite or zinc blende is an important zinc ore, also providing cadmium, gallium and indium as by-products. Zinc is mostly used as sheets for galvanizing iron, and alloyed with copper to make brass. Sphalerite can be mistaken for galena, hence its name, from the Greek for 'treacherous'. The colour of sphalerite tends to darken as the iron content increases. A content of about 10 per cent imparts a black colour; any higher, and the ore may be called marmatite. Sphalerite forms in pegmatites and hydrothermal veins accompanying galena, acanthite, barite and chalcopyrite. It is found at Alston Moor (England), the Tri-State area (USA), Broken Hill (NSW, Australia), Kapnik (Hungary), Santander (Spain) and Sullivan (Canada).

## ZnS

| | |
|---|---|
| Colour: | usually brown or black, also yellow or reddish, rarely colourless |
| Lustre; opacity: | resinous, greasy; transparent to translucent to opaque |
| Streak: | brownish white |
| Hardness: | 3.5–4 |
| Specific gravity: | 3.9–4.2 |
| Cleavage; fracture: | perfect; conchoidal, brittle |
| Habit: | dodecahedral and octahedral crystals common; massive, compact, botryoidal or fibrous |
| Crystal system: | isometric |

# Chalcopyrite

Chalcopyrite, or copper pyrites, is the most important copper ore. By-products from copper extraction include silver and gold. It can be distinguished from pyrite by the fact that it does not produce sparks when hit by a hammer and also because it crumbles when cut with a knife due to poor cleavage. It can be distinguished from pyrrhotite because it is non-magnetic, and from gold because it is brittle. Chalcopyrite occurs mainly in hydrothermal veins associated with cassiterite, galena, pyrite, quartz, calcite and/or sphalerite, and in metamorphosed volcanic rocks. It is found in the Copper Belt of Zambia, Rio Tinto (Spain), Katanga (Congo), Cyprus, the Urals (Russia), and Montana, Arizona and Utah (USA).

## $CuFeS_2$

| | |
|---|---|
| Colour: | brass yellow, honey yellow |
| Lustre; opacity: | metallic; opaque |
| Streak: | greenish black |
| Hardness: | 3.5 |
| Specific gravity: | 4.1–4.3 |
| Cleavage; fracture: | indistinct; conchoidal, uneven |
| Habit: | pseudo-tetrahedral crystals, uncommon; usually massive and compact, sometimes reniform or mammilated |
| Crystal system: | tetragonal |

# Tetrahedrite-Tennanite

Tetrahedrite and tennanite form a continuous series. The replacement of sulphur for tellurium in goldfieldite and of silver for iron in freibergite also occurs. It can act as a geothermometer because the silver content rises as the temperature of formation falls. Most mineral specimens are antimony-rich tetrahedrite. The group have been called fahlerz minerals, and are copper ores that have also been used for silver, mercury and antimony recovery. They occur in hydrothermal veins associated with copper, lead, zinc and silver minerals. Tetrahedrite-tennanite is found in Botés and Kapnik (Romania), Boliden (Sweden), Pribram (Czech Republic), Tsumeb (Namibia) and Butte (Montana, USA).

## $(Cu,Fe)_{12}Sb_4S_{13} - (Cu,Fe)_{12}As_4S_{13}$

| | |
|---|---|
| Colour: | steel grey to brown, occasionally twinned |
| Lustre; opacity: | metallic; opaque |
| Streak: | dark grey |
| Hardness: | 3–4.5 |
| Specific gravity: | 4.6–5.2 |
| Cleavage; fracture: | none; conchoidal, uneven |
| Habit: | crystals often modified tetrahedral; massive, granular, compact |
| Crystal system: | isometric |
| Other: | melt easily on heating; soluble in nitric acid |

# Stannite

Stannite, named from the Latin *stannum* for tin, is also known as tin pyrites, bolivianite or bell metal ore. It has been worked as a tin ore in Cornwall and forms part of silver deposits in Bolivia. It is a fairly rare mineral found in hydrothermal veins and pegmatites associated with cassiterite, wolframite, pyrite and arsenopyrite. It may contain other metals such as silver, cadmium and indium, and is called zincian stannite when zinc-rich. Stannite is found at Etna Mine (South Dakota, USA), Seward Peninsula (Alaska, USA), Llallagua (Bolivia), Cinovec (Czech Republic), Zeehan (Tasmania, Australia) and Wheal Rock (Cornwall, England), the last being the type locality for the mineral.

## $Cu_2FeSnS_4$

| | |
|---|---|
| Colour: | greyish black, steel grey; often has an iridescent olive green or blue surface |
| Lustre; opacity: | metallic; opaque |
| Streak: | black |
| Hardness: | 3.5–4 |
| Specific gravity: | 4.3–4.5 |
| Cleavage; fracture: | imperfect; conchoidal, uneven |
| Habit: | crystals rare, tetrahedral or more often pseudooctahedral due to twinning; massive, granular, disseminated |
| Crystal system: | tetragonal |

# Wurtzite

Wurtzite is dimorphic with sphalerite, the more common form of zinc sulphide. The zinc can be replaced partially by iron, giving a darker colour. A rarer trigonal polymorph exists, called matraite. Crystals are usually quite small, but can be delightful shapes of somewhat elongated six-sided pyramids on a flat hexagonal base. Wurtzite is found in hydrothermal veins associated with sphalerite, pyrite, chalcopyrite, barite and marcasite. It is named after the French chemist Charles Wurtz (1817–1884). Locations include Thomaston Dam (Connecticut, USA), Butte (Montana, USA), Frisco (Utah, USA), Cornwall (England), Pribram (Czech Republic), Baia Sprie (Romania) and Oruro and Potosi (Bolivia).

## ZnS

| | |
|---|---|
| Colour: | light to dark brown |
| Lustre; opacity: | adamantine, greasy; translucent to opaque |
| Streak: | light brown |
| Hardness: | 3.5–4 |
| Specific gravity: | 3.98–4.08 |
| Cleavage; fracture: | good; uneven |
| Habit: | rare crystals usually hemimorphic pyramids, sometimes hexagonal tabular crystals or short prisms; usually concentrically banded crusts, fibrous or columnar |
| Crystal system: | hexagonal |

# Greenockite

Greenockite is a cadmium ore named after Lord Greenock, on whose land near Glasgow it was first found. Other cadmium ore minerals are cadmoselite (CdSe) and otavite (CdCO$_3$), and all are quite rare. Commercial production of cadmium, however, is mostly as a by-product in the smelting of zinc sulphide ores. Cadmium is used in rechargeable batteries, alloys and pigments. Greenockite is a secondary mineral formed on the surface of cadmium-rich sphalerites. It is brightly coloured when fresh, but becomes dull on weathering. Tiny crystals are found at Llallagua (Bolivia), Bishopstown (Scotland) and Paterson (New Jersey, USA); encrustations are found at Příbram (Czech Republic), Joplin (Missouri, USA) and Sardinia (Italy).

## CdS

| | |
|---|---|
| Colour: | yellow, orange, red |
| Lustre; opacity: | adamantine, resinous; translucent |
| Streak: | orange yellow |
| Hardness: | 3–3.5 |
| Specific gravity: | 4.9–5 |
| Cleavage; fracture: | distinct, imperfect |
| Habit: | prismatic, hexagonal crystals rare, sometimes twinned; usually powdery encrustations or coatings |
| Crystal system: | hexagonal |

# Enargite

Enargite is a minor ore of copper and arsenic named from the Greek *enarges*, meaning 'obvious', because of its notably distinct cleavage. It is a dimorph of the mineral luzonite and is often mixed with the analogous antimony mineral stibioluzonite ($Cu_3SbS_4$). Twinning can give rise to attractive star shapes called 'trillings'. Enargite occurs in hydrothermal veins associated with chalcopyrite, tetrahedrite, bornite, pyrite, barite, quartz and covellite. It is found at Bor (Serbia), Chuquicamata (Chile), Bingham and Tintic (Utah, USA), Butte (Montana, USA), Luzon Island (Phillipines), Morococha, Quiruvilca and Cerro de Pasco (Peru), and Freiberg (Germany). Prisms up to 8cm (3in) have been found at Tsumeb (Namibia).

## $Cu_3AsS_4$

| | |
|---|---|
| **Colour:** | grey to black, can have violet or rose-brown internal reflections |
| **Lustre; opacity:** | metallic; opaque |
| **Streak:** | black |
| **Hardness:** | 3 |
| **Specific gravity:** | 4.4–4.5 |
| **Cleavage; fracture:** | perfect; uneven |
| **Habit:** | crystals rare tabular, blocky or prismatic often pseudohexagonal and striated ; usually as aggregates or granular masses |
| **Crystal system:** | orthorhombic |

# Galena

G alena is a common sulphide and is the main ore for lead, used and named by
the ancient Greeks. Lead is used in batteries, glass, solder and radiation shields.
Up to 1 per cent silver is found in galena, which makes it an important silver ore. It
is a natural semiconductor and was one of the favourite 'crystals' used as crude
diodes in crystal radio sets. Galena occurs in hydrothermal veins associated with
chalcopyrite, pyrite, sphalerite barite, calcite, fluorite and quartz. It is mined in the
Tri-State area of Missouri, Oklahoma and Kansas (USA), Broken Hill (Australia) and
Santa Eulalia (Mexico); crystals are found at Pribram (Czech Republic), Isle of Man
(UK) and Sardinia (Italy).

## PbS

| | |
|---|---|
| Colour: | light lead grey, dark lead grey |
| Lustre; opacity: | metallic; opaque |
| Streak: | greyish black |
| Hardness: | 2.5 |
| Specific gravity: | 7.2–7.6 |
| Cleavage; fracture: | perfect; soft no fracture |
| Habit: | well-formed crystals; massive, granular |
| Crystal system: | cubic |

# Cinnabar

Cinnabar is a toxic, dense red mineral formerly used as a pigment known as vermilion, the use of which began in ancient times. Free mercury can be produced by heating cinnabar above 580°C (1076°F). Mercury compounds are used in fine chemicals and paints, and mercury itself in thermometers and scientific instruments. Cinnabar is found in a variety of rocks often associated with volcanic activity, such as hot springs. It also occurs in hydrothermal veins and as placer deposits. The three most important locations are Almadén (Spain), Monte Amiato (Italy) and Idrija (Slovenia). Other locations include Nikotawa (Russia), Hunan Province (China) and the Altai Mountains of Central Asia.

## HgS

| | |
|---|---|
| Colour: | bright scarlet to brick red |
| Lustre; opacity: | adamantine; translucent |
| Streak: | bright red |
| Hardness: | 2–2.5 |
| Specific gravity: | 8.1 |
| Cleavage; fracture: | perfect; uneven, splintery |
| Habit: | rare rhombohedral or thick tabular crystals; earthy films; massive or granular |
| Crystal system: | trigonal |

# Pyrrhotite

Pyrrhotite is distinguishable from pyrite in being magnetic, hence the alternative name magnetic pyrites. It is somewhat deficient in iron, there being approximately 11 sulphur atoms per 10 iron atoms. The mineral corresponding exactly to the formula FeS, which has been found only in meteorites, is called troilite. Named after the Greek *pyrrotes*, for 'red coloured', pyrrhotite is not a major iron ore, but nickel-rich pyrrhotite deposits are used to extract nickel, cobalt and platinum. It is found in mafic and ultramafic igneous rocks, hydrothermal veins and some high-grade metamorphic rocks. Good crystals come from Trepca (Serbia), Kysbanya (Romania), New York (USA) and Freiberg (Germany).

## FeS

| | |
|---|---|
| Colour: | bronze, bronze red, dark brown |
| Lustre; opacity: | metallic; opaque |
| Streak: | grey black |
| Hardness: | 3.5–4 |
| Specific gravity: | 4.58–4.65 |
| Cleavage; fracture: | imperfect; uneven |
| Habit: | prismatic or tabular crystals; massive, granular |
| Crystal system: | monoclinic (hexagonal when low in sulphur, close to FeS) |

# Miargyrite

Miargyrite, common among silver ore deposits, is named from the Greek for 'smaller' and 'silver', alluding to its silver content, which is lower than the mineral pyrargyrite. Easily confused with other silver minerals, miargyrite may be distinguished by its unusual deep red streak. Crystals usually grow to only about 1cm (½in), but the red internal reflections seen in this mineral make it appealing. It is found in hydrothermal veins associated with pyrargyrite, silver, galena, sphalerite, quartz, calcite and barite. Miargyrite is found at Baia Sprie (Romania), Pribram and Trebsko (Czech Republic), Randsberg (California, USA), Owyhee (Idaho, USA), Copiapo and Tarapaca (Chile), Potosi and Huanchaka (Peru), and Freiberg (Germany).

## AgSbS$_2$

| | |
|---|---|
| Colour: | grey to black with dark red internal reflections |
| Lustre; opacity: | metallic; opaque |
| Streak: | cherry red |
| Hardness: | 2.5 |
| Specific gravity: | 5.25 |
| Cleavage; fracture: | imperfect/fair; subconchoidal |
| Habit: | well-formed crystals, often coarse plates, blades, equant or wedge-shaped; granular, massive aggregates, disseminated |
| Crystal system: | monoclinic |

# Nickeline

Nickeline, or niccolite, is the first mineral from which nickel was extracted, but is now only a minor ore. The names of both mineral and element come from the German *kupfernickel*, or devil's nickel, because it was impossible to extract copper from the mineral, despite its copper-like appearance. It occurs in hydrothermal veins or is disseminated in basic igneous rocks such as gabbros, and is associated invariably with sulphides of silver, nickel and cobalt. Specimens are often coated with a pale to dark green film of annabergite. Nickeline is found at Eisleben and Freiberg (Germany), Schladming (Austria), Cobalt and Eldorado (Canada), Natsume (Japan), Bou Azzer (Morocco), Anarak (Iran) and La Rioja (Argentina).

## NiAs

| | |
|---|---|
| Colour: | copper-red |
| Lustre; opacity: | metallic; opaque |
| Streak: | brownish black |
| Hardness: | 5.5 |
| Specific gravity: | 7.78–7.8 |
| Cleavage; fracture: | imperfect; uneven to conchoidal |
| Habit: | crystals stocky, tabular or pyramidal, rare; columnar; massive; reniform |
| Crystal system: | hexagonal |

# Millerite

Millerite is a widespread but uncommon minor ore of nickel, also found in iron-nickel meteorites, albeit in minute quantities. Named after the English mineralogist W.H. Miller (1801–1880), it is also known as hair pyrites after its fine acicular crystals, or capillary pyrite after its occurrence as fine hollow crystals. It is a hydrothermal deposit found in cavities in limestones and dolomites, on barite and as an alteration product of nickel minerals. Millerite is found at Ramsbeck and Kamsdorf (Germany), Kotalahti (Finland), Keokuk (Iowa, USA), St Louis (Missouri, USA), Temagami (Ontario, Canada), Thompson (Manitoba, Canada), Onllwyn (Wales) and Kambalda and Leinster (Australia).

## NiS

| | |
|---|---|
| Colour: | brassy yellow, iridescent on tarnishing |
| Lustre; opacity: | metallic; opaque |
| Streak: | greenish black |
| Hardness: | 3–3.5 |
| Specific gravity: | 5.2–5.6 |
| Cleavage; fracture: | perfect; uneven |
| Habit: | acicular crystals, often in tufts or felted masses; rarely granular or massive |
| Crystal system: | trigonal |

# Covellite

Covellite is a rare mineral, also called indigo copper, occasionally found as flat, hexagonal crystals up to 10cm (4in) large and attractive rosettes of platy crystals. Covellite crystals are indigo blue and show pleasing iridescent yellow and red flashes. Strongly tarnished samples are coloured purple or black. It was discovered on Vesuvius by the Italian mineralogist N. Covelli (1790–1829). Covellite usually occurs in the oxidized zones of copper deposits and in volcanic sublimates, associated with chalcopyrite, chalcocite, bornite and pyrite. Covellite is found at the Calabona mine (Sardinia) and Vesuvius (Italy), Salzberg (Austria), Butte (Montana, USA), Kennicott (Alaska, USA), Bor (Serbia) and Bou Azzer (Morocco).

## CuS

| | |
|---|---|
| Colour: | indigo blue, strongly iridescent |
| Lustre; opacity: | metallic; opaque |
| Streak: | black grey |
| Hardness: | 1.5–2 |
| Specific gravity: | 4.6–4.76 |
| Cleavage: | perfect |
| Habit: | foliated, platy crystal aggregates; rarely hexagonal, flattened crystals; compact masses |
| Crystal system: | hexagonal |

# Pyrite

Pyrite, also called iron pyrite or simply pyrites, is also well known as fool's gold. It has often been mistaken for gold due to its yellow metallic lustre. Unlike gold, however, pyrite is hard, brittle and often unmistakably crystalline. Pyrite is used as a source of sulphur, especially for sulphuric acid manufacture. It occurs in igneous rocks, and is found in hydrothermal veins associated with sphalerite, galena, quartz, copper sulphides and gold, the latter two sometimes being commercially extracted from pyrite-rich ores. Pyrite also occurs in some metamorphic rocks and as pseudomorphs infilling the shapes of fossils. Excellent crystals are to be found in many locations. Pyritized fossils are found in Germany, England and Italy.

## $FeS_2$

| | |
|---|---|
| **Colour:** | pale brass yellow |
| **Lustre; opacity:** | metallic; opaque |
| **Streak:** | greenish black |
| **Hardness:** | 6.5 |
| **Specific gravity:** | 5–5.02 |
| **Cleavage; fracture:** | poor; uneven to conchoidal |
| **Habit:** | striated cubes, octahedra or pyritohedra, sometimes as 'iron cross' twins; compact granular aggregates, nodules, concretions and stalactitic forms, pseudomorphs after fossils |
| **Crystal system:** | cubic |

# Pyrite Varieties

Pyrite is very popular as large cubes and distorted dodecahedra called pyritohedra. Large crystals, especially cubes in metamorphic rocks, can make intriguing specimens with a bright, golden cube embedded incongruously in a contrasting granular or schistose matrix. Discs of sectioned nodules showing a radiating internal structure make attractive ornamental pieces. Pyrite used in jewellery is sometimes called marcasite by jewellers, especially when used as faceted stones set in silver. Pyrite is difficult to cut for jewellery because of its brittleness. It has been used by the ancient Greeks to adorn earrings and pins, and for jewellery in Victorian times. The Incas are said to have used pyrite tablets as mirrors.

## $FeS_2$

| | |
|---|---|
| Colour: | pale brass yellow |
| Lustre; opacity: | metallic; opaque |
| Streak: | greenish black |
| Hardness: | 6.5 |
| Specific gravity: | 5–5.02 |
| Cleavage; fracture: | poor; uneven to conchoidal |
| Habit: | striated cubes, octahedra or pyritohedra, sometimes as 'iron cross' twins; compact granular aggregates, nodules, concretions and stalactitic forms, pseudomorphs after fossils |
| Crystal system: | cubic |

# Stibnite

Stibnite, also known as antimonite, is the major ore of antimony. The name is derived from the old Greek word for antimony, *stibi*. Widely distributed but in small deposits, stibnite is mostly found in hydrothermal veins, but can occur in association with hot springs, associated with sulphides of silver, lead and mercury, pyrite, galena and quartz. Stibnite can form striking arrays of roughly aligned or radiating elongated prisms. The largest deposits of stibnite are in Hunan province (China); others locations include Shikoku Island (Japan) and Baia Sprie and Kapnik (Romania). Antimony is used in alloys to harden other metals, especially lead in storage batteries. It is increasingly used in semiconductors.

## $Sb_2S_3$

| | |
|---|---|
| Colour: | lead grey, bluish lead grey, steel grey, black |
| Lustre; opacity: | metallic; opaque |
| Streak: | blackish grey |
| Hardness: | 2 |
| Specific gravity: | 4.63 |
| Cleavage; fracture: | perfect; conchoidal |
| Habit: | granular, prismatic crystals, striated surface or cleavage face |
| Crystal system: | orthorhombic |

# Cobaltite

Cobaltite is a major ore of cobalt, the name of which comes from the German *kobold*, meaning 'underground spirit' or 'goblin', in reference to the difficulty of smelting it. Crystal forms of cobaltite are similar to those of pyrite, but the two are easily distinguished by colour. Cobaltite is often weathered to give crusts of pink to bright purple erythrite, called cobalt bloom by miners (evidence of underlying cobalt minerals). It is found in hydrothermal veins or contact-metamorphosed rocks. Excellent crystals come from Tunaberg (Sweden), Skutterud (Norway), Cornwall (England), Española, Cobalt and Sudbury (Ontario, Canada), Broken Hill and Torrington (NSW, Australia), and Bou Azzer (Morocco).

## CoAsS

| | |
|---|---|
| Colour: | reddish silver white, violet steel grey, black |
| Lustre; opacity: | metallic; opaque |
| Streak: | greyish black |
| Hardness: | 5.5 |
| Specific gravity: | 6.33 |
| Cleavage; fracture: | good; uneven |
| Habit: | cubes, octahedra or pyritohedra, usually striated; granular or compact masses, disseminated |
| Crystal system | orthorhombic |

# Bismuthinite

Bismuthinite is similar in appearance and properties to stibnite, but can be distinguished by its inability to melt in a match flame. Sprays of steel grey prismatic crystals resemble those of stibnite. It is the major ore of bismuth, but the free metal is mostly obtained as a by-product of lead and copper smelting. Substitution of bismuth for lead and copper gives the mineral aikinite ($CuPbBiS_3$), which forms a series with bismuthinite. It occurs in hydrothermal veins associated with tin, silver and cobalt minerals. Bismuthinite is found at Haddam (Connecticut, USA), Llallagua and Tasno (Bolivia), Cerro de Pasco (Peru), Cornwall (England) and Mount Biggenden (Australia).

## $Bi_2S_3$

| | |
|---|---|
| Colour: | grey, silver white, tin white |
| Lustre; opacity: | metallic; opaque |
| Streak: | grey |
| Hardness: | 2 |
| Specific gravity: | 6.8–7.2 |
| Cleavage; fracture: | perfect; uneven |
| Habit: | prismatic, acicular crystals, finely striated; granular and compact aggregates |
| Crystal system: | orthorhombic |

# Sylvanite

Sylvanite is one of the few ores of gold, other than native gold itself, and also of silver and tellurium. Gold, normally very unreactive, has a particular affinity for tellurium. Sylvanite is named after Transylvania, where the mineral was first discovered. It is rare and not commercially mined. Tellurium is obtained from the anode slime in copper refining. Although less than 0.1 per cent is usually added to steels, more than half of the tellurium production is used in this way. Sylvanite occurs in hydrothermal veins, associated with calaverite ($AuTe_2$) and petzite ($Ag_3AuTe_2$). It is found at Baia de Aries (Romania), Kalgoorie (Australia), Bereznyakov and Yaman-Kasy, Ural Mountains (Russia), and Cripple Creek (Colorado, USA).

## $AgAuTe_4$

| | |
|---|---|
| Colour: | yellowish silver white, white |
| Lustre; opacity: | metallic, opaque |
| Streak: | steel grey |
| Hardness: | 1.5–2 |
| Specific gravity: | 7.9–8.3 |
| Cleavage; fracture: | perfect; uneven |
| Habit: | stubby, prismatic or arborescent crystals; branching encrustations resembling script; granular or bladed masses |
| Crystal system: | monoclinic |

# Hauerite

H auerite is a rare form of manganese disulphide named after the Austrian geologists J. and F. von Hauer. The finest specimens are large octahedral crystals sometimes modified by cubic faces, from the Destricella mine (Raddusa, Sicily). Specimens often comprise hauerite with associated rambergite (MnS). Hauerite occurs in sulphur-rich clay deposits and altered lavas associated with sulphur, realgar, gypsum, aragonite and calcite, and in the ferromanganese deposits in the Pacific Ocean. It is found at Kalinka and Banská Stiavnica (Slovakia), Bohemia (Czech Republic), Jezyorko and Grzybow (Poland), Raddusa (Italy), Yazovsk and Podgornensk (Ural Mountains, Russia) and in salt domes in Texas (USA).

## $MnS_2$

| | |
|---|---|
| Colour: | brownish grey to brownish black, reddish tints |
| Lustre; opacity: | metallic; opaque |
| Streak: | reddish brown |
| Hardness: | 4 |
| Specific gravity: | 3.46 |
| Cleavage; fracture: | perfect; uneven |
| Habit: | octahedral and cubo-octahedral crystals up to 5 cm (2 in), often fractured unevenly; rounded aggregates |
| Crystal system: | isometric |

# Ullmannite

Ullmannite is a rare form of nickel antimony sulphide of the cobaltite group, named after the German chemist J. Ullmann (1771–1821). It is closely related to gersdorfite (NiAsS) and will almost invariably contain some arsenic. Ullmannite also forms a series with willyamite, $(Co,Ni)SbS$. Crystals grow to about 3cm (1¼in) and resemble those seen in pyrite. Ullmannite occurs in hydrothermal veins associated with minerals such as skutterudite, galena, nickeline, pyrrhotite and tetrahedrite. It is found at Siegerland, Harzgerode and Lobenstein (Germany), Waldenstein and Lolling (Austria), Fourstones (Northumberland, England), Durham (England), Broken Hill (NSW, Australia) and Sarrabus (Sardinia, Italy).

## NiSbS

| | |
|---|---|
| **Colour:** | steel grey, silver white, tin white |
| **Lustre; opacity:** | metallic; opaque |
| **Streak:** | greyish black |
| **Hardness:** | 5–5.5 |
| **Specific gravity:** | 6.65 |
| **Cleavage; fracture:** | good; uneven |
| **Habit:** | crystals as cubes, octahedra, dodecahedra and tetrahedra; massive, granular |
| **Crystal system:** | cubic |

# Marcasite

Marcasite is a polymorph of pyrite, and is used, like pyrite, for sulphuric acid production, not as an iron ore. It is called spear pyrites after the arrow- or spear-head shape of twinned crystals; it is also known as white iron pyrite, as it has a paler colour than pyrite. Marcasite was formerly used in jewellery, but is now likely to be pyrite. Marcasite forms in hydrothermal veins, often in lead and zinc ores, is precipitated in sedimentary rocks and can be found replacing fossils. Marcasite is found at Carlsbad and Rammelsberg (Germany), Karlovy Vary (Czech Republic), Derbyshire (England) and the Tri-State mining area (USA). Nodules with a radiating internal structure are found in the chalk of Southeast England.

## $FeS_2$

| | |
|---|---|
| Colour: | steel grey, silver white |
| Lustre; opacity: | metallic; opaque |
| Streak: | greyish black |
| Hardness: | 5.5 |
| Specific gravity: | 6.65 |
| Cleavage; fracture: | good; uneven |
| Habit: | crystals as flat prisms, occasionally as rosettes, often twinned in shapes described as cockscombs and spearheads; massive, granular, crusty aggregates, concretions |
| Crystal system: | cubic |

# Arsenopyrite

Arsenopyrite is common in sulphide deposits and is the major ore of arsenic, and is often also rich in silver, gold, cobalt and tin. Arsenic, however, is obtained commercially as a by-product during the refining of sulphide ores. Arsenopyrite has a silvery colour that distinguishes it from pyrite and marcasite, although it can tarnish on exposure. Mispickel and arsenical pyrites are alternative names. It occurs in sulphide deposits, in hydrothermal veins and in some metamorphic rocks. Good crystals are found at Roxbury (Connecticut, USA), Leadville (Colorado, USA) and Valle Anzasca and Val Sugana (Italy). Large deposits are at Boliden (Sweden), Freiberg (Germany), Deloro (Canada), Sulitjelma (Norway) and Cornwall (England).

## FeAsS

| | |
|---|---|
| Colour: | tin white, light steel grey, can have a pink tint |
| Lustre; opacity: | metallic; opaque |
| Streak: | black |
| Hardness: | 5 |
| Specific gravity: | 6.07 |
| Cleavage; fracture: | distinct; uneven |
| Habit: | crystals as elongated, striated prisms and cruciform twins; granular masses |
| Crystal system: | monoclinic |

# Glaucodot

Glaucodot contains up to 25 per cent cobalt, but is not a commercially important ore. It is regarded by some as a member of the arsenopyrite-cobaltite (FeAsS-CoAsS) series, but these crystallize in different systems. The name comes from the Greek for 'blue', after its use in a dark blue glass called smalt. It occurs in hydrothermal veins associated with sulphides and in metamorphosed lavas. Weathering and alteration often produce a bloom of erythrite. Good crystals come from Hakansbö (Sweden) and Huasco (Tarapaca, Chile). Other localities include Cobalt (Ontario, Canada), Oravita (Romania), Skutterud (Norway), Sumpter (Oregon, USA), Franconia (New Hampshire, USA) and Alston (Cumbria, England).

## (Cu,Fe)AsS

| | |
|---|---|
| Colour: | greyish or reddish silver-white |
| Lustre; opacity: | metallic; opaque |
| Streak: | black |
| Hardness: | 5 |
| Specific gravity: | 5.9–6.01 |
| Cleavage; fracture: | perfect; uneven, fragile |
| Habit: | prismatic or elongate crystals; granular or radiating fibrous masses |
| Crystal ystem: | orthorhombic |

# Skutterudite

Skutterudite, also known as smaltite, is one of the major ores of cobalt. The cobalt is invariably partially replaced by other elements, such as copper, zinc, silver and particularly nickel. When nickel forms the major component, it is referred to as nickel-skutterudite. It forms fine crystals resembling those of pyrite, but with a silvery colour, and is often altered to crimson red erythrite. Skutterudite is formed in hydrothermal veins associated with arsenopyrite, calcite and sulphides of cobalt and nickel. It is named after Skutterud in Norway, where it occurs as fine crystals; it is also found at Cobalt (Canada), Huelva (Spain), Schneeberg (Germany) and Bou Azzer (Morocco). Deposits are mined in Germany, Austria and the Czech Republic.

## $(Co,Ni)As_3$

| | |
|---|---|
| Colour: | white, light steel grey, sometimes with a an iridescent film |
| Lustre; opacity: | metallic; opaque |
| Streak: | black |
| Hardness: | 5.5–6 |
| Specific gravity: | 6.1–6.9 |
| Cleavage; fracture: | distinct; conchoidal |
| Habit: | crystals are cubic, octahedral or pyritohedral; compact granular masses |
| Crystal system: | cubic |

# Molybdenite

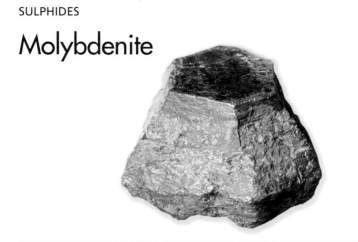

**M**olybdenite forms two-dimensional sheets, and these, like micas and graphite, give rise to flaky crystals. It is an excellent high-temperature dry lubricant and the main ore of molybdenum. Similar in appearance to graphite, it has a higher density and a more metallic bluish appearance. The name is derived from the Greek *molybdos*, for lead having been mistaken for galena. It mostly occurs in granitic rocks, in pegmatites and pneumatolytic veins, and in contact-metamorphosed rocks. Good crystals are found at Edison (New Jersey, USA), Climax (Colorado, USA), Arendal (Norway), Temikaming (Quebec, Canada) and Kingsgate (NSW, Australia), the latter providing crystals 70 x 5mm (2¾ x ¼in).

## $MoS_2$

| | |
|---|---|
| **Colour:** | bluish-grey |
| **Lustre; opacity:** | metallic; opaque |
| **Streak:** | bright blue-grey |
| **Hardness:** | 1–1.5 |
| **Specific gravity:** | 4.7 |
| **Cleavage; fracture:** | perfect |
| **Habit:** | tabular hexagonal crystals; usually as bladed, foliated or interwoven masses |
| **Crystal system:** | hexagonal |

# Proustite

Proustite forms beautiful translucent cinnabar-red crystals, but exposure to light and air causes them to darken, becoming semi-opaque with a grey streak. Rarely for a sulphide mineral, it is not metallic or opaque. Resembling pyrargyrite, it was identified only by analysis by the French chemist J. Proust (1755–1826). Proustite is also known as ruby silver ore or light red silver ore. It is found in oxidized zones of hydrothermal veins associated with other silver and sulphide minerals. Proustite crystals of up to 15cm (6in) have been found at Chañarcillo (Chile); other locations are Jáchymov and Pribram (Czech Republic), Chihuahua and Zacatas (Mexico), Annaberg and Wittichen (Germany), and Sarrabus (Sardinia).

## $Ag_3AsS_3$

| | |
|---|---|
| Colour: | dark red, darkening on exposure to light and air |
| Lustre; opacity: | adamantine; semi-transparent to translucent |
| Streak: | brick red, becoming grey in altered specimens |
| Hardness: | 2–2.5 |
| Specific gravity: | 5.57 |
| Cleavage; fracture: | good, rhombohedral; conchoida |
| Habit: | crystals rare, as rhombohedra or scalenohedra, usually striated and distorted; usually massive |
| Crystal system: | trigonal |

# Pyrargyrite

Pyrargyrite is related to proustite, with antimony replacing arsenic, both in the hexagonal system. To distinguish it from proustite, pyrargyrite has been called dark red silver ore, but is also referred to as ruby silver. Pyrargyrite crystals can be striking and attractive, but darken fairly quickly on exposure to light and become opaque, posing problems with storage and display. It is formed in hydrothermal veins associated with other silver minerals and by alteration of argentite and silver-rich galena. Good hexagonal crystals occur at St Andreasberg and Freiberg (Germany), and Colquechaca (Bolivia); other localities are Sarrabus (Sardinia), Pribram (Czech Republic), Zacetas (Mexico) and Chañarcillo (Chile).

## $Ag_3SbS_3$

| Colour: | black with dark red tints, darkening on exposure to light |
|---|---|
| Lustre; opacity: | adamantine, submetallic; translucent, becoming opaque on exposure to light |
| Streak: | purple-red |
| Hardness: | 2.5–3 |
| Specific gravity: | 5.85 |
| Cleavage; fracture: | good, rhombohedral; uneven to conchoidal |
| Habit: | crystals hemimorphic being prisms with varying terminations; granular aggregates, compact masses, disseminated grains |
| Crystal system: | trigonal |

# Stephanite

Named after Archduke Victor Stephan (1817–1867), Mining Director for Austria, stephanite is also called black silver ore or brittle silver ore. It is a major ore of silver, alongside acanthite in importance. Good crystals are rare, but can grow to about 6cm (2¼in) and display a brilliant metallic lustre. Twinning often occurs to give pseudohexagonal crystals. Stephanite is found in hydrothermal veins associated with silver, proustite, pyrargyrite, polybasite, tetrahedrite and acanthite. Excellent crystals have been found at St Andreasberg and Freiberg (Germany), and at Zacatecas and Arizpe (Mexico). It is mined at Cobalt in Ontario and Elsa in Yukon (Canada) and is an important ore at the famous Comstock Lode (Nevada, USA).

## $Ag_5SbS_4$

| | |
|---|---|
| Colour: | iron-black |
| Lustre; opacity: | metallic; opaque |
| Streak: | black, shiny |
| Hardness: | 2–2.5 |
| Specific gravity: | 6.3 |
| Cleavage; fracture: | poor; uneven |
| Habit: | crystals rare, prismatic to tabular; granular aggregates, massive, disseminated |
| Crystal system: | orthorhombic |

# Polybasite

Polybasite is a minor silver ore and yet another that has been called ruby silver. It forms a series with pearceite, $(Ag,Cu)_{16}As_2S_{11}$, although the antimony-rich polybasite is much more common. Good crystals are rare, but can grow to about 6cm (2¼in) and have a reddish tinge due to internal reflections. Fine crystals are found at Husky Mine (Yukon, Canada) and rosettes of hexagonal plates at Guanajuata (Mexico). Polybasite occurs in hydrothermal veins usually accompanied by quartz, calcite, barite or other silver minerals. Other good localities include St Andreasberg and Freiberg (Germany), and Pribram (Czech Republic). It is mined at Chañarcillo (Chile), Sarrabus (Sardinia) and Colorado (USA).

## $(Ag,Cu)_{16}Sb_2S_{11}$

| | |
|---|---|
| Colour: | iron black, rarely cherry red |
| Lustre; opacity: | metallic; opaque |
| Streak: | black |
| Hardness: | 2–3 |
| Specific gravity: | 6–6.2 |
| Cleavage; fracture: | poor; uneven |
| Habit: | bevelled, tabular, pseudohexagonal crystals; bladed, in rosettes, granular compact aggregates, crusts |
| Crystal system: | monoclinic |

# Bournonite

Bournonite, also known as endellionite, forms crystals that have a good metallic lustre and interesting shapes. Twinning often produces shapes resembling worn cog wheels, hence the name wheel ore. Such twinned crystals are called 'trillings' and frequently are striated along the 'teeth' of the cog. Some crystals can develop a greyish tarnish, so some care with storage is advised. Bournonite occurs in hydrothermal veins, associated with galena, tetrahedrite, pyrite and especially silver. Excellent crystals are found at Harz (Germany), St Endellion and Lanreath (Cornwall, England), Pribram (Czech Republic), Kapnik-Bnya (Hungary), Sarrabus (Sardinia), Broken Hill (NSW, Australia) and Park City (Utah, USA).

## $PbCuSbS_3$

| | |
|---|---|
| Colour: | dark grey to black |
| Lustre; opacity: | metallic; opaque |
| Streak: | steel grey |
| Hardness: | 2.5–3 |
| Specific gravity: | 5.7–5.9 |
| Cleavage; fracture: | good; fragile |
| Habit: | crystals as stubby, tabular, multi-faceted prisms; granular aggregates, disseminated grains |
| Crystal system: | orthorhombic |

61

# Hutchinsonite

Hutchinsonite is an ore of the metal thallium, others being crooksite ($Cu_7TlSe_4$), thalcusite ($Cu_3FeTl_2S_4$) and lorandite ($TlAsS_2$). It was named to honour Arthur Hutchinson (1866–1937), Professor of Mineralogy at Cambridge University. Thallium is obtained as a by-product of the smelting of thallium-rich zinc and lead ores (which are likely to contain hutchinsonite). Thallium is very toxic, but is used in some specialist glass manufacture. Hutchinsonite occurs in hydrothermal deposits associated with orpiment, realgar, pyrite, sphalerite and galena. It is found at the Lengenbach Quarry (Binnental, Switzerland), Segen Gottes (Black Forest, Germany), Quiluvrilca (Peru) and Toya-Takarada (Hokkaido, Japan).

## $(Tl,Pb)_2As_5S_9$

| | |
|---|---|
| Colour: | scarlet–vermilion to deep cherry red, strong red internal reflections |
| Lustre; opacity: | submetallic; subtranslucent to opaque |
| Streak: | red |
| Hardness: | 1.5–2 |
| Specific gravity: | 4.6 |
| Cleavage; fracture: | good; conchoidal, brittle |
| Habit: | acicular or prismatic crystals; granular masses |
| Crystal system: | orthorhombic |

# Boulangerite

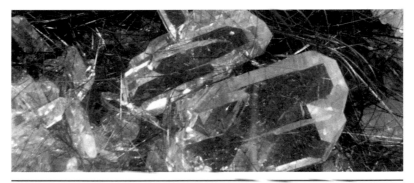

Boulangerite is a minor ore of lead named after the French mining engineer C. Boulanger (1810–1849). It can form thin, acicular crystals up to 2cm (¾in) long, resembling fibres. Boulangerite and jamesonite have been called feather ores or plumosite, after the feathery habit of some varieties. Thin fibres of boulangerite are flexible, unlike the brittle jamesonite. Disseminated boulangerite can easily be overlooked, being mistaken for stray hairs. Boulangerite occurs in hydrothermal veins in lead, zinc and antimony deposits. It is found at Pribram (Czech Republic), Molières (France), Bottino (Italy), Noche Buena Mine (Zacatecas, Mexico), Boliden (Sweden), Claustal (Germany) and Stevens County (Washington, USA).

## $Pb_5Sb_4S_{11}$

| | |
|---|---|
| Colour: | grey |
| Lustre; opacity: | dull, metallic; opaque |
| Streak: | black |
| Hardness: | 2.5–3 |
| Specific gravity: | 5.8–6.2 |
| Cleavage; fracture: | good; brittle but flexible as thin needles |
| Habit: | acicular crystals; fibrous masses or tufts, disseminated |
| Crystal system: | monoclinic |
| Other: | melts easily |

# Realgar

Realgar, named from the Arabic *rahj al jahr* for 'mine powder', is often found with yellow orpiment ($As_2S_3$), to which it alters on exposure to light and air. Its colour and transparency contrast with the grey, opaque nature of most other sulphides. Realgar has been used in fireworks (to give a white colour) and paints. Like sulphur, which occurs as rings of eight atoms, it is in the form of alternating sulphur and arsenic atoms $As_4S_4$. Realgar mostly occurs in veins with orpiment, cinnabar or stibnite, but may be found in limestones, clays, volcanic rocks and hot springs. Crystals are rare, but are found at Nagyag (Romania), Binnental (Switzerland), Matra (Corsica), Manhattan (Nevada, USA) and King County (Washington, USA).

## AsS

| | |
|---|---|
| Colour: | orange-red to red |
| Lustre; opacity: | resinous; semi-transparent |
| Streak: | yellow-orange |
| Hardness: | 1.5–2 |
| Specific gravity: | 3.5–3.6 |
| Cleavage; fracture: | perfect; conchoidal |
| Habit: | rare small, stubby, prismatic crystals; compact aggregates; films |
| Crystal system: | monoclinic |

# Orpiment

Orpiment is a rare mineral often found in association with realgar. Its name comes from the Latin *auripigmentum*, meaning 'golden pigment'. On standing, orpiment will slowly turn into a powder, a process accelerated by light. Orpiment was traded as a pigment throughout the Roman Empire and used as a medicine in China. Orpiment is deposited around hot springs and volcanic fumaroles, associated with realgar and, sometimes, cinnabar. It also occurs in metamorphosed dolerites and in hydrothermal veins. The major deposits of orpiment are in Zashuran (Iran), Kurdistan (Turkey), Georgia and Manhattan (Nevada, USA). Large crystals have been found at Shimen (Hunan, China) and Quiruvica (La Libertad, Peru).

## As$_2$S$_3$

| | |
|---|---|
| Colour: | orange-yellow to yellow |
| Lustre; opacity: | greasy, pearly on fracture surfaces; translucent to transparent |
| Streak: | yellow |
| Hardness: | 1.52 |
| Specific gravity: | 3.48 |
| Cleavage; fracture: | perfect; flaky |
| Habit: | crystals rare, as small, flat prisms, occasionally fibrous; crusts or bladed masses, earthy, powdery |
| Crystal system: | monoclinic |

# Rammelsbergite

Rammelsbergite, named after the German chemist Karl Rammelsberg
(1813–1899), is rare and difficult to distinguish from other sulphides, often
being mistaken for gersdorfite (NiAsS). It occurs in hydrothermal veins together
with nickel and cobalt minerals. Associated minerals include skutterudite,
lollingtonite, safflorite, nickeline, bismuth and silver. Rammelsberg is found at
Franklin and Sterling Hill (New Jersey, USA), Mohawk Mine (Michigan, USA),
Coniston (Cumbria, England), St Marie-aux-Mines (France), Legnica (Poland),
Löllington-Hüttenberg (Austria) and the type locality, Schneeberg (Saxony,
Germany). Large crystals come from Bou Azzer (Morocco).

## $NiAs_2$

| | |
|---|---|
| Colour: | tin white with a faint pinkish hue, darker tarnish |
| Lustre; opacity: | metallic; opaque |
| Streak: | black |
| Hardness: | 5.5 |
| Specific gravity: | 7.1 |
| Cleavage; fracture: | indistinct; uneven |
| Habit: | small crystals as imperfect prisms; granular, massive, radiating aggregates |
| Crystal system: | orthorhombic |

# Jordanite

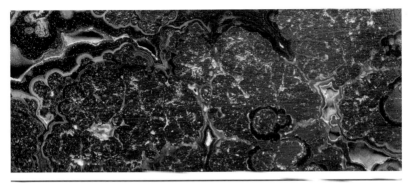

Jordanite is a rare mineral, named after the German mineralogist H. Jordan (1808–1887). It forms a series with antimony-rich geocronite, $Pb_{14}(Sb,As)_6S_{23}$. It occurs in hydrothermal veins and metamorphosed lead-arsenic deposits in dolomite, and may be associated with galena, sphalerite, pyrite and anatase. The most important occurrence is at Lengenbach (Binnental, Switzerland). In the Seravezza marble in Tuscany, Italy, jordanite occurs in cavities, as lustrous, lead-grey hexagonal crystals up to 1cm (½in). Other localities include Săcărîmb (Romania), Wiesloch (Germany), Zuni Mine (Colorado, USA) and Sinking Valley (Pennsylvania, USA). It has also been found in 'black smoker' chimneys on ocean floors.

## $Pb_{14}(As,Sb)_6S_{23}$

| | |
|---|---|
| Colour: | lead-grey, commonly tarnished and iridescent |
| Lustre; opacity: | metallic; opaque |
| Streak: | black |
| Hardness: | 3 |
| Specific gravity: | 6.4 |
| Cleavage; fracture: | perfect; conchoidal, brittle |
| Habit: | crystals deeply striated prismatic, and tabular, pseudohexagonal twins; granular, globular and botryoidal aggregates |
| Crystal system: | monoclinic |

# Jamesonite

J amesonite, also known as antimony glance or grey antimony, was named for the Scottish mineralogist Robert Jameson (1774–1854). It is characterized by hair-like fibres, which may be thick and felted, or may occur as individual 'hairs', and is sometimes also known as feather ore. Jamesonite may be distinguished from the acicular mineral boulangerite because it has brittle rather than flexible crystals and from acicular yellow millerite by colour. It occurs in hydrothermal lead-silver-zinc veins. It may be associated with pyrite, sphalerite, arsenopyrite, siderite, dolomite, calcite, rhodochrosite or quartz. Notable localities are Cornwall (England), Herja Mine (Maramures, Romania) and Zacatecas (Mexico).

## $Pb_4FeSb_6S_{14}$

| | |
|---|---|
| Colour: | lead grey, iridescent tarnish |
| Lustre; opacity: | metallic or silky; opaque |
| Streak: | grey–black |
| Hardness: | 2.5 |
| Specific gravity: | 5.63–5.78 |
| Cleavage; fracture: | perfect basal (perpendicular to length); uneven |
| Habit: | very elongated acicular or fibrous crystals, occasionally prismatic; usually compact or felted masses, may be radial or plumose |
| Crystal system: | monoclinic |

# Cosalite

Cosalite is a rare mineral named after the Cosalá Mine (Sinaloa, Mexico). It occurs in hydrothermal deposits in lead sulphide ores, in contact skarns and in pegmatites. Associated minerals include chalcopyrite, pyrite, sphalerite, skutterudite, bismuth, tremolite, diopside, epidote and quartz. It forms hairlike crystals (found at Carrock Fell Mine, in Cumbria, England) or elongated prisms (as at Limestone Quarry in Saxony, Germany). Other good localities are Kara Oba (Kazakhstan), Braichyroen (Snowdon, Wales), Cobalt (Ontario, Canada) and Hecla Mine, Dundas (Tasmania, Australia). Kudriavite, $(Cd,Pb)Bi_2S_4$, is a closely related mineral found around fumaroles (e.g. Kudriavy Volcano, Kuril Islands, Russia).

## $Pb_2Bi_2S_5$

| | |
|---|---|
| **Colour:** | lead grey or steel grey to silver-white |
| **Lustre; opacity:** | metallic; opaque |
| **Streak:** | black |
| **Hardness:** | 2.5–3 |
| **Specific gravity:** | 6.86–6.99 |
| **Cleavage; fracture:** | very rare; uneven |
| **Habit:** | long prisms, vertically striated, hairlike; radial and granular aggregates |
| **Crystal system:** | orthorhombic |

# Halite

H alite, or rock salt, typically forms through the evaporation of enclosed bodies of sea water. It may form a thick, stratified deposit, or domes where the low-density salt has risen through overlying sediments, as along the Gulf Coast (USA). Halite also forms as a volcanic sublimate or as a cave deposit. It is associated with other evaporites, such as sylvite (KCl), gypsum, anhydrite and dolomite. Rock salt is used as common table salt, and its taste is characteristic. It is an important raw material in the chlor-alkali industry, drilling muds, aluminium purification and many other industries. Well-known deposits include those at Stassfurt (Germany) and in Texas and New Mexico (USA). Good crystals are found at Wieliczka (Galicia, Poland).

## NaCl

| | |
|---|---|
| **Colour:** | white when pure, greyish, pinkish, bluish, violet, orange |
| **Lustre; opacity:** | vitreous, greasy; transparent to translucent |
| **Streak:** | white |
| **Hardness:** | 2.5 |
| **Specific gravity:** | 2.1–2.2 |
| **Cleavage; fracture:** | perfect cubic; conchoidal |
| **Habit:** | crystals cubic or as octahedra, skeletal 'hopper' crystals; granular, massive, rarely stalactitic or fibrous |
| **Crystal system:** | cubic |

# Villiaumite

Villiaumite is a rare mineral named after the French explorer Maxime Villiaume, who collected the mineral from cavities in nepheline syenites at Rouma (Islands of Los, Guinea). It is strongly coloured, with some shades of red being unique in minerals. It is found in nepheline syenites and their pegmatites, in which alkali metals such as sodium, lithium and potassium are concentrated. Associated minerals include nepheline, aegerine, sodalite and zeolites. Villiaumite is soluble in water and displays weak red fluoresecence under shortwave ultraviolet light. Most specimens come from the Kola Peninsula (Russia); good crystals are found at Mont Saint-Hilaire (Quebec, Canada) and Windhoek (Namibia).

## NaF

| | |
|---|---|
| Colour: | carmine red, lavender pink to light orange |
| Lustre; opacity: | vitreous; transparent |
| Streak: | white, pinkish |
| Hardness: | 2.5 |
| Specific gravity: | 2.79 |
| Cleavage; fracture: | perfect in three directions forming cubes; conchoidal |
| Habit: | rarely cubic or octahedral crystals; granular aggregates, massive |
| Crystal system: | cubic |

# Chlorargyrite

Chlorargyrite, a silver chloride mineral, was named after the Latin *argentum* (silver) and the Greek *chloro* (pale green). Also called cerargyrite or horn silver, it forms a complete solid-solution with bromargyrite (AgBr). It is pale when fresh, but darkens to brownish-purple on exposure to light. Chlorargyrite dissolves in ammonia, but not in nitric acid. It forms as a secondary mineral in the weathered and enriched zones of silver deposits, especially in arid regions, and can form very rich albeit small silver ore deposits. The type locality is Saxony (Germany); it occurs elsewhere at Lake Valley District (New Mexico, USA), Atonopah (Nevada, USA), Broken Hill (NSW, Australia), Freiburg (Saxony, Germany) and Atacama (Chile).

## AgCl

| | |
|---|---|
| **Colour:** | colourless when fresh, pale grey, yellowish; can darken |
| **Lustre; opacity:** | resinous, waxy, adamantine; transparent to translucent |
| **Streak:** | white, shining |
| **Hardness:** | 1.5–2.5 |
| **Specific gravity:** | 5.55 (6.5 in bromargyrite) |
| **Cleavage; fracture:** | absent; uneven to subconchoidal, sectile, ductile |
| **Habit:** | crystals rare, as cubes, or modified by octahedra; usually massive or in crusts, columnar |
| **Crystal system:** | cubic |

# Iodargyrite

Iodargyrite, or iodyrite, was named after its chemical composition (from the Greek *iodes* meaning 'violet') and the Greek *argyros* for 'silver'. A very rare secondary mineral, it forms in the oxidized parts of silver deposits. The type locality is Albarradón Mine (Zacatecas, Mexico), but the best place for specimens is Broken Hill (NSW, Australia), the world's largest silver-lead-zinc deposit. Iodargyrite is also important for other halides, such as the very rare iodides marshite (copper), miersite (silver and copper), perroudite (a mercury silver halide), and bright yellow crystals of bromargyrite (a silver halide). Other locations include Atacama (Chile), Dzhezkazgan (Kazakhstan) and Nevada (USA).

## AgI

| | |
|---|---|
| Colour: | colourless, becomes yellowish on exposure to light |
| Lustre; opacity: | greasy to adamantine, pearly on cleavage surfaces; transparent |
| Streak: | white or yellow, shiny |
| Hardness: | 1–1.5 |
| Specific gravity: | 5.7 |
| Cleavage; fracture: | perfect basal; conchoidal, sectile and flexible |
| Habit: | crystals prismatic, platy, barrel-shaped; scales, powdered |
| Crystal system: | hexagonal |

# Fluorite

Fluorite, or fluorspar, is a popular mineral, which can fluoresce as a result of impurities such as yttrium. Some specimens phosphoresce; others thermoluminesce (glow when heated, as at Franklin in New Jersey, USA, and Mont Saint-Hilarie in Quebec, Canada) or triboluminesce (glow when crushed or struck). Fluorite forms in hydrothermal veins as a gangue mineral associated with sulphides (e.g. galena or sphalerite), barite and quartz, and as an accessory in granite and granite pegmatites. It is an important industrial mineral, used as a flux in iron smelting, as a source of fluorine, as special optical lenses, and as a rare gemstone. The main mining areas are Canada, USA, Russia, Mexico and Italy.

## $CaF_2$

| | |
|---|---|
| **Colour:** | colourless, white, yellow, green, purple and blue |
| **Lustre; opacity:** | vitreous; transparent to translucent |
| **Streak:** | white |
| **Hardness:** | 4 |
| **Specific gravity:** | 3.18 |
| **Cleavage; fracture:** | perfect octahedral; subconchoidal to uneven |
| **Habit:** | crystals common, as cubes, octahedra or rarely dodecahedra; nodular, granular aggregates, earthy masses |
| **Crystal system:** | cubic |

# Fluorite: Gem Varieties

Fluorite shows a wide range of colours. The most famous variety is Blue John, a purple and yellow banded variety from Castleton (Derbyshire, England), which has been used for ornaments and jewellery. The Ancient Greeks and the Ancient Egyptians, and the Chinese have used it for decorative purposes for over 300 years. Rather soft for general use as a gemstone and too well cleaved to be easily cut, it can nonetheless be brightly polished and cut into cabochons, protected by rock crystal (quartz). A deposit of colourful highly silicated fluorite discovered quite recently in Utah has been given a number of fanciful names, such as bertandite and Picasso stone. More properly called opalized fluorite, it makes attractive cabochon gems.

## $CaF_2$

| | |
|---|---|
| **Colour:** | colourless, white, yellow, green, purple and blue |
| **Lustre; opacity:** | vitreous; transparent to translucent |
| **Streak:** | white |
| **Hardness:** | 4 |
| **Specific gravity:** | 3.18 |
| **Cleavage; fracture:** | perfect octahedral; subconchoidal to uneven |
| **Habit:** | crystals common, as cubes, octahedra or rarely dodecahedra; nodular, granular aggregates, earthy masses |
| **Crystal system:** | cubic |

# Sal-ammoniac

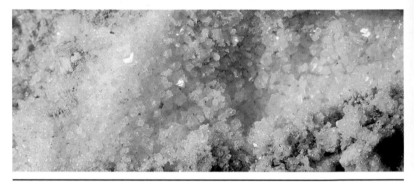

Sal-ammoniac forms in volcanic regions around fumaroles, with solid white crystals forming directly from the bluish ammonium chloride vapour as a sublimate (i.e. there is no liquid phase). It has a pungent, cool and saline taste. Sal-ammoniac forms on Vesuvius (Campania), Etna (Sicily), and other southern Italian volcanoes, Mont Pelée (Martinique), Parícutin (Mexico) and Kilauea (Hawaii). Associated minerals include sulphur, realgar and orpiment. Crystals must be collected quickly, as they will dissolve in the first rain shower. Sal-ammoniac formation is also associated with burning coal seams, as at Duttweiler (Saarland, Germany), and, unusually, with guano on Cicna and Guanape Islands (Peru).

## $NH_4Cl$

| | |
|---|---|
| Colour: | colourless, white, yellow, reddish or brown |
| Lustre; opacity: | vitreous; transparent to translucent |
| Streak: | white |
| Hardness: | 1–2 |
| Specific gravity: | 1.53 |
| Cleavage; fracture: | poor; conchoidal to earthy |
| Habit: | crystals as cubes, octahedra or dodecahedra, also skeletal or dendritic; generally efflorescent or encrusting |
| Crystal system: | cubic |

# Cryolite

Cryolite is an uncommon mineral of very restricted distribution. It possesses the unusual property that, if submerged in water, it becomes almost invisible, since it has a refractive index of 1.33, close to that of water. It is soluble in sulphuric acid, producing fumes of hydrofluoric acid. Cryolite occurs only in pegmatites, probably formed as a precipitate from fluoride-rich solutions. The most notable occurrence is in a granitic pegmatite at Ivigtut (Greenland), where it is associated with topaz, siderite, galena, microcline, fluorite and other unusual fluorides. It is also found in a topaz mine at Miask (Urals, Russia). Artificial cryolite has now replaced the natural mineral as a flux in the extraction of aluminium from bauxite.

## $Na_3AlF_6$

| | |
|---|---|
| Colour: | usually colourless to white, or grey, reddish, brownish |
| Lustre; opacity: | vitreous to greasy, pearly; transparent |
| Streak: | white |
| Hardness: | 2.5–3 |
| Specific gravity: | 2.95 |
| Cleavage; fracture: | absent, although has three partings; uneven, brittle |
| Habit: | pseudo-cubic crystals, commonly twinned; granular aggregates often arranged in a parquet-like pattern |
| Crystal system: | monoclinic |

# Carnallite

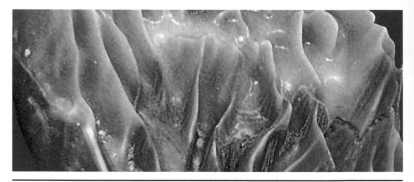

Carnallite is a rare mineral that sometimes fluoresces, and will colour a flame violet due to its potassium content. It has a bitter, salty taste, will readily dissolve in water (emitting a creaking sound), and must be kept in sealed containers. Carnallite is one of the last minerals to precipitate in an evaporating basin, in particular conditions that do not exist today. It occurs with other potassium and magnesium evaporites such as sylvite, kainite and kieserite. It is a valuable source of potash (for fertilizers) and magnesium. The most famous locality is the Stassfurt potash deposit (Germany); it also occurs in Carlsbad (New Mexico, USA), Paradox Basin (Colorado and Utah, USA) and the Perm Basin (Russia).

## $KMgCl_3.6H_2O$

| | |
|---|---|
| Colour: | colourless, milky white, yellow, pink, brown, rarely blue |
| Lustre; opacity: | vitreous to greasy; transparent to translucent |
| Streak: | white |
| Hardness: | 2.5 |
| Specific gravity: | 1.6 (very light) |
| Cleavage; fracture: | absent; conchoidal |
| Habit: | pseudo-hexagonal pyramidal crystals, rare; granular and fibrous aggregates forming layers |
| Crystal system: | orthorhombic |

# Atacamite

A tacamite is named from the Atacama Desert in Chile, which is one of the most arid regions in the world. Dark green itself, atacamite is often associated with other coloured minerals such as green malachite, red cuprite, blue-green chrysocolla, and also gypsum. It generally forms through the oxidation of copper minerals in arid, salty conditions, and is found in many places in Chile. It occurs as a fumarolic deposit on Vesuvius (Italy) and Etna (Sicily, Italy), and through the weathering of sulphides formed as black smoker deposits around volcanic vents on the ocean floor. It also forms through the alteration of bronze and copper antiquities, and is found in the slag heaps at Laurion (Attica, Greece).

## $Cu_2Cl(OH)_3$

| | |
|---|---|
| Colour: | bright green, dark emerald green to black-green |
| Lustre; opacity: | vitreous to adamantine; transparent to translucent |
| Streak: | apple green |
| Hardness: | 3–3.5 |
| Specific gravity: | 3.76 |
| Cleavage; fracture: | good; conchoidal, brittle |
| Habit: | crystals acicular, striated, or tabular; massive, as fibrous aggregates or granular |
| Crystal system: | orthorhombic |

# Cotunnite

Cotunnite forms as a volcanic sublimate, its type locality being Monte Somma-Vesuvius (Italy). It was named in honour of Domenico Cotugno (Cottunius) (1736–1822), an Italian physician and professor of anatomy from Naples (Italy). It was formed during the 1975–76 fissure eruption of Tolbachik volcano (Kamchatka Peninsula, Russia), where it is associated with halite, silver, gold, tenorite, and rare minerals such as burnsite and ponomarevite. It also forms by the alteration of galena in saline environments, and as an alteration product of lead-bearing slag or other archaeological material after immersion in sea water. Hence, like diaboleite, cotunnite occurs in the ancient slag heaps of Laurion (Greece).

## $PbCl_2$

| | |
|---|---|
| Colour: | colourless, pale green, pale yellow, white |
| Lustre; opacity: | adamantine, silky, pearly; transparent to translucent |
| Streak: | white |
| Hardness: | 2.5 |
| Specific gravity: | 5.8 |
| Cleavage; fracture: | perfect; conchoidal to uneven |
| Habit: | prismatic or acicular crystals, or skeletal; in aggregates of radiating sprays, massive, granular, crusts, pseudomorphs |
| Crystal system: | orthorhombic |

# Boleite

Boleite is an unusual indigo blue colour, and makes a most attractive collector's item, although crystals are rarely cut as gems. It was named after its type locality, Boleó (Baja California, Mexico). Although tetragonal, it is always twinned, and as a result appears as cubes, with corners sometimes cut by octahedral faces. A secondary mineral, it forms from the alteration of sulphide deposits by chlorine-bearing aqueous solutions. It may be associated with atacamite, anglesite, cerussite or gypsum. Noted localities include Broken Hill (NSW, Australia), Mammoth District (Arizona, USA) and the Mendip Hills (Somerset, England). It also forms in Laurion (Greece), where smelter slag has been immersed in the sea.

## $Pb_9Cu_8Ag_3Cl_{21}(OH)_{16} \cdot H_2O$

| | |
|---|---|
| Colour: | light indigo blue, azure-blue, dark blue |
| Lustre; opacity: | weakly vitreous to pearly on cleavage surfaces; translucent to transparent |
| Streak: | light green, light blue |
| Hardness: | 3.5 |
| Specific gravity: | 4.8–5.1 |
| Cleavage; fracture: | perfect; uneven |
| Habit: | normally as pseudo-cubic twinned crystals |
| Crystal system: | tetragonal |

# Diaboleite

Diaboleite comes from the Greek *dia* ('difference') and boleite (the mineral); it should not be confused with pseudoboleite, $(Pb_5Cu_4Cl_{10}(OH)_8.2H_2O)$, meaning false boleite. Diaboleite is a very rare secondary mineral, its type locality being the Mendip Hills (Somerset, England). The other main locality is in the copper porphyry deposits of Mammoth Mine (Arizona, USA), associated mainly with cerussite, wulfenite, quartz and hemimorphite, and also with boleite, linarite and pseudoboleite. It occurs in the 2000-year-old mineral slags of Laurion (Greece), many of which are now in the sea. This has led to the production of many new minerals, including laurionite, the first slag mineral to be described (in 1887).

## $Pb_2CuCl_2(OH)_4$

| | |
|---|---|
| **Colour:** | dark blue |
| **Lustre; opacity:** | adamantine; transparent to translucent |
| **Streak:** | blue |
| **Hardness:** | 2.5 |
| **Specific gravity:** | 5.48 (extremely heavy for a translucent mineral) |
| **Cleavage; fracture:** | perfect; conchoidal |
| **Habit:** | very small tabular crystals; also as platy aggregates, grains, or as encrustations |
| **Crystal system:** | tetragonal |

# Zincite

Although zinc oxide itself is colourless, zincite is almost invariably coloured, due to manganese and iron impurities. The more attractive deep red crystals have earned it the name ruby zinc (at Franklin, where it is mined); the red colour is due to the presence of manganese dioxide or hematite. It was one of the first minerals described in an American mineralogy journal. Zincite is found as a primary mineral in metamorphosed ore deposits and as a secondary mineral in weathered zinc ore deposits. It is associated with franklinite, willemite and calcite at Sterling Hill and Franklin (New Jersey, USA): other locations are Tsumeb (Namibia), Kapushi, (Katanga, Congo) and in the ash from Mt St Helens (Washington, USA).

## ZnO

| | |
|---|---|
| Colour: | yellow, orange, red, brown, rarely green or colourless |
| Lustre; opacity: | subadamantine; transparent, more often translucent |
| Streak: | yellow–orange |
| Hardness: | 4 |
| Specific gravity: | 5.68 |
| Cleavage; fracture: | perfect; irregular |
| Habit: | hemimorphic crystals, hexagonal prisms terminated differently at either end; granular, massive and foliated in veins |
| Crystal system: | hexagonal |

# Cuprite

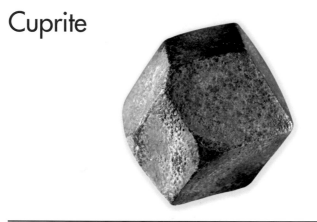

Cuprite is known as red copper oxide, which distinguishes it from CuO, or black copper oxide. Cuprite oxidizes slowly in air, tarnishing the surface. It is an important copper ore, mainly being found in dull massive bodies. Fine, fibrous crystals are called chalcotricite; ruby copper is a gem-quality crystal found at Santa Rita (New Mexico, USA) and Onganyo (Namibia). It occurs as a secondary mineral in the oxidized zones of copper ore deposits, accompanied typically by malachite, azurite, chalcocite and native copper. Cuprite often occurs with oxides of iron as an earthy red-brown material known as tile ore. It is found at Tsumeb (Namibia), Cornwall (England), Chessy (France) and Bisbee (Arizona, USA).

## $Cu_2O$

| | |
|---|---|
| Colour: | red to dark red |
| Lustre; opacity: | submetallic, adamantine, earthy; translucent |
| Streak: | brownish-red |
| Hardness: | 3.5–4 |
| Specific gravity: | 5.8–6.1 |
| Cleavage; fracture: | poor; irregular, conchoidal |
| Habit: | crystals usually octahedral, sometimes dodecahedral or cubes, rarely needles; mostly massive, granular or earthy |
| Crystal system: | cubic |

# Perovskite

Perovskite is mined not for titanium, but for rare earths in it such as niobium and cerium. Named after the Russian mineralogist L. Perovski (1792–1856), perovskite has a structure well known among crystallographers adopted by superconducting ceramics and high-pressure minerals in the Earth's mantle. It occurs in silica-poor igneous rocks and metamophic rocks. Associations include rare earth minerals such as loparite ($(Na,Ce)TiO_3$), as well as pyrochlore, ilmenite, leucite and titanite. Good crystals have been obtained from Alnö (Sweden), Magnet Cove (Arkansas, USA) and the Urals (Russia); other locations include Val Malenco and Vesuvius (Italy), Bagagem (Brazil), Kaiserstuhl (Germany) and Quebec (Canada).

## $CaTiO_3$

| | |
|---|---|
| Colour: | red-brown, grey-black, yellow |
| Lustre; opacity: | adamantine, submetallic; translucent |
| Streak: | pale yellow |
| Hardness: | 5.5 |
| Specific gravity: | 4.0 |
| Cleavage; fracture: | none; subconchoidal to indistinct |
| Habit: | crystals pseudocubic, often striated parallel to edges; granular aggregates and reniform masses |
| Crystal system: | orthorhombic |

# Tenorite

Tenorite, or black copper oxide, is a rare mineral named after the Italian botanist Michel Tenore (1781–1861). Earthy specimens containing tenorite are called melaconite. It is formed in the oxidized zones of copper deposits, associated with azurite, malachite, chalcocite, cuprite and limonite, and occasionally found in volcanic sublimates. The bladed crystals are collectable specimens, and botryoidal tenorite provides a contrasting dull, grey setting as a matrix for bright blue-green chrysocolla. Tenorite occurs at Val d'Ossola (Italy), Cornwall (England), Leadhills (Scotland), Rio Tinto (Spain), the Urals and Kamchatka (Russia), Bisbee (Arizona, USA), Chuquicamata (Chile) and Tsumeb (Namibia).

## CuO

| | |
|---|---|
| **Colour:** | steel-grey to black |
| **Lustre; opacity:** | metallic, dull; opaque |
| **Streak:** | black, greenish |
| **Hardness:** | 3–4 |
| **Specific gravity:** | 5.8–6.4 |
| **Cleavage; fracture:** | indistinct; conchoidal to irregular |
| **Habit:** | crystals usually elongated plates, often striated and serrated edges; scaly and earthy aggregates; encrustations |
| **Crystal system:** | monoclinic |

# Gahnite

Gahnite, known as automolite or zinc-spinel, is named after its discoverer, J. Gahn (1745–1818), the Swedish chemist who discovered manganese. It occurs in granite pegmatites and metamorphic rocks and as a placer deposit. It is associated with galena, sphalerite and magnetite. Gahnite is usually found as small crystals in the type localities Falun (Sweden), Silberberg (Bavaria, Germany) and Tiriolo (Calabria, Italy), but larger crystals have been obtained from mines in Franklin and Sterling Hill (New Jersey, USA). Other deposits are in Connecticut (USA), Minas Gerais (Brazil), Smilovne (Bulgaria) and Victoria Range (New Zealand). A lead-bearing variety called limaite is found at Ponto de Lima (Portugal).

## $ZnAl_2O_4$

| | |
|---|---|
| Colour: | green to bluish green |
| Lustre; opacity: | vitreous, greasy; translucent, opaque on edges |
| Streak: | grey |
| Hardness: | 7.5–8 |
| Specific gravity: | 4.6 |
| Cleavage; fracture: | indistinct; conchoidal |
| Habit: | crystals; granular aggregates, grains |
| Crystal system: | cubic, but twinning is ubiquitous and crystals may appear trigonal |

# Spinel

The term 'spinel' is also used as a general term for minerals of formula $AB_2O_4$ such as gahnite, hercynite ($FeAl_2O_4$) and galaxite ($MnAl_2O_4$). Spinel has been mistaken for ruby and sapphire; the so-called Timur Ruby in the British Crown jewels is a ruby spinel. Spinel is found in contact-metamorphosed rocks, in igneous rocks and as a placer deposit. Synthetic spinels have been produced as artificial gemstones since 1910. The word spinel comes from the Latin *spina*, for 'little thorn', after the sharpness of its crystals. The best gem-quality spinels come from gravels in Sri Lanka, Myanmar and Madagascar. Good crystals are found at Vesuvius and Lazio (Italy), Orange County (New York, USA) and Sterling Hill (New Jersey, USA).

## $MgAl_2O_4$

| | |
|---|---|
| **Colour:** | colourless pure; red, blue, green, black |
| **Lustre; opacity:** | vitreous; transparent to translucent |
| **Streak:** | white to grey or brown |
| **Hardness:** | 7.5–8 |
| **Specific gravity:** | 3.5–4.1 |
| **Cleavage; fracture:** | none, octahedral parting; conchoidals |
| **Habit:** | octahedral crystals; granular aggregates; grains |
| **Crystal system:** | cubic |

# Magnetite

**M**agnetite, or magnetic oxide of iron, is the essential constituent of lodestone, known since ancient times. It is a major iron ore and is mined in vast quantities for the iron and steel industries; slag is further worked to recover vanadium and phosphorus. Swedish magnetite, containing some silicates, is used to make a very hard silicon steel. Magnetite is widespread among many igneous and metamorphic rocks, especially mafic and ultramafic rocks in high temperature mineral veins. It is also found in river and marine sediments and in dune deposits. Good crystals come from Val Malenco and Val de Vizze (Italy), Binnental (Swizerland) and Pfitschtal (Austria). Lodestone is famously found at Magnet Cove (Arkansas, USA).

## $Fe_3O_4$

| | |
|---|---|
| **Colour:** | black |
| **Lustre; opacity:** | lustre, submetallic, dull; opaque |
| **Streak:** | black |
| **Hardness:** | 5.5–6.5 |
| **Specific gravity:** | 5.2 |
| **Cleavage; fracture:** | none, octahedral parting; conchoidal |
| **Habit:** | crystals octahedral, sometimes dodecahedral; granular or massive |
| **Crystal system:** | cubic |

# Chromite

Chromite is chemically related to magnetite, chromium atoms replacing those of iron; it is also magnetic, but weaker than magnetite. It is the only commercial ore of chromium, which is used in steels, especially stainless steel. Chromium salts are used in electroplating, leather tanning, fireproofing fabrics and in paints. Chromite is used as a refractory for lining furnaces in the ceramic industry. The range in specific gravity is a reflection of its contamination with magnesiochromite ($MgCr_2O_4$), spinel ($MgAl_2O_4$) and related minerals. Chromite occurs in ultrabasic rocks and serpentinites, and as a placer deposit. Large deposits are mined in South Africa, Russia, Albania, Turkey, Zimbabwe and the Philippines.

## $FeCr_2O_4$

| | |
|---|---|
| **Colour:** | brownish black to black |
| **Lustre; opacity:** | metallic to submetallic; opaque |
| **Streak:** | dark brown |
| **Hardness:** | 5.5 |
| **Specific gravity:** | 4.1–5.1 |
| **Cleavage; fracture:** | none; uneven, conchoidal |
| **Habit:** | crystals octahedral, rare; usually massive, granular |
| **Crystal system:** | cubic |
| **Other:** | weakly magnetic; insoluble in acids |

# Franklinite

Franklinite is a spinel group mineral named after its type locality of Franklin. White calcite, green willemite and red zincite often accompany franklinite, and specimens displaying combinations of these are very collectable. Franklinite occurs in beds and veins in high temperature metamorphosed dolomites, associated with calcite, zincite, willemite, rhodonite, magnetite and garnet. It is also found in some manganese and iron deposits. The most famous and most mined location is that at Franklin and Sterling Hill (New Jersey, USA), which has produced crystals up to 30cm (12in) large. Other locations are Långban (Sweden), Hranicna (Czech Republic), Atasui (Khazakstan), Sayan (Siberia, Russia) and Western Australia.

## $ZnFe_2O_4$

| | |
|---|---|
| Colour: | black |
| Lustre; opacity: | metallic, with reddish internal reflections; opaque |
| Streak: | red–brown |
| Hardness: | 5.5–6.5 |
| Specific gravity: | 5.1–5.2 |
| Cleavage; fracture: | imperfect; conchoidal |
| Habit: | octahedral, sometimes dodecahedral crystals; massive aggregates |
| Crystal system: | cubic |

# Minium

Minium, red oxide of lead or simply red lead, has been used as a pigment, especially in anti-rusting paints, although lead's toxicity has lowered demand. Its unusual name comes from the river Minius in northwest Spain. It is formed by the alteration of galena and cerrussite, under extreme oxidizing conditions, and its presence may function as an indicator of the degree of oxidation. Some specimens from Broken Hill (NSW, Australia) are particularly good, but are said to have been the result of a mine fire. Its powdery form can disguise its high density. Minium is found at Badenweiler and Horhausen (Germany), Monteponi (Sardinia, Italy), Bolaños and Zimapan (Mexico), Leadhills (Scotland) and Broken Hill (Australia).

## $Pb_3O_4$

| | |
|---|---|
| **Colour:** | light red to red-brown |
| **Lustre; opacity:** | dull to greasy; opaque |
| **Streak:** | orange-yellow |
| **Hardness:** | 2–3 |
| **Specific gravity:** | 8.2 |
| **Cleavage; fracture:** | perfect; earthy |
| **Habit:** | rare, scaly crystals; usually powdered or massive aggregates |
| **Crystal system:** | tetragonal |

# Chrysoberyl

Chrysoberyl is hard and durable, making a fine stone that is used in jewellery, though somewhat lacking in 'fire'. A rare, much valued variety is alexandrite, which is green in daylight, but appears reddish in artificial (tungsten filament) light. Cat's eye has inclusions of fine needles of rutile and is most prized when golden yellow-brown. Chrysoberyl is found in pegmatites and mica schists around granite intrusions, and in alluvial and marine deposits. It has been obtained from the Ural Mountains for thousands of years. Alexandrite crystals 1–10cm (½–4in) in length occur in the Urals' Takowaja River. Alluvial deposits in Brazil and Sri Lanka produce cat's eye. Fine transparent yellow-green crystals occur at Espirito Santo (Brazil).

## BeAl$_2$O$_4$

| | |
|---|---|
| Colour: | colourless, grey, brown, green, yellow |
| Lustre; opacity: | subadamantine, silky; transparent to translucent |
| Streak: | white |
| Hardness: | 8.5 |
| Specific gravity: | 3.7 |
| Cleavage; fracture: | good; conchoidal |
| Habit: | prismatic, tabular crystals, often pseudohexagonal twins; grains and pebbles in alluvial deposits |
| Crystal system: | orthorhombic |

# Corundum

Extremely hard (equal to silicon carbide and second only to diamond), corundum is a gem mineral (ruby and sapphire) and is used as an abrasive in the form of emery for cutting, grinding and drilling. Grey-coloured masses are often forms that have been altered by hydrothermal solutions to margarite or zoisite. Corundum occurs in igneous rocks, in contact metamorphosed shales and bauxite, in pegmatites and metamorphosed limestones and as a placer deposit. Emery deposits are granular masses, often with magnetite, hematite and spinel. Good localities are Mogok (Myanmar), Sri Lanka, Madagascar, Glebe Hill (South Africa), Ardnamurchan (Scotland), Naxos (Greece) and the central Urals (Russia).

## $Al_2O_3$

| | |
|---|---|
| Colour: | colourless, grey or brown granular mass; can be red, blue, yellow, green, purple or colourless gems |
| Lustre; opacity: | adamantine; transparent to semi-opaque |
| Streak: | white |
| Hardness: | 9 |
| Specific gravity: | 4 |
| Cleavage; fracture: | none; uneven to conchoidal |
| Habit: | rough prisms or barrel shaped crystals bounded by steep pyramids; massive, granular |
| Crystal system: | trigonal |

# Corundum: Gem Varieties

$R$uby is red, gem-quality corundum widely used in jewellery. The red colour varies with the content of chromium and iron oxides. A very rare pink-orange coloured stone is called papdaradscha. All other corundum gem varieties are called sapphire; the most popular is coloured shades of blue by iron and titanium impurities. Yellow sapphire, formerly known as oriental topaz, occurs alone or banded with blue sapphire to give a green form of sapphire known since medieval times as oriental peridot. Star rubies and sapphires are opalescent and reflect light in the form of three- or six-pointed stars, an effect called asterism. Fine rubies and sapphires come from Myanmar (Burma) Sri Lanka and India.

## $Al_2O_3$

| | |
|---|---|
| Colour: | colourless, grey or brown granular mass; can be red, blue, yellow, green, purple or colourless gems |
| Lustre; opacity: | adamantine; transparent to semi-opaque |
| Streak: | white |
| Hardness: | 9 |
| Specific gravity: | 4 |
| Cleavage; fracture: | none; uneven to conchoidal |
| Habit: | rough prisms or barrel shaped crystals bounded by steep pyramids; massive, granular |
| Crystal system: | trigonal |

# Arsenolite

A rsenolite or white arsenic, produced as a by-product of sulphide smelting, is widely used for preparing arsenic compounds, but quite rare in nature. Usually dull in appearance, crystal specimens – e.g. from White Caps (Nevada, USA) and St Etienne (France) – can be quite beautiful under magnification. A dimorphic form of arsenolite is the monoclinic clauditite. Arsenolite is toxic and should be handled with care. Arsenolite is formed by alteration of arsenic minerals, including by mine fires. Associated minerals are realgar, orpiment and erythrite. It is found at Annaberg (Germany), Jáchymov (Czech Republic), Cornwall (England), Laurion (Greece), St Marie-aux-Mines (France) and Smolnik (Slovakia).

## $As_2O_3$

| | |
|---|---|
| Colour: | white, pale blue, pale pink or yellow if contaminated with realgar or orpimiment |
| Lustre; opacity: | vitreous |
| Streak: | white |
| Hardness: | 1.5 |
| Specific gravity: | 3.7 |
| Cleavage; fracture: | perfect; conchoidal |
| Habit: | rare octahedral crystals; encrustations, earthy |
| Crystal system: | cubic |

# Senarmontite

Senarmontite is dimorphic with the orthorhombic valentinite – also called antimony bloom, with which it is commonly associated. Senarmontite is named after the French mineralogist H. de Sénarmont (1808–1862), whereas valentinite is more intriguingly named after the sixteenth-century alchemist B. Valentinus. Commercially obtained from other antimony-bearing minerals, senarmontite is used in paints, plastics, medicines and especially as a flame-retardant for PVC in aircraft and motor vehicles. It occurs in oxidized antimony-bearing hydrothermal deposits. Large crystals are found at Hamimate Mine (Sensa, Algeria); other locations are Pernek (Slovakia), Mopung Hills (Nevada, USA) and Cornwall (England).

## $Sb_2O_3$

| | |
|---|---|
| Colour: | colourless to grey |
| Lustre; opacity: | resinous; translucent to transparent |
| Streak: | white |
| Hardness: | 2 |
| Specific gravity: | 5.3 |
| Cleavage; fracture: | conchoidal; irregular |
| Habit: | well-formed octahedral crystals; granular, encrusting, massive |
| Crystal system: | cubic |

# Ilmenite

Ilmenite is a major ore of titanium. Pure ilmenite is black with a metallic lustre, but its properties can be altered by incorporated giekielite ($MgTiO_3$) and pyrophanite ($MnTiO_3$). Resistant to weathering, it often appears in sands such as at Menaccan Sands (Cornwall, England), where menaccanite was an early reported form of the mineral. The streak is useful to distinguish it from hematite and, unlike magnetite, it is non-magnetic. It is found in igneous rocks, where it settles in magma intrusions with other dense minerals such as hematite and magnetite. Good crystals are found at Kragerö (Norway), Val Devero (Italy), St Gotthard (Switzerland) and Orange County (New York, USA), and in sands at Travancore (India).

## $FeTiO_3$

| | |
|---|---|
| Colour: | iron black |
| Lustre; opacity: | metallic to submetallic; opaque |
| Streak: | black to brownish black |
| Hardness: | 5–6 |
| Specific gravity: | 4.5–5 |
| Cleavage; fracture: | none, basal partings; conchoidal |
| Habit: | crystals flat tabular rhombohedra; massive, compact; grains disseminated in igneous rocks |
| Crystal system: | trigonal |

# Hematite

H ematite, or red oxide of iron, is named after the Greek for 'blood'. On oxidation of iron-rich fluids, it precipitates, to give rocks a rusty appearance. Red ochre is an earthy clay-rich mixture containing hematite. Rounded opaque bodies, such as kidney ore, have been carved into figures that take a high polish. Rare crystalline forms are petal-shaped aggregates called 'iron roses' and shiny specular hematite. Powdered, it is an abrasive for polishing as jewellers' rouge. It occurs in oxidized igneous rocks and veins, and as a sedimentary cement. Huge quantities are mined at Lake Superior (USA), Quebec (Canada), Brazil and Australia. Beautiful crystals occur at Rio Marino (Elba, Italy), Bahia (Brazil) and Cumbria (England).

## $Fe_2O_3$

| | |
|---|---|
| Colour: | steel–grey to iron–black, can be iridescent; dull to bright red when massive or earthy |
| Lustre; opacity: | metallic, dull, earthy; opaque |
| Streak: | dark red to red-brown |
| Hardness: | 5–6 |
| Specific gravity : | 4.9–5.3 |
| Cleavage; fracture: | none; conchoidal |
| Habit: | crystals tabular or rhombohedral, sometimes with striated or curved faces; massive, laminated or earthy |
| Crystal system: | trigonal |

# Quartz

Quartz is the most abundant mineral on the Earth's surface. It forms beautiful crystals as hexagonal prisms, weighing up to 130kg (287lb). Quartz is used in glass-making, ceramics, refractories and abrasives. It produces electricity when strained (piezoelectric) or heated (pyroelectric), used in electrical sensors. Quartz is an essential mineral of many acid igneous and metamorphic rocks, and occurs in most clastic sediments. Some sandstones and their metamorphic equivalent, both called quartzites, are almost entirely quartz. It often occurs veins and fissures; these provide the best crystals. Good specimens occur in the Alps in Switzerland and Austria, at Carrara (Italy), Bourg d'Oisans (France) and the Urals (Russia).

## $SiO_2$

| | |
|---|---|
| Colour: | colourless or white; tinted many shades |
| Lustre; opacity: | vitreous; transparent to opaque |
| Streak: | white |
| Hardness: | 7 |
| Specific gravity: | 2.65 |
| Cleavage; fracture: | absent; conchoidal, splintery |
| Habit: | usually six-sided prismatic crystals terminated by six faces, the prisms faces often horizontally striated; massive, compact, drusy |
| Crystal system: | trigonal |

# Quartz: Gem Varieties

Clear, colourless crystals are called rock crystal. The opacity of milky quartz is caused by small, gas or liquid bubbles. Colours are produced by iron hydrates in yellow citrine, ferric oxide in violet amethyst, and titanium or manganese in pink rose quartz. Brown or smoky quartz, found as huge crystals in Brazil, can be produced artificially by irradiating rock crystal. Quartz cat's eye, tiger's eye and hawk's eye have inclusions giving a wavy, striped effect. Rutilated quartz contains rutile needles intersecting at 60° angles. Minute reflective scales in aventurine quartz give a green or brown spangled appearance. Many varieties are used in jewellery and specimens of amethyst are widely collected.

## $SiO_2$

| Colour: | colourless or white; tinted many shades |
| --- | --- |
| Lustre; opacity: | vitreous; transparent to opaque |
| Streak: | white |
| Hardness: | 7 |
| Specific gravity : | 2.65 |
| Cleavage; fracture: | absent; conchoidal, splintery |
| Habit: | usually six-sided prismatic crystals terminated by six faces, the prisms faces often horizontally striated; massive, compact, drusy |
| Crystal system: | trigonal |

# Cristobalite

Cristobalite is a much rarer form of silicon dioxide than quartz and rarer than tridymite. It has two forms: tetragonal cristobalite, which is stable up to 270°C (518°F), and cubic cristobalite, which is stable above 1470°C (2678°F). Between these temperatures, both forms can exist. Beautiful specimens found at Cerro San Cristobal (Portugal) comprise octahedral cristobalite embedded in transparent but dark, glassy obsidian. Cristobalite occurs in intermediate igneous rocks and as recrystallized opals. Associated minerals are opal, chalcedony and tridymite. Other locations are Monte Dore (France), Glass and Sugarloaf mountains (California, USA), Crater Lake (Oregon, USA), Eiffel (Germany), Sarospatak (Hungary) and Tokatoka (New Zealand).

## $SiO_2$

| | |
|---|---|
| Colour: | white to yellowish |
| Lustre; opacity: | vitreous; translucent to transparent |
| Streak: | white |
| Hardness: | 6.5 |
| Specific gravity: | 2.2 |
| Cleavage; fracture: | absent; conchoidal |
| Habit: | rare crystals; microcrystalline as small balls, fibres (called lussatite), crusts |
| Crystal system: | tetragonal |

# Tridymite

Tridymite is stable between 870°C (1598°F) and 1470°C (2678°F) and is a high-temperature polymorph of quartz. Although in a metastable state at normal temperatures, it is widespread and possibly underestimated in abundance due to the difficulty in identification. Tridymite will change into quartz, but the process is very slow. Tridymite is prepared synthetically for use in heat-resistant porcelain and as refractory material in furnaces. Tridymite is found as a sublimate in acid volcanic rocks and in contact metamorphosed sandstones. Tridymite is found in the Eiffel district (Germany), Cerro San Cristobal (Portugal), Pomona (California, USA), Mule Springs (Oregon, USA) and Kamomoto (Japan). It has been found in stony meteorites.

## SiO$_2$

| | |
|---|---|
| Colour: | colourless, white |
| Lustre; opacity: | vitreous to pearly; transparent to translucent |
| Streak: | white |
| Hardness: | 6.5–7 |
| Specific gravity: | 2.27 |
| Cleavage; fracture: | absent; conchoidal |
| Habit: | small pseudo-hexagonal blades; spherical aggregates |
| Crystal system: | monoclinic |

# Chalcedony

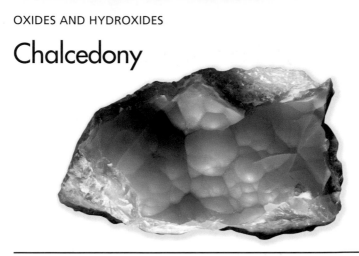

Chalcedony is made of microscopic quartz crystals and is mostly banded, which imparts much of its appeal as an ornamental stone. Flints and cherts are impure forms, the former being well known as nodules in chalk. It is named from the Ancient Greek town of Kalchedon in Asia Minor. Chalcedony is usually produced by precipitation from aqueous solutions, often associated with hot springs or volcanoes. It can be produced by dehydration of opal. Chalcedony is found as the variety agate in Rio Grande de Sul (Brazil) and Idar-Oberstein (Germany), as carnelian in Brazil, Uruguay and California (USA), as chrysoprase in the Urals (Russia), California and Queensland (Australia), and flint in Southern England.

## $SiO_2$

| | |
|---|---|
| Colour: | variable, white through shades of brown, red and grey to black |
| Lustre; opacity: | waxy to vitreous; translucent |
| Streak: | white |
| Hardness: | 6.5 |
| Specific gravity : | 2.6 |
| Cleavage; fracture: | absent; uneven, splintery, conchoidal |
| Habit: | no crystals; botryoidal or stalactitic, often banded; in fissures and veins, massive or nodular |
| Crystal system: | none, microcrystalline |

# Chalcedony: Gem Varieties

Chalcedony, like quartz, has a number of attractive forms coloured by various impurities, but shows different patterns of banding. Agate has curved, often semi-concentric bands. Moss agate is a pale translucent stone with dendritic moss- or tree-like inclusions of iron oxides. The translucent carnelian is orange-red and jasper is a more massive, sometimes striped opaque stone of varying colour, but often red. Chrysoprase is a fine translucent, apple-green; heliotrope, or bloodstone, is dark green and opaque with red spots; and plasma has yellow spots. Onyx has white and black or brown bands, with straight bands rather than curved. Sard is a variety of onyx, and sardonyx has white bands like onyx and red-brown bands like sard.

## $SiO_2$

| | |
|---|---|
| Colour: | variable, white through shades of brown, red and grey to black |
| Lustre; opacity: | waxy to vitreous; translucent |
| Streak: | white |
| Hardness: | 6.5 |
| Specific gravity: | 2.6 |
| Cleavage; fracture: | absent; uneven, splintery, conchoidal |
| Habit: | no crystals; botryoidal or stalactitic, often banded; in fissures and veins, massive or nodular |
| Crystal system: | none, microcrystalline |

# Opal

Opal, named from the Sanskrit for 'precious stone', is amorphous hydrated silica. It is made of tiny spheroids, giving internal reflections of light and a play of colours, or 'fire'. Precious opal is beautifully iridescent. Red fire opal and black opal are the most sought-after varieties; the latter has been more expensive than diamond. Opal is produced by the low-temperature weathering and alteration of silica-rich rocks, especially around geysers and hot springs. The skeletons of diatoms, sponges and radiolaria are composed of opal. Opals have been obtained from White Cliffs (NSW, Australia) since the nineteenth century. Mines in the Czech Republic have been worked since Roman times. An artificial form is called Slocum stone.

## $SiO_2.nH_2O$

| | |
|---|---|
| Colour: | white when pure; can be yellow, red, blue, brown or others |
| Lustre; opacity: | waxy or resinous; transparent to opaque |
| Streak: | white |
| Hardness: | 5.5–6.5 |
| Specific gravity: | 1.8–2.3 |
| Cleavage; fracture: | none; conchoidal, uneven |
| Habit: | massive, often nodular, stalactitic, cavity-filling, concretions or crusts |
| Crystal system: | none, amorphous |

# Pyrolusite

Pyrolusite is an important ore of manganese, a metal used widely in steel-making. It is also used in glass-making for removing coloration due to impurities of iron oxides, hence the name from the Greek words for 'fire' and 'wash'. Pyrolusite occurs with manganite and psilomelane, in a dark earthy ore called wad. Found on the surface of rocks in joints, it forms dendritic markings, often picturesque or fanciful. Pyrolusite is formed by chemical precipitation in lakes or oxidation of manganese ores. Large nodules are found at the bottom of seas and oceans. Mined localities include Platten (Bavaria, Germany), Epleny (Hungary), Cornwall (England), Nikepol (Ukraine), Deccan (India), Minas Gerais (Brazil), Cuba and South Africa.

## $MnO_2$

| | |
|---|---|
| Colour: | grey or grey-black |
| Lustre; opacity: | metallic; opaque |
| Streak: | black to bluish-black |
| Hardness: | 6–6.5 |
| Specific gravity: | 4.7–5.1 |
| Cleavage; fracture: | poor; uneven |
| Habit: | rare prismatic crystals; usually concretionary aggregates and earthy masses |
| Crystal system: | tetragonal |

107

# Cassiterite

Cassiterite, named after the Greek for 'tin', is its major ore. Tin is widely used for metal plating in food canning and for alloys, famously in bronze (one of the earliest metals known to the ancients). Twinned crystals known as knee twins are popularly collected. Radiating, fibrous concretions are known as wood tin. Cassiterite is found in hydrothermal veins and pegmatites associated with minerals such as fluorite, scheelite, topaz and tourmaline. Placer deposits are called stream tin. Rarely occurring in workable quantities in the USA, it is found at Erzgebirge, Altenberg and Zinnwald (Germany), Cornwall (England), Brittany (France), Bolivia, Sumatra, Yunnan (China) and Elba and Lake Como (Italy).

## $SnO_2$

| | |
|---|---|
| **Colour:** | brown to black |
| **Lustre; opacity:** | adamantine; opaque |
| **Streak:** | white to yellow |
| **Hardness:** | 7 |
| **Specific gravity:** | 6.8–7.1 |
| **Cleavage; fracture:** | imperfect; conchoidal |
| **Habit:** | crystals as prisms, bipyramids and needles |
| **Crystal system:** | tetragonal |

# Rutile

Rutile is a form of titanium dioxide often embedded in other minerals as needle-like inclusions of metallic appearance. Such inclusions have been named maiden hair, cat's eye and star forms. Quartz crystals with embedded rutile needles intersecting at angles of 60° are called sagenite or rutilated quartz. Rutile is durable and cuts well, having a high 'fire', but its colour is usually unattractive. Twinning is common, giving elbow-shaped crystals. Pure powdered titanium dioxide is brilliant white and used as a pigment in white paints. Rutile is found in igneous intrusions, pegmatites and metamorphic rocks and placer deposits. Good crystals are found at Binnental (Switzerland) and in Grove Mountain (Georgia, USA).

## $TiO_2$

| | |
|---|---|
| Colour: | yellow, red, brown, black |
| Lustre; opacity: | metallic; translucent to opaque |
| Streak: | yellow browns |
| Hardness: | 6–6.5 |
| Specific gravity : | 4.3 |
| Cleavage; fracture: | perfect; uneven, conchoidal |
| Habit: | crystals usually elongate prisms, often striated; grains, fibrous aggregates and inclusions |
| Crystal system: | tetragonal |

# Anatase

A natase is named from the Greek for 'elongated', after the sharp crystals it often forms. It is a polymorph of titanium dioxide and is formed, like brookite, at lower temperatures than rutile, to which it can be converted by heating. Anatase mostly forms as transparent to opaque 1–3mm (up to ⅛in) isolated crystals embedded in a matrix of accessory minerals. It is easily distinguished from rutile by crystal form and specific gravity. It is found as a secondary mineral in titanium-bearing rocks, in igneous rocks, in metamorphic rocks and as a placer deposit. Associated minerals are brookite, albite, quartz and titanite. Excellent specimens are found at Binnental and Tavetschal (Switzerland) and Val Devero and Vatellina (Italy).

## $TiO_2$

| | |
|---|---|
| **Colour:** | yellow to brown, deep blue, black |
| **Lustre; opacity:** | adamantine; translucent to opaque |
| **Streak:** | white to light brown |
| **Hardness:** | 5.5–6 |
| **Specific gravity:** | 3.8–3.9 |
| **Cleavage; fracture:** | perfect; conchoidal |
| **Habit:** | usually sharp, bipyramidal crystals, sometimes tabular |
| **Crystal system:** | tetrahedral |

# Brookite

Named after the English mineralogist H. Brike (1771–1857), brookite is the third polymorph of titanium dioxide. Like anatase, it forms at lower temperatures than rutile. The larger crystals, especially heart-shaped twins, are popular. Brookite is found in veins and fissures in altered igneous and metamorphic rocks, such as granites and gneisses. Associated minerals include anatase, albite, quartz and rutile. It also occurs as a placer deposit. Fine crystals are found at Bourg d'Oisans (Dauphiné, France), Grisons and Uri cantons (Switzerland) and Tyrol and Untersulzbachtal (Austria). The site at Prenteg (Wales) produced some of the finest specimens in the nineteenth century.

## $TiO_2$

| | |
|---|---|
| Colour: | brown to black |
| Lustre; opacity: | adamantine, submetallic; transparent to translucent |
| Streak: | yellow, yellow-brown |
| Hardness: | 5.5–6 |
| Specific gravity: | 3.9–4.2 |
| Cleavage; fracture: | imperfect; subconchoidal |
| Habit: | tabular or lamellar crystals, sometimes striated |
| Crystal system: | orthorhombic |

# Columbite

Columbite is the major ore of niobium, which is used in high-strength steels and superconducting alloys. The term columbite can also refer to the series of minerals from ferrocolumbite to manganocolumbite, $(Fe,Mn)Nb_2O_6$. Columbite also forms a series with tantalite, $(Fe,Mn)(Ta,Nb)_2O_6$. Niobium, named from Niobe, daughter of Tantalus, was chosen over columbium (after Columbus) as the preferred name in the 1950s, after much debate. Columbite and tantalite are found in granite pegmatites rich in lithium and phosphorus, associated with albite, spodumene, tourmaline, cassiterite, apatite and beryl. It is found at Haddam (Connecticut, USA), Rabenstein (Germany), Ilmen Mountains (Urals, Russia) and Greenland.

## $FeNb_2O_6$

| | |
|---|---|
| **Colour:** | brown or black |
| **Lustre; opacity:** | metallic; nearly opaque, transparent in thin lamellae |
| **Streak:** | black to dark red |
| **Hardness:** | 6 |
| **Specific gravity:** | 5.1 |
| **Cleavage; fracture:** | good; subconchoidal |
| **Habit:** | crystals as complex, stubby prisms, aggregates of thin, tabular crystals; granular, massive |
| **Crystal system:** | orthorhombic |

# Furgusonite

Furgusonite, named after the Scottish politician and landowner Robert Furguson (1767–1840), is an ore of yttrium found widespread but in small amounts. Specimens are usually radioactive and often metamict. Yttrium is used to give red colours on TV screens, in X-ray filters, in superconductors and in alloys. Invariably substituted by a number of the other rare-earth elements, the term furgusonite-Y is used for the yttrium-rich mineral. Fergusonite occurs in rare earth-bearing granite pegmatites and as a placer deposit. The type locality where it was first discovered is Qeqertaussaq Island (Greenland). Major mining areas include Arendal (Norway), Blum mine (Ilmen Mountains, Russia) and Ytterby (Sweden).

## $YNbO_4$

| | |
|---|---|
| Colour: | black, brown, grey, yellow |
| Lustre; opacity: | submetallic; translucent to opaque |
| Streak: | brown |
| Hardness: | 5.5–6 |
| Specific gravity: | 4.3–5.8 |
| Cleavage; fracture: | indistinct; subconchoidal |
| Habit: | crystals as prismatic to acicular dipyramids, usually powdery; granular, massive |
| Crystal system: | tetragonal |

# Brucite

Brucite, an ore of magnesium, is used to produce magnesia (MgO), magnesium compounds and refractories. Brucite can be quite rich in manganese, weathering to dark brown. Brucite occurs in marbles by alteration of periclase, in hydrothermal veins in metamorphic limestones and chlorite schists, and in serpentinized dunites. Associated minerals include calcite, aragonite, dolomite, magnesite, talc and chrysotile. It is found at Castle Point (Hoboken, New Jersey, USA), Gabbs (Nevada, USA), Asbestos (Quebec, Canada), Vesuvius and Sardinia (Italy), Shetland Islands and Isle of Muck (Scotland), and the Ethyl Mine (Mutorashanga, Zimbabwe). It was first described by Archibald Bruce (1777–1818), an American mineralogist.

## $Mg(OH)_2$

| | |
|---|---|
| Colour: | white, shades of grey, blue and green |
| Lustre; opacity: | waxy, pearly on cleavage faces; transparent |
| Streak: | white |
| Hardness: | 2–2.5 |
| Specific gravity: | 2.4 |
| Cleavage; fracture: | perfect; uneven, separates into flexible plates |
| Habit: | tabular crystals in platy or foliate masses, rosettes, sometimes fibrous; granular, massive |
| Crystal system: | hexagonal |

# Goethite

Goethite is a major constituent of limonite and ochres, and an important ore mineral. Named after the famous German poet J. Goethe (1749–1832), it is also known as iron hydroxide, needle ironstone or acicular iron ore. Black crystals are attractive but rare. Sprays of acicular crystals are found at Příbram. Goethite often forms an attractive matrix in specimens of other minerals such as vanadite. Its perfect cleavage gives it a soft and greasy feel. Goethite is formed by oxidation of iron-rich minerals, usually pyrite, siderite and magnetite. Large amounts are mined at Příbram (Czech Republic) and in Cuba, Alsace-Lorraine (France), Westphalia (Germany), Lake Superior (USA) and Labrador (Canada).

## FeO(OH)

| | |
|---|---|
| **Colour:** | brown to black |
| **Lustre; opacity:** | adamantine, submetallic, silky; translucent to opaque |
| **Streak:** | yellow-brown |
| **Hardness:** | 5–5.5 |
| **Specific gravity:** | 4.3 |
| **Cleavage; fracture:** | perfect; uneven to hackly |
| **Habit:** | rare prisms with vertical striations; usually stalactitic, massive or earthy aggregates of radiating fibrous forms |
| **Crystal system:** | orthorhombic |

# Diaspore

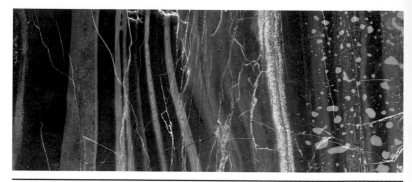

Diaspore is most widely found in bauxite, the major ore of aluminium. Other minerals constituting bauxite are closely related, especially boehmite (AlO(OH)) and gibbsite (Al(OH)$_3$). Bauxite is formed by extreme weathering of aluminosilicate rocks in tropical regions. Purer forms of diaspore are rare relative to the abundance of bauxite and good crystals rarer still. Other important associations are with corundum and margarite among emery deposits and with chlorite and chloritoid in metamorphic rocks. The name from the Greek 'to disperse' alludes to its easy disintegration in a flame. Crystals are found in Chester (Massachusetts, USA), Naxos (Greece), Campolongo (Switzerland) and Mramorskoi (Urals, Russia).

## AlO(OH)

| | |
|---|---|
| Colour: | white; greenish, grey or pink as aggregates |
| Lustre; Opacity: | vitreous or pearly; transparent to translucent |
| Streak: | white |
| Hardness: | 6.5–7 |
| Specific Gravity : | 3.3–3.5 |
| Cleavage; Fracture: | perfect; conchoidal |
| Habit: | crystals tabular or acicular; foliated or stalactitic aggregates |
| Crystal System: | orthorhombic |

# Limonite

Named from the Latin *limus* for 'mud', limonite has been variously called brown ironstone, brown iron and brown haematite. It is a term used to describe a rock made of an ill-defined mixture of mostly amorphous hydrated iron oxides, microcrystalline goethite (FeOOH) and lepidocrocite (FeOOH). Not strictly a mineral, but not quite seen as a rock, limonite is usually included among minerals. It is used as a pigment as yellow ochre and in modelling clay. It is quite hard, but very fragile, easily disintegrating into grains and powders. It is formed by surface oxidation of iron deposits or is left after the dissolution of iron-rich rocks in tropical regions. Limonite is often found as a cubic polymorph after pyrite.

## hydrated iron oxides

| | |
|---|---|
| Colour: | yellow-brown to black |
| Lustre; opacity: | subvitreous, dull, earthy; opaque |
| Streak: | yellow brown |
| Hardness: | 5–5.5 |
| Specific gravity: | ca. 4 |
| Cleavage; fracture: | absent; conchoidal, splintery |
| Habit: | botryoidal, stalactitic, oolitic earthy or porous masses; loose yellow-brown crusts to dark, iridescent bodies when compact |
| Crystal system: | none, amorphous |

# Manganite

Manganite, or brown ore of manganese, is a minor ore of manganese. It usually forms rather dull bodies similar to other manganese minerals, but when crystalline it is easier to identify and is quite collectable. Such specimens include lustrous feathery crystals (up to 8mm/⅓in), found in the Kalahari manganese field. Pyrolusite, which can resemble manganite, is softer and has a bluish streak. It is formed by the alteration of other manganese minerals in low-temperature hydrothermal veins, associated with calcite and barite, and in hot springs, associated with psilomelane and pyrolusite. Crystals up to 7–8cm (2¾–3in) large are found in Harz (Germany), Como (Italy) and Negaunee and Marquette (Michigan, USA).

## MnO(OH)

| | |
|---|---|
| Colour: | black, opaque |
| Lustre; opacity: | metallic; opaque, red, translucent in thin plates |
| Streak: | dark brown |
| Hardness: | 4 |
| Specific gravity: | 4.3–4.4 |
| Cleavage; fracture: | perfect; uneven |
| Habit: | elongate prisms with deep striations lengthwise, usually in bundles; microcrystalline, granular, radially fibrous, oolitic |
| Crystal system: | monoclinic |

# Pyrochlore

Pyrochlore is the generic name usually applied to the series from pyrochlore, $(Na,Ca)_2Nb_2O_6(OH,F)$, to microlite, $(Na,Ca)_2Ta_2O_6(OH,F)$. Pyrochlore turns green on heating and is named from the Greek for 'fire' and 'green'; microlite is named from the Greek for 'small stone'. This compositionally diverse mineral is a source of a number of rare earth elements and uranium, and is usually radioactive. It is found in pegmatites and carbonatites, associated with apatite, nepheline, zircon, biotite and forsterite. It is rare and found at Mbeya (Tanzania), Fen (Norway), Kaiserstuhl (Germany), Oka (Canada), Newry (Maine), Haddam (Connecticut, USA), Betanima (Madagascar), Minas Gerais (Brazil) and Varutrask (Sweden).

## $(Na,Ca)_2(Nb,Ta,Ti)_2O_6(OH,F,O)$

| | |
|---|---|
| Colour: | usually brown; greenish, reddish |
| Lustre; Opacity: | greasy; translucent to opaque |
| Streak: | yellowish brown |
| Hardness: | 5–5.5 |
| Specific Gravity : | 4.3–4.5 |
| Cleavage; Fracture: | distinct, octahedral; conchoidal, uneven |
| Habit: | crystals usually octahedral, disseminated; granular |
| Crystal System: | cubic |

# Thorianite

Thorianite forms a series with uraninite ($UO_2$) and contains other elements substituting for thorium; a $ThO_2$ content of about 70 per cent would be typical. It is an ore of thorium, which is used in nuclear fuel elements, refractory materials and incandescent gas mantles. Like all thorium and uranium minerals, thorianite contains radiogenic elements such as lead, which have been formed by radioactive decay. It is found in pegmatites, carbonatites and serpentinites, and as a placer deposit. Thorianite is found at Taolañaro (Madagascar), Transvaal (South Africa), Kola Peninsula (Siberia, Russia) and Easton (Pennsylvania, USA). Thorium is named after the old Scandinavian god of war, Thor.

## $ThO_2$

| | |
|---|---|
| Colour: | brownish black, greenish, yellow |
| Lustre; opacity: | metallic; opaque |
| Streak: | greenish-grey |
| Hardness: | 6.5–7 |
| Specific gravity: | 9.7–9.8 |
| Cleavage; fracture: | imperfect; subconchoidal, brittle |
| Habit: | cubic crystals, often as interpenetrant twins; granular |
| Crystal system: | cubic |

# Uraninite

O res containing uraninite, known as pitchblende, are major ores not only of uranium, but also of radium. Uranium is a major source of energy via nuclear fission. Uraninite is radioactive and found in pegmatites, in sandstones and conglomerates, and in hydrothermal veins in sulphide ores. Pitchblende from Yáchymov (Czech Republic) was used by the Curies in the discovery of polonium and radium in 1898. Radium and uranium are also sources of radioactivity for various uses in industry, science and medicine. Large crystals are found at Wilberforce (Canada). Mining areas include Great Bear Lake (Canada), Shinkolobwe (Zaire), the Colorado Plateau (USA) and Witwatersrand (South Africa).

## $UO_2$

| | |
|---|---|
| Colour: | brown, grey, black |
| Lustre; opacity: | greasy, submetallic; opaque |
| Streak: | black |
| Hardness: | 5.5–6 |
| Specific gravity: | 4.3–4.5 |
| Cleavage; fracture: | difficult; conchoidal |
| Habit: | rare modified cubes; usually dense botryoidal, reniform, massive, colloform; sometimes dendritic |
| Crystal system: | cubic |

# Billietite

Billietite is a radioactive mineral found as rare but attractive amber yellow crystals. It is an uncommon alteration product of uraninite, named after the Belgian crystallographer Valère Billiet (1903–1945). Billietite is similar to becquerelite $(Ca(UO_2)_6O_4(OH)_6.6\text{-}8H_2O)$, and related to compreignacite $(K_2(UO_2)_6O_4(OH)_6.6\text{-}8H_2O)$. Associated minerals are barite, calcite, chalcopyrite, hematite and other rare species such as uranophane, fourmarierite, metabernite, rutherfordine and becquerelite. Billietite is found in Shaba Province (Congo), the La Crouzille, Margnac and Rabéjac mines (France), Menzenschwand (Black Forest, Germany) and the Delta mine (Utah, USA).

## $Ba(UO_2)_6O_4(OH)_6.6\text{-}8H_2O$

| | |
|---|---|
| Colour: | yellow-brown |
| Lustre; opacity: | adamantine; transparent to translucent |
| Streak: | yellow |
| Hardness: | not determined |
| Specific gravity: | 5.3 |
| Cleavage; fracture: | perfect; brittle |
| Habit: | crystals pseudohexagonal, tabular |
| Crystal system: | orthorhombic |

# Plattnerite

Plattnerite is an uncommon dense mineral composed of lead oxide. It mostly occurs as masses, but specimens comprising drusy crusts showing many shiny crystals are fairly common. Specimens of plattnerite with contrasting minerals such as calcite and wulfenite are popular. Plattnerite is named after the German metallurgist K. Plattner (1800–1858). It occurs in oxidized, weathered hydrothermal lead deposits, typically in arid climates, associated with cerussite, smithsonite, hemimorphite, calcite and quartz. It is found in Leadhills and Wanlockhead (Scotland), Anarak and Anjireh (Iran), Tsumeb (Namibia), Idaho, Arizona, Nevada and New Mexico (USA), and Durango and Chihuahua (Mexico).

## $PbO_2$

| | |
|---|---|
| Colour: | black |
| Lustre; opacity: | adamantine to submetallic; opaque |
| Streak: | dark brown |
| Hardness: | 5.5 |
| Specific gravity: | 9.6 |
| Cleavage; fracture: | good; conchoidal to uneven |
| Habit: | small, prismatic crystals, sometimes acicular; nodular or botryoidal, fibrous or concentrically zoned, massive |
| Crystal system: | tetragonal |

# Betafite

Betafite is named after the type locality of Betafo in Madagascar. The hardness, specific gravity and other properties vary widely as composition changes. It is an ore of uranium and consequently radioactive; also used to obtain niobium, tantalum, other rare earth elements and associated thorium. Although black in colour, the surface is invariably altered (metamict), making it appear greenish or yellowish. It is found in pegmatites and adjacent metamorphosed limestones. Crystals up to 100kg (220lb) have been reported. Associated minerals are quartz, feldspars, biotite, zircon and rare earth minerals. Betafite is found at Tangen (Norway), Sludianka (Baikal, Russia), Bancroft (Ontario, Canada) and Val d'Ossola (Italy).

## $(Ca,Na,U)_2(Ti,Nb,Ta)_2O_6(OH)$

| | |
|---|---|
| Colour: | black, with a tint of yellow, brown or green |
| Lustre; opacity: | waxy, greasy to adamantine; translucent to opaque |
| Streak: | yellowish white |
| Hardness: | 3–5.5 |
| Specific gravity: | 3.7–4.9 |
| Cleavage; fracture: | none; conchoidal to uneven |
| Habit: | octahedral and dodecahedral crystals, sometimes elongated; granular masses common; crusts |
| Crystal system: | cubic |

# Psilomelane

Psilomelane is a term given to a collection of poorly defined hydrated barium-bearing manganese ores, the main component probably being romanechite ($BaMn_5O_{10}.H_2O$). The term wad is used for earthy mixtures of psilomelane, pyrolusite and others. Psilomelane is found in weathed ores and as a replacement deposit in limestones and dolomites. It also forms desert varnish, a dark coating of rocks in dry regions. Romanechite was authenticated at Romanèche (France) and occurs as crystals at Schneeberg (Saxony, Germany) and Oberwolfach (Black Forest, Germany). Psilomelane occurs at Cornwall (England), Virginia, Nevada and New Mexico (USA), Pilbara (Western Australia) and Chihuahua (Mexico).

## No fixed formula

| | |
|---|---|
| Colour: | iron black to steel grey |
| Lustre; opacity: | dull; opaque |
| Streak: | brownish black |
| Hardness: | 5–5.5 (6 for romanechite) |
| Specific gravity: | 4.4–4.5 |
| Cleavage; fracture: | absent; conchoidal to uneven |
| Habit: | rare euhedral crystals (romanechite); massive, fibrous, botryoidal, stalactitic, concretionary, earthy, powdery |
| Crystal system: | monoclinic (romanechite) |

# Nitratine

The nitrates as a whole readily dissolve in water, so nitratine (or soda nitre) should be kept in an airtight container with a desiccant. It has a bitter, cooling taste, and colours a flame yellow. It can be distinguished from nitre (salt-petre, KNO3) by the flame test, as nitre turns a flame violet. Nitratine is used in the chemical industry, for fertilizers and in fireworks. It occurs as a bedded deposit in playa lakes in arid regions, associated with halite, gypsum and other evaporites. It may also precipitate from nitrate-bearing ground water. Economically valuable deposits of billions of tons occur in regions adjacent to the type locality of Tarapacá (Chile). It also occurs in arid regions of the Persian Gulf.

## NaNO$_3$

| | |
|---|---|
| **Colour:** | colourless, white, sometimes greyish, yellowish brown |
| **Lustre; opacity:** | vitreous; transparent to translucent |
| **Streak:** | white |
| **Hardness:** | 1.5–2 |
| **Specific gravity:** | 2.2–2.3 |
| **Cleavage; fracture:** | perfect, rhombohedral; conchoidal, sectile |
| **Habit:** | crystals rare; granular or massive encrustations, stalactitic |
| **Crystal system:** | trigonal |

# Calcite

Calcite is a major rock-forming mineral, the principal component of limestone and marble, and an important constituent of igneous carbonatite. It effervesces strongly in cold, dilute hydrochloric acid. Crystals show a wide variety of forms, such as nail-head spar (flat-topped rhombohedra) or dog-tooth spar (sharply pointed). Fine sand-covered crystals come from Fontainebleau (France); calcite with hematite inclusions from Chihuahua (Mexico); and fluorescent calcite from Franklin (New Jersey, USA). An image appears double when viewed through transparent rhombs of Iceland spar, a property known as 'double refraction'. This was used to produce nicol prisms for petrological microscopes.

## $CaCO_3$

| Colour: | usually colourless or white; may be brown, red, green or black |
|---|---|
| Lustre; opacity: | vitreous, dull, pearly; transparent to translucent |
| Streak: | white to greyish |
| Hardness: | 3 |
| Specific gravity: | 2.71 |
| Cleavage; fracture: | perfect, rhombohedral; subconchoidal |
| Habit: | wide variety of crystal forms; stalactitic, granular, massive, fibrous or many other habits |
| Crystal system: | trigonal |

# Magnesite

$M$agnesite, or bitter spar, is much less common than calcite, and will only dissolve with effervescence in hydrochloric acid on warming. It forms when limestone is altered by magnesian solutions, often accompanied by the formation of dolomite, and during the hydrothermal metamorphism of ultramafic rocks to talc schists and serpentinite. An important ore of magnesium, it is heated to produce magnesium oxide (MgO), used in the manufacture of cements and refractory bricks. Powdered magnesia is used in the rubber, paper and pharmaceutical industries. Large deposits are found in Styria (Austria), Manchuria (China), Silesia (Poland), Madras (India) and Euboea (Greece).

## $MgCO_3$

| | |
|---|---|
| Colour: | white or colourless, also greyish or yellowish brown |
| Lustre; opacity: | vitreous or dull when compact; transparent to translucent |
| Streak: | white |
| Hardness: | 3.5–4.5 |
| Specific gravity: | 3.0–3.2 |
| Cleavage; fracture: | perfect rhombohedral; conchoidal fracture |
| Habit: | crystals rare and usually rhombohedral; massive, lamellar, granular or fibrous |
| Crystal system: | trigonal |

# Siderite

Siderite is a common carbonate, forming series with magnesite, rhodochrosite and smithsonite. It dissolves slowly with effervescence in cold hydrochloric acid, and becomes magnetic on heating. It usually forms in sedimentary deposits, such as in coalfields, as nodules and beds of impure iron carbonate called clay ironstone, and as oolitic ironstone. It is also found in metamorphic iron formations (as at Biwabik, Minnesota, USA). Magnesite-siderite series carbonates occur in carbonatites at Nkombwa (Zambia) and Newania (Rajasthan, India). It also forms in hydrothermal veins associated with barite, fluorite and galena. Large crystals occur at Mont Saint-Hilaire (Quebec, Canada) and Mosojllacta (Colavi, Bolivia).

## $FeCO_3$

| | |
|---|---|
| Colour: | shades of brown, tan, greenish grey |
| Lustre; opacity: | vitreous, silky, pearly on cleavage; translucent |
| Streak: | white |
| Hardness: | 3.5–4.5 |
| Specific gravity: | 3.96 when pure |
| Cleavage; fracture: | perfect rhombohedral; uneven to conchoidal |
| Habit: | crystals rhombohedral, often with curved faces made up of overlapping scales; massive, granular, concretionary, botryoidal |
| Crystal system: | trigonal |

# Smithsonite

Smithsonite is very attractive and popular, and can fluoresce pale green or blue in ultraviolet light. A secondary mineral, it forms in the weathered zone of zinc deposits and may replace adjacent carbonate rocks. Associated minerals include malachite, azurite, aurichalcite, anglesite and hemimorphite. Pale pink twinned crystals are found in Ojuela Mine (Durango, Mexico); pale green botryoidal smithsonite at Broken Hill (NSW, Australia); and blue-green botryoidal specimens from the Kelly Mine (New Mexico, USA). Cream or yellow globular turkey-fat ore is found in Rush Mine (Arkansas, USA). Other good specimens come from Laurion (Greece), Tsumeb (Namibia) and Chessy (France).

## $ZnCO_3$

| | |
|---|---|
| **Colour:** | white, grey, yellow, brown, shades of green, pink, purple |
| **Lustre; opacity:** | vitreous or pearly; translucent |
| **Streak:** | white |
| **Hardness:** | 4–4.5 |
| **Specific gravity:** | 4.4–4.5 |
| **Cleavage; fracture:** | perfect rhombohedral; subconchoidal to uneven |
| **Habit:** | crystals rare, rhombohedral, with curved faces; massive, botryoidal, reniform, stalactitic, granular or encrustations |
| **Crystal system:** | trigonal |

# Rhodochrosite

Rhodochrosite is a beautiful rose colour, but darkens on exposure through oxidation. A minor ore of manganese, it dissolves with effervescence in hot dilute hydrochloric acid, and can luminesce light pink in long-wave ultraviolet light. Its prime commercial source is the USA. Crystals can be cut as gems, and the banded rock is very attractive when polished; the type known as Ina Rose comes from the oldest mines in Argentina. Rhodochrosite occurs as a metasomatic deposit, as a primary mineral in hydrothermal veins, associated with sulphides and manganese-bearing minerals, and more rarely in pegmatites. It is found in Freiburg (Germany), Las Cabesses (France), Pasto Bueno (Peru) and Colorado (USA).

## $MnCO_3$

| | |
|---|---|
| Colour: | pale to deep rose pink, yellowish grey, brownish or orange |
| Lustre; opacity: | vitreous to pearly; transparent to translucent |
| Streak: | white |
| Hardness: | 3.5–4 |
| Specific gravity: | 3.5–3.7 |
| Cleavage; fracture: | perfect rhombohedral; uneven |
| Habit: | crystals rhombohedral, prismatic, scalenohedral or tabular, often curved faces; massive, granular, stalactitic, globular or botryoidal |
| Crystal system: | trigonal |

# Dolomite

Dolomite is a major rock-forming mineral. It typically forms rhombohedral crystals, the faces of which may be curved, and can form a saddle-shape. Unlike calcite, it bubbles only weakly in dilute hydrochloric acid. Dolomite is the major constituent of the sedimentary rock called dolomite, most of which has formed from the passage of magnesium-bearing solutions through limestone. It also occurs in marbles, associated with talc, tremolite, diopside or wollastonite, in hydrothermal veins with metallic ores, and in igneous carbonatites. Dolomite has many uses, e.g. in the manufacture of cement, and as a source of magnesium oxide. Very good crystals are found at Eugui (Navarra Province, Spain) and at Touissite (Morocco).

## $CaMg(CO_3)_2$

| | |
|---|---|
| **Colour:** | colourless, white to cream, pale pink, grey or brown |
| **Lustre; opacity:** | vitreous to pearly; transparent to translucent |
| **Streak:** | white |
| **Hardness:** | 3.5–4 |
| **Specific gravity:** | 2.85 |
| **Cleavage; fracture:** | perfect rhombohedral; subconchoidal |
| **Habit:** | crystals rhombohedral, often composed of overlapping scales; massive or granular |
| **Crystal system:** | trigonal |

# Ankerite

Ankerite (brown-spar) is a common mineral that forms a series with dolomite, from which it can be distinguished by colour, which darkens on heating. It effervesces in hydrochloric acid and may fluoresce in long-wave ultraviolet light. Ankerite forms in sedimentary rocks through hydrothermal alteration and low temperature metasomatism; as a gangue mineral in sulphide veins; and in low-grade metamorphic ironstones and sedimentary banded iron formations. It can be associated with dolomite, siderite, quartz, copper sulphides and occasionally gold. The type locality is Styria (Austria). Sharply pointed 'dog-tooth' crystals occur in Chihuahua (Mexico) and crystals up to 5cm (2in) long at Mlynky (Slovakia).

## $CaFe(CO_3)_2$

| | |
|---|---|
| Colour: | white, grey, yellow, yellow-brown, weathers dark brown |
| Lustre; opacity: | vitreous to pearly; translucent |
| Streak: | white |
| Hardness: | 3.5–4 |
| Specific gravity: | 2.9–3.1 |
| Cleavage; fracture: | perfect rhombohedral; subconchoidal |
| Habit: | crystals rhombohedral; massive or granular |
| Crystal system: | trigonal |

# Witherite

Witherite forms a series with strontianite ($SrCO_3$), from which it is distinguished by a flame test; witherite colours the flame green rather than crimson. It dissolves with effervescence in dilute hydrochloric acid; it sometimes fluoresces light blue, and may phosphoresce. It forms in hydrothermal veins, often by the alteration of barite. Associated minerals include barite, fluorite and galena. It also forms as an anoxic sediment, the barium being sourced through hot springs. An ore of barium, it is used in speciality glasses, in the production of rat poison, and was formerly used for refining sugar. Good crystals are found at Alston Moor (Cumbria) and at Hexham (Northumberland, England).

## $BaCO_3$

| | |
|---|---|
| Colour: | colourless, white, grey, yellow, green or brown |
| Lustre; opacity: | vitreous or resinous; transparent to translucent |
| Streak: | white |
| Hardness: | 3–3.5 |
| Specific gravity: | 4.29 |
| Cleavage; fracture: | one distinct; uneven |
| Habit: | twinned crystals of pseudo-hexagonal form, commonly striated; massive, botryoidal, granular, fibrous, columnar |
| Crystal system: | orthorhombic |

# Aragonite

Aragonite is less widespread than its polymorph calcite. It also dissolves with effervescence in dilute hydrochloric acid, but lacks the excellent rhombohedral cleavage of calcite. Aragonite crystals are often twinned, giving a hexagonal appearance. It is the main constituent of shells of many recent and fossil organisms. Although precipitating from warm marine waters, it inverts to calcite over time. It occurs as sinter from hot springs, or as dripstone in caves, and is the constituent of pearls in oysters. It occurs in amygdales in basalt, and is the stable polymorph in high-pressure metamorphic rocks. Aragonite is an ornamental stone: onyx is a popular banded variety, and flos-ferri is a coral-like form.

## $CaCO_3$

| | |
|---|---|
| **Colour:** | colourless to white, or yellowish |
| **Lustre; opacity:** | vitreous; transparent to translucent |
| **Streak:** | white |
| **Hardness:** | 3.5–4 |
| **Specific gravity:** | 2.95 |
| **Cleavage; fracture:** | distinct; subconchoidal |
| **Habit:** | crystals prismatic, elongated, often in radiating groups; coral-like form known as flos-ferri; columnar, stalactitic or encrusting |
| **Crystal system:** | orthorhombic |

# Strontianite

Strontianite was named after Strontian in Scotland, and is the mineral from which Sir Humphrey Davy separated strontium in 1807. It is common in carbonatites (e.g. Kola Peninsula, Russia); forms in hydrothermal veins in limestone, marl and chalk; occurs rarely in sulphide-rich veins associated with galena, sphalerite and chalcopyrite; and can form concretions in limestones and marls, occasionally replacing celestite. Fine crystals occur at Strontian (Scotland) and Oberdorf (Styria, Austria). It used to be mined from veins in limestones at Drensteinfurt (Westphalia, Germany). It is a principal ore of strontium, used for special glass for televisions and VDUs; strontium salts are used for the red colour in fireworks.

## $SrCO_3$

| | |
|---|---|
| Colour: | white, colourless, yellow, greenish or brownish |
| Lustre; opacity: | vitreous to resinous; transparent to translucent |
| Streak: | white |
| Hardness: | 3.5 |
| Specific gravity: | 3.78 |
| Cleavage; fracture: | perfect in one direction; subconchoidal to uneven |
| Habit: | crystals prismatic, pseudohexagonal twins, or radiating aggregates; massive, fibrous, granular or concretionary |
| Crystal system: | orthorhombic |

# Cerussite

Cerussite is a popular mineral due to its high sparkle and its yellow fluorescence. It often forms chevron twins, star-shaped pseudo-hexagonal twins, or complex twins of snowflake appearance. It forms in the oxidation zones of lead veins, associated with galena, sphalerite, pyromorphite, smithsonite, anglesite or goethite. Cerussite is toxic, but was used as a cosmetic by Queen Elizabeth I. It was formerly mined at the Llanfur nach silver-lead mine in Wales and large deposits were worked in southern Kazakhstan. It is mined today at Anguran Mine (Zanjan, Iran). Beautiful 'snowflake' twins occur at Mt Isa Mine (Queensland, Australia) and at Tsumeb (Namibia), where they are known as Jack Straw.

## $PbCO_3$

| | |
|---|---|
| **Colour:** | colourless, white or greyish |
| **Lustre; opacity:** | adamantine, vitreous, resinous; transparent to translucent |
| **Streak:** | white |
| **Hardness:** | 3–3.5 |
| **Specific gravity:** | 6.56 (high for a transparent mineral) |
| **Cleavage; fracture:** | two directions, distinct; conchoidal or uneven, very brittle |
| **Habit:** | crystals common, often tabular but may be acicular; massive, granular, compact or stalactitic |
| **Crystal system:** | orthorhombic |

# Malachite

Malachite is a highly regarded semi-precious mineral, mined for about 6000 years. Its light and dark green banding make it extremely popular for carvings and jewellery, and it was used both in the Winter Palace in Leningrad and the Taj Mahal, India. Malachite is a common secondary mineral, formed by the weathering of copper deposits. Associated minerals are often very colourful: striking blue azurite and chrysocolla, black mottramite and red limonite. Good crystals are rare, but occur at Chessy (France) and at Onganja mine (Namibia). It has been mined in the Urals (Russia), individual blocks weighing many kilograms, but the most famous ore deposit is in Katanga Province (Democratic Republic of Congo).

## $Cu_2CO_3(OH)_2$

| | |
|---|---|
| Colour: | bright green and commonly banded |
| Lustre; opacity: | vitreous to silky; translucent to opaque |
| Streak: | pale green |
| Hardness: | 3.5–4 |
| Specific gravity: | 3.9–4 |
| Cleavage; fracture: | perfect; subconchoidal to uneven |
| Habit: | acicular crystals or tabular pseudomorphs after azurite, twinning common; botryoidal with concretionary structure |
| Crystal system: | monoclinic |

# Azurite

Azurite is a striking azure blue mineral, popular with collectors, but rarely faceted. It was used as a pigment during the Middle Ages and Renaissance (blue verditer). It forms as a secondary mineral in the oxidized zone of copper deposits associated with carbonate rocks, occurring with malachite, chrysocolla, cerussite or smithsonite. It forms better crystals than malachite, which sometimes pseudomorphs it through hydration of the azurite. There are more than a hundred different crystal forms, good crystals are found at Chessy (France), hence the synonym chessylite, Sardinia (Italy), Broken Hill (NSW, Australia), Tsumeb (Namibia), Laurion (Greece) and Oujda (Morocco).

## $Cu_3(CO_3)_2(OH)_2$

| | |
|---|---|
| Colour: | intense azure blue, paler when earthy, darker in crystals |
| Lustre; opacity: | vitreous, adamantine or dull; transparent to opaque |
| Streak: | pale blue |
| Hardness: | 3.5–4 |
| Specific gravity: | 3.78 |
| Cleavage; fracture: | perfect, prismatic; conchoidal |
| Habit: | crystals complex, often tabular or short prismatic, twinning common; massive, nodular or earthy |
| Crystal system: | monoclinic |

# Hydrozincite

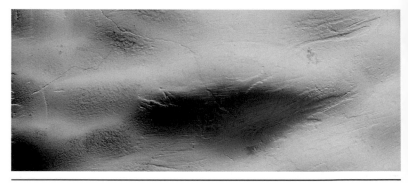

Hydrozincite, or zinc bloom, forms in the oxidation zones of zinc deposits through the alteration of sphalerite, zincite and other zinc minerals. It usually occurs as masses or crusts with internal fibrous structures, frequently with smithsonite. It readily dissolves in hydrochloric acid and often fluoresces strongly. When visited at night and with ultraviolet lights, the Trotter mine dump at Franklin (New Jersey, USA) makes a most unusual sight, with willemite fluorescing bright green, calcite bright red, and hydrozincite blue-white. Hydrozincite has been mined as a zinc ore, such as in the Picos de Europa near Santander (Spain), Nevada (USA) and currently at Mae Sod (Thailand) and Skorpion Mine (Namibia).

## $Zn_5(CO_3)_2(OH)_2$

| | |
|---|---|
| Colour: | usually white to grey, may be yellowish or brownish |
| Lustre; opacity: | crystals pearly, silky or dull; transparent to translucent |
| Streak: | white, dull to shining |
| Hardness: | 2–2.5 |
| Specific gravity: | 4 |
| Cleavage; fracture: | perfect; uneven |
| Habit: | crystals small and very rare, sharply pointed; usually massive, earthy, botryoidal, encrusting or stalactitic |
| Crystal system: | monoclinic |

# Rosasite

Rosasite is a very attractive rare bluish green mineral discovered in 1908 at Rosas Mine (Sardinia, Italy). A rare secondary mineral, it occurs in the oxidation zone of zinc-copper deposits, typically formed by the action of zinc-bearing solutions on primary copper minerals, but it can also be of post-mine origin. It may be associated with colourful minerals, such as limonite, hydrozincite, malachite, aurichalcite, smithsonite, cerussite or hemimorphite. Single crystals can be found at the Summit Mine (Montana); elsewhere in the USA it is found in California and New Mexico. Rosasite occurs in Kisil Espe (Turkestan), Ojuela Mine (Durango, Mexico), and Tsumeb (Namibia). It is a minor ore of copper.

## $(Cu,Zn)_2CO_3(OH)_2$

| | |
|---|---|
| Colour: | green to bluish green or sky blue |
| Lustre; opacity: | silky, vitreous or dull; translucent to opaque |
| Streak: | paler than colour |
| Hardness: | 4.5 |
| Specific gravity: | 4.0–4.2 |
| Cleavage; fracture: | in two directions at right angles; fibrous, splintery |
| Habit: | commonly radiating tufts of fibrous crystals; as crusts, or botyroidal masses or nodules |
| Crystal system: | monoclinic |

# Aurichalcite

A urichalcite is a popular mineral characterized by delicate acicular crystals, and great care must be taken when handling. It was named either after the Greek word *oreichalchos*, which means 'mountain copper', or possibly after *aurichalcum* which means 'yellow copper ore'. Aurichalcite effervesces in cold hydrochloric and nitric acids, and in ammonia. It forms in the oxidized zones of zinc-copper deposits, and is occasionally used as an ore. It can be associated with red limonite and other colourful minerals such as azurite, smithsonite and malachite. Localities include Rosas Mine (Sardinia, Italy), Chessy (Rhône, France), Laurion (Attica, Greece), Tsumeb (Namibia) and notably Ojuela Mine (Mapimi, Durango, Mexico).

## $(Zn,Cu)_5(CO_3)_2(OH)_6$

| | |
|---|---|
| **Colour:** | pale green to greenish blue and sky blue |
| **Lustre; opacity:** | silky or pearly; transparent to translucent |
| **Streak:** | pale green or blue |
| **Hardness:** | 1–2 |
| **Specific gravity:** | 3.6–3.9 (above average for non-metallic minerals) |
| **Cleavage; fracture:** | perfect; uneven or fibrous, fragile |
| **Habit:** | delicate acicular crystals, often striated, radiating tufts; as feathery encrustations or columnar, laminated, granular |
| **Crystal system:** | orthorhombic |

# Phosgenite

Phosgenite is a rare lead mineral of high lustre, which fluoresces yellow. It dissolves with effervescence in dilute nitric acid. It forms in the oxidation zone of hydrothermal lead ore deposits, especially in the presence of sea water. It has also been found in slag heaps from the ancient lead-silver mines at Laurion (Attica, Greece), which are now in the sea. Phosgenite was used as a white pigment in ancient Egyptian cosmetics, but it was probably synthesized from smelted lead oxides, as there was no access to the natural mineral. Enormous crystals occur at Monteponi and Montevecchio (Sardinia, Italy), in association with cerussite and anglesite; other notable localities are Tsumeb (Namibia), and Dundas (Tasmania).

## $Pb_2(CO_3)Cl_2$

| | |
|---|---|
| **Colour:** | colourless, white, pale brown or pale yellowish brown |
| **Lustre; opacity:** | adamantine; transparent to translucent |
| **Streak:** | white |
| **Hardness:** | 2.5–3 |
| **Specific gravity:** | 6.13 |
| **Cleavage; fracture:** | two distinct, prismatic; conchoidal, sectile and flexible |
| **Habit:** | crystals usually prismatic, may be tabular, weakly striated; also massive or granular |
| **Crystal system:** | tetragonal |

143

# Trona

Trona is deposited from saline lakes in arid regions, associated with halite, natron, gypsum or thenardite. It has an alkaline taste, is soluble and fluoresces white or blue. A natural source of sodium carbonate (soda ash), it is used to make paper, detergents, soap, glass, food and paper. The world's biggest reserves are in Wyoming (USA) and Lake Magadi (Kenya). In ancient Egypt, salt deposits in the lower Nile delta were exploited for natrum (largely trona), and used in medicine, mummification and to make cement (when mixed with caustic soda from silicate minerals and Nile silt). Notable occurrences include Searles Lake (California), Soda Lake (Nevada, USA) and the Otjiwalundo salt pan (Namibia).

## $Na_3(CO_3)(HCO_3).2H_2O$

| | |
|---|---|
| Colour: | colourless, grey, white, yellowish, brown |
| Lustre; opacity: | vitreous to dull, earthy; translucent |
| Streak: | white |
| Hardness: | 2.5–3.0 |
| Specific gravity: | 2.17 |
| Cleavage; fracture: | perfect; uneven to subconchoidal |
| Habit: | crystals prismatic or tabular, fibrous to compact aggregates; earthy crusts or efflorescences |
| Crystal system: | monoclinic |

# Gaylussite

Gaylussite, also known as natrocalcite, is a rare mineral named after the French scientist J.L. Gay-Lussac (1778–1850). It dehydrates when exposed to air, slowly crumbling and leaving calcium carbonate. It is slightly soluble in water, and effervesces in hydrochloric acid; it may luminesce creamy white. It is found in clay, shales and evaporites from soda lakes, along with natron, borax or calcite. Large crystals occur in the desert sands of Namibia and at Lake Amboseli (Kenya). It has also formed as an alteration product at Oldoinyo Lengai (Tanzania), the only volcano erupting natrocarbonatite lava. It occurs at Searles Lake (California, USA), Mt Erebus (Antarctica) and the Gobi Desert (Mongolia).

## $Na_2Ca(CO_3)_2.5H_2O$

| | |
|---|---|
| Colour: | white, yellowish-white |
| Lustre; opacity: | vitreous, dull; transparent to translucent |
| Streak: | grey–white |
| Hardness: | 2.5–3 |
| Specific gravity: | 1.99 (well below average) |
| Cleavage; fracture: | very good; conchoidal |
| Habit: | crystals prismatic or wedge-shaped; massive and encrusting |
| Crystal system: | monoclinic |

# Borax

Borax desiccates on exposure to air, turning to a white powder, tincalconite $(Na_2B_4O_7.5H_2O)$. It dissolves in water, has a bittersweet taste and may fluoresce blue-green. One of four main ores of boron, it forms in arid regions on the edges of playa lakes and is associated with other evaporites, especially borates. The source of the boron is probably thermal springs of volcanic origin. Commercially important deposits are exploited in California (USA); huge crystals can be found at Clear Lake and Borax Lake. Borax is used in cleaning products, water softeners, pesticides, timber preservatives and agriculture. It readily converts to boric acid, which is used as , for example, a mild antiseptic and in nuclear power plants.

## $Na_2B_4O_7.10H_2O$

| | |
|---|---|
| Colour: | colourless, white, tinged with grey, blue or green |
| Lustre; opacity: | vitreous, resinous, dull; transparent to opaque |
| Streak: | white |
| Hardness: | 2–2.5 |
| Specific gravity: | 1.7 |
| Cleavage; fracture: | perfect; conchoidal |
| Habit: | crystals short, prismatic; massive |
| Crystal system: | monoclinic |

# Ulexite

Ulexite forms as an evaporite in boron-rich lake basins in arid regions, associated with other borate minerals. It sometimes forms rounded masses of fine fibrous crystals known as cotton balls, as found in Death Valley (California, USA), or as parallel fibrous aggregates. Light is transmitted up each fibre, thus displaying fibre optics. If a specimen is polished flat at both ends (perpendicular to the fibres) and placed over a print, for example, the image appears at the top of the specimen. This unusual property has made it very popular, and it is sometimes referred to as television stone. The best locality for compact fibres is Boron, Kern County (California, USA). Turkey is the leading producer of boron ore, followed by the USA.

## $NaCaB_5O_9.8H_2O$

| | |
|---|---|
| Colour: | white or colourless |
| Lustre; opacity: | vitreous or silky |
| Streak: | white |
| Hardness: | 2.5 |
| Specific gravity: | 1.96 |
| Cleavage; fracture: | perfect; uneven |
| Habit: | crystals very rare; rounded aggregates with fibrous internal structure, tufted masses |
| Crystal system: | triclinic |

# Colemanite

Colemanite is one of the main ores of boron (see also borax, kernite and ulexite). It forms in warm and arid regions in alkaline playa lakes deficient in sodium and carbonate; the boron is probably sourced from geothermal springs. One boron mineral may change to another during diagenesis, e.g. colemanite can form from ulexite through contact with calcium-bearing ground water. Associated minerals include other borates, gypsum, celestine and calcite. More than 80 per cent of the world production of borates comes from the USA (including colemanite from Death Valley, California) and Turkey. Boron is used in the chemical industry and in the manufacture of steel, paints, heat-resistant glass and fluxes for welding.

## $Ca_2B_6O_{11}.5H_2O$

| | |
|---|---|
| Colour: | colourless, white, yellowish or grey |
| Lustre; opacity: | vitreous, adamantine; transparent to translucent |
| Streak: | white |
| Hardness: | 4–4.5 |
| Specific gravity: | 2.44 |
| Cleavage; fracture: | perfect; uneven or conchoidal |
| Habit: | crystals short, prismatic; compact, granular |
| Crystal system: | monoclinic |

# Kernite

Kernite is a rare mineral, the last of the four principal ores of boron. Specimens are difficult to keep because they effloresce (lose water), becoming opaque and dull. Kernite forms in intermittent lakes, supplied with boron from geothermal springs. It can form from borax with a rise in temperature and pressure, thus tending to concentrate at the base of stratified borate deposits. It can be associated with colemanite, ulexite and borax. Crystals up to 8.75m (29ft) long have been reported from Boron (Kern County, California, USA), a commercial source of kernite. Crystals up to 2.5m (8ft) occur at Tincalayu Mine (Salta, Argentina). Other important occurrences include Catalonia (Spain) and the Kirka deposit (Eskişehir, Turkey).

## $Na_2B_4O_7.4H_2O$

| | |
|---|---|
| Colour: | colourless when fresh, turning white |
| Lustre; opacity: | vitreous, dull, silky; transparent to opaque |
| Streak: | white |
| Hardness: | 2.5–3 |
| Specific gravity: | 1.9 |
| Cleavage; fracture: | perfect; splintery |
| Habit: | rare short, prismatic crystals; usually cleaved masses with fibrous habit |
| Crystal system: | monoclinic |

# Thenardite

**N**amed after the French chemist L.J. Thénard (1777–1857), thenardite is anhydrous sodium sulphate. In damp air, samples will absorb water to give the hydrated form, mirabilite or Glauber salt ($Na_2SO_4.10H_2O$). This requires that the mineral be stored in closed containers. It is used in the manufacture of sodium salts and as a desiccant in the chemical industry. Mostly found in salt lakes in especially hot and dry tropical areas and deserts, thenardite is associated with minerals, including mirabilite, gypsum, glauberite, epsomite and halite. It is common in the deserts of the USA (California, Arizona, Nevada), the Sahara, Chile, Central Asia, Egypt and Sudan. Sometimes it is found in fumaroles, such as in Vesuvius (Italy).

## $Na_2SO_4$

| | |
|---|---|
| Colour: | colourless, white or grey-white; yellowish or reddish tinges |
| Lustre; opacity: | vitreous; transparent to translucent |
| Streak: | white |
| Hardness: | 2.5–3 |
| Specific gravity: | 2.7 |
| Cleavage; fracture: | perfect; uneven to hackly |
| Habit: | crystals, sometimes large, are usually bipyramidal, occasionally prismatic with striated faces; crusts |
| Crystal system: | orthorhombic |

# Gypsum

The most common sulphate mineral, gypsum has relatively poor water-solubility and is often the first mineral deposited on evaporation of sea water. Varieties include selenite (colourless and transparent), satin spar (fibrous) and alabaster (massive and granular). Alabaster, usually white or in pastel shades, has been widely used for ornamental carvings for thousands of years. Satin spar is cut into cabochons and polished to give a 'cat's eye' effect. Its low thermal conductivity is utilized to insulate buildings ('drywalling'). Gypsum usually occurs as massive beds among other evaporites. It is often found as a cap rock on salt domes. It is found at Stassfurt (Germany), Paris basin (France) and Nova Scotia (Canada).

## $CaSO_4.2H_2O$

| | |
|---|---|
| Colour: | colourless or white; shades of grey, yellow or pink |
| Lustre; opacity: | vitreous, pearly on cleavage faces; transparent to translucent |
| Streak: | white |
| Hardness: | 2 |
| Specific gravity: | 2.32 |
| Cleavage; fracture: | perfect; conchoidal, splintery |
| Habit: | simple tabular crystals, often with curved faces; rosette-shaped aggregates and fibrous or granular masses |
| Crystal system: | monoclinic |

# Anhydrite

Anhydrite is formed by evaporation of sea water above 42°C (108°C); gypsum forms below this. It is mostly produced by dehydration of buried gypsum, which causes the rock to shrink, forming crevices and caverns. Anhydrite and gypsum are also the names of rocks comprising large masses of these minerals. Such rocks are used for producing sulphuric acid and ammonium sulphate (for fertilizer), paper fillers and plasters (notably plaster of Paris). Anhydrite often forms thick beds in the lower strata of evaporite deposits and is abundant as the cap to salt domes. It is found at Stassfurt (Germany), the Paris basin (France) and Louisiana and Texas (USA). Unusual purple crystals are found at Bex (Switzerland).

## $CaSO_4$

| | |
|---|---|
| **Colour:** | colourless to bluish when transparent, white, pink or mauve when massive; may be further discoloured by impurities |
| **Lustre; opacity:** | vitreous to pearly; transparent to translucent |
| **Streak:** | white |
| **Hardness:** | 3–3.5 |
| **Specific gravity:** | 2.9–3 |
| **Cleavage; fracture:** | good; uneven, splintery |
| **Habit:** | usually massive or granular; sometimes fibrous or lamellar; rarely crystals |
| **Crystal system:** | orthorhombic |

# Celestine

Celestine, or celestite, named after the Latin for 'celestial', is the main ore of strontium. The most attractive crystals are a beautiful pale sky blue, but colourless celestine is also common. Large crystals (2–3kg/4½–6½lb) occur at Put-in-Bay (Ohio, USA). Strontium gives a strong crimson colour to a flame, useful in fireworks and flares. It is distinguished from barite by its lower density and very different flame test (barium gives green). Celestine occurs in impure limestones associated with sulphur, and in evaporites with gypsum, anhydrite or halite. Good crystals of celestine come from Lake Erie (USA), Bristol (England) and Sicily (Italy). Celestine, as a strontium ore, is mined in England, Russia and Tunisia.

## $SrSO_4$

| | |
|---|---|
| Colour: | colourless or pale blue |
| Lustre; opacity: | vitreous, pearly on cleavage; transparent to translucent |
| Streak: | white |
| Hardness: | 3–3.5 |
| Specific gravity: | 3.9–4 |
| Cleavage; fracture: | perfect; uneven |
| Habit: | tabular or prismatic crystals; can be fibrous or granular |
| Crystal system: | orthorhombic |

# Anglesite

As with most lead minerals, anglesite is notably dense. Anglesite, named after Anglesey, Wales, is an ore of lead formerly much used as a pigment in white paints, but now largely superseded by titanium oxide. Attractive yellow crystals are popular, but are quite soft and fragile. Anglesite occurs in the oxidized zones of galena deposits, associated with cerussite, mimetite and pyromorphite; and rarely as a sublimate in volcanoes. Good crystals come from Tsumeb (Namibia), Anglesey (Wales), Musen (Germany), Phoenixville (USA) and Monteponi (Sardinia). Sulphur-covered crystals are from Los Lamentos (Chihuahua, Mexico). It is mined in Leadhills (Scotland), Derbyshire (England) and Arizona and Utah (USA).

## $PbSO_4$

| | |
|---|---|
| Colour: | colourless or white; can be tinged brown, grey, blue, green, purple or more usually pale yellow |
| Lustre; opacity: | adamantine, sometimes resinous; transparent to opaque |
| Streak: | white |
| Hardness: | 2.5–3 |
| Specific gravity : | 6.2–6.4 |
| Cleavage; fracture: | perfect; conchoidal |
| Habit: | crystals prismatic, tabular or pyramidal; massive, compact or granular |
| Crystal system: | orthorhombic |

# Barite

Barite (also baryte, barytes or heavy spar) is notable for its high density, the Greek *baros* meaning 'heavy'. Large crystals (up to 1m/3¼ft) and roseate clusters of grains called desert roses are popular among collectors. Stalagmitic barite may be sectioned to reveal attractive concentric zoning. Large quantities are mined for paint and paper manufacture, as drilling muds in the oil industry and as a source of metallic barium. Barite is found in lead and zinc mines as a gangue mineral (mining waste) with calcite, fluorite and quartz, occurring in veins in lead, zinc, silver, iron and nickel ores. Good desert roses come from Oklahoma and Kansas (USA); large crystals are to be found in Cumbria and Cornwall (England).

## $BaSO_4$

| | |
|---|---|
| **Colour:** | colourless or white; red, brown, yellow or blue |
| **Lustre; opacity:** | vitreous, pearly on cleavage; transparent to translucent |
| **Streak:** | white |
| **Hardness:** | 3–3.5 |
| **Specific gravity:** | 4.3–4.6 |
| **Cleavage; fracture:** | perfect; uneven |
| **Habit:** | crystals tabular, sometimes prismatic; often massive, sometimes fibrous or lamellar clusters, or granular stalagmites |
| **Crystal system:** | orthorhombic |

155

# Spangolite

A beautiful rare blue-green mineral, spangolite usually occurs as aggregates of small crystals on a matrix; specimens with minerals such as azurite, brochantite and chrysocolla make pleasing displays. Spangolite is named after the engineer and avid mineral collector Norman Spang (1843–1922), who owned the original specimen. Spangolite is widespread, but found only in small quantities. Spangolite occurs in oxidized copper sulphide ores associated with azurite, malachite, adamite and tyrolite. It is found at Blanchard mine (New Mexico, USA), Tintic (Utah, USA), Mujaba Hill (Nevada, USA), St Day (Cornwall, England), Fontana Rossa (Corsica), Broken Hill (NSW, Australia), Laurion (Greece) and Arenas (Sardinia).

## $Cu_6AlSO_4(OH)_{12}Cl.3H_2O$

| | |
|---|---|
| Colour: | green or greeny-blue |
| Lustre; opacity: | vitreous; transparent |
| Streak: | pale yellow-green |
| Hardness: | 3 |
| Specific gravity: | 3.1 |
| Cleavage; fracture: | perfect; conchoidal |
| Habit: | short prisms and hexagonal plates |
| Crystal system: | hexagonal |

# Brochantite

Brochantite, named after the French geologist A. Brochant de Villiers (1772–1840), is a bright green mineral popular as a micromount. It is very difficult to distinguish from fibrous forms of antlerite and atacamite, although the latter is softer. Brochantite is formed as a secondary mineral in the oxidized zone of copper deposits, usually in dry climates. It is associated with malachite, atacamite, antlerite, limonite, cuprite, chrysocolla and cyanotrichite. Popular localities are Chuquicamata (Chile), Tsumeb (Namibia), Sardinia, Rezbanya (Romania), Ain Barbar (Algeria) and Broken Hill (NSW, Australia). Artificial brochantite is produced, so collectors should be careful with sources.

## $Cu_4SO_4(OH)_6$

| | |
|---|---|
| Colour: | bright green |
| Lustre; opacity: | vitreous to pearly; transparent to translucent |
| Streak: | light green |
| Hardness: | 3.5–4 |
| Specific gravity: | 3.97 |
| Cleavage; fracture: | perfect; uneven to conchoidal |
| Habit: | small, stubby or acicular, striated crystals, sprays of small needles; fibrous or granular crusts and nodules; rarely massive |
| Crystal system: | monoclinic |

# Alunite

Alunite is the main constituent of the rock alum stone, mined for alum production since the fifteenth century. Alum has the formula $KAl(SO_4)2.12H_2O$ and is used for papermaking and treating skins. Alum and alunite have been used to stem bleeding of small cuts. Most deposits were formed when rocks rich in alkali feldspar (pegmatites, syenites, trachytes) were altered by sulphate-rich water, in turn produced from altered pyrite. Sometimes alunite occurs in veins cutting across schists and in fumaroles. It is often found with halloysite and kaolinite. Alunite is mined at La Tolfa (Italy), Nevada (USA), France, Hungary, Greece, Almeria (Spain) and Bullah Delah (NSW, Australia).

## $KAl_3(SO_4)_2(OH)_6$

| | |
|---|---|
| Colour: | white; can be grey, yellowish or reddish |
| Lustre; opacity: | vitreous; transparent to translucent |
| Streak: | white |
| Hardness: | 3.5–4 |
| Specific gravity: | 2.6–2.9 |
| Cleavage; fracture: | good; conchoidal |
| Habit: | crystals as rhombohedra or plates; usually granular or earthy masses |
| Crystal system: | hexagonal |

# Linarite

Linarite is a rare mineral usually occurring with copper and lead ores. The name is derived from Linares, where it was first recognized in 1839. Linarite can be distinguished from the similar mineral azurite, as the latter fizzes with acids. Linarite is found in the oxidized zones of mixed lead and copper deposits, associated with aurichalcite, cerrussite, malachite and hemimorphite. The best crystals, more than 10cm (4in) in length, come from Mammoth Mine (Tiger, Arizona, USA); others come from Kisamori (Akita, Japan), Linares plateau (Jean, Spain), Tsumeb (Namibia), Red Gill (Cumbria, England), Serra de Capitillas (Argentina), Rosas and San Giovani (Sardinia), Leadhills (Scotland).

## $PbCuSO_4(OH)_2$

| | |
|---|---|
| Colour: | royal blue |
| Lustre; opacity: | vitreous; transparent to translucent |
| Streak: | blue |
| Hardness: | 2.5 |
| Specific gravity: | 5.3–5.5 |
| Cleavage; fracture: | perfect; conchoidal |
| Habit: | acicular or tabular crystals, often slender prisms like tourmaline; encrustations, aggregates |
| Crystal system: | monoclinic |

# Glauberite

G lauberite is used for the extraction of Glauber salt ($Na_2SO_4.10H_2O$), after which it is named, as a mordant in textile dying and in pharmaceuticals. Glauberite is very water-soluble and can be dissolved out of rocks and infilled with other mineral pseudomorphs. Glauberite may be found in buried sediments of geological age or in modern salt lakes and other evaporites. Associated minerals include halite, thenardite, calcite and gypsum. Occasionally it is a sublimate in fumaroles. Good crystals of glauberite are found in Villarubia (Spain), Lorraine (France) and salt lakes in California and Arizona (USA). Large masses occur around Saltzburg (Austria), Ruthenia (Russia), Texas (USA) and New Mexico (USA).

## $Na_2Ca(SO_4)_2$

| | |
|---|---|
| Colour: | white, tinged yellow or brick-red |
| Lustre; opacity: | vitreous; transparent to translucent |
| Streak: | white |
| Hardness: | 2.5–3 |
| Specific gravity : | 2.8 |
| Cleavage; fracture: | perfect; conchoidal |
| Habit: | tabular, prismatic or bipyramidal crystals, sometimes with striated faces and rounded edges; compact masses and crusts |
| Crystal system: | monoclinic |

# Halotrichite

Halotrichite is isomorphous with pickeringite ($MgAl_2(SO_4)_4.22H_2O$), which is present in most specimens. Masrite is a variety containing manganese and cobalt; apjohnite, dietrichite, redingtonite, wupatkiite and bilinite variously have cobalt, manganese, zinc, nickel and/or chromium replacing the iron or aluminium. Halotrichite, also known as iron alum or feather alum, is named from the Latin for 'hair salt' because of its form as fine fibrous needles. It is found as a pyrite alteration product in aluminous rocks and in fumaroles. It occurs at Sulfatara (Naples, Italy), Falun (Sweden), Recsk (Hungary), Istria (Croatia), Dubnik (Slovakia), Copiapo (Atacama, Chile) and Alum Mountain (New Mexico, USA).

## $FeAl_2(SO_4)_4.22H_2O$

| | |
|---|---|
| Colour: | colourless, white, yellowish, greenish |
| Lustre; opacity: | vitreous; transparent to translucent |
| Streak: | white |
| Hardness: | 1.5 |
| Specific gravity: | 1.9 |
| Cleavage; fracture: | imperfect; conchoidal |
| Habit: | acicular, prismatic crystals; crusts and aggregates |
| Crystal system: | monoclinic |

161

# Cyanotrichite

Cyanotrichite is named from the Greek for 'blue hair', after the appearance of felted masses of crystalline needles. Related to but rarer than halotricite, it is also known as lettsomite or velvet copper. Specimens as attractive blue tufts on a matrix are best viewed magnified, as the crystals are usually small. Cyanotrichite occurs in the oxidized zones of copper deposits, associated with minerals such as azurite, malachite and limonite. It is found at Cap Garonne (France), Laurion (Greece), Nemaqualand (South Africa), Mednorudnyansk (Russia), Bisbee (New Mexico, USA), Grandview (Arizona, USA), Moldova Noua (Romania), Traversella (Piedmont) and Rio Marina (Elba, Italy) and St Day (Cornwall, England).

## $Cu_4Al_2SO_4(OH)_{12}.2H_2O$

| | |
|---|---|
| Colour: | orange-red, hyacinth red |
| Lustre; opacity: | vitreous; transparent to translucent |
| Streak: | ochre yellow |
| Hardness: | 2.5 |
| Specific gravity: | 2.1 |
| Cleavage; fracture: | perfect; conchoidal, irregular |
| Habit: | elongated prismatic crystals as radiating fibrous aggregates of botryoidal or reniform shape |
| Crystal system: | monoclinic |

# Botryogen

**B**otryogen is a rare dark orange mineral named from the Greek *botrys* for 'grape' and *genos* for 'yield', after its characteristic habit. A popular variety with small aggregates of botryogen on halotrichite needles is found at Smolník (Slovakia). Botryogen, also known as red iron vitriol, is formed by the action of sulphate-rich fluids on mafic minerals. It often occurs near pyrite deposits in arid regions, associated with epsomite, copiapite and voltaite. It is found at Rammelsberg (Germany), Falun (Sweden), Villé Valley (France), Chuquicamata (Chile), Knoxville (Tennessee, USA), San Juan (Argentina), Queensland (Australia), Madeni-Zakli (Iran) and Paracutin (Mexico).

## MgFe(SO$_4$)$_2$OH.7H$_2$O

| | |
|---|---|
| Colour: | orange-red, hyacinth red |
| Lustre; opacity: | vitreous; transparent to translucent |
| Streak: | ochre yellow |
| Hardness: | 2.5 |
| Specific gravity: | 2.1 |
| Cleavage; fracture: | perfect; conchoidal, irregular |
| Habit: | elongated prismatic crystals as radiating fibrous aggregates of botryoidal or reniform shape |
| Crystal system: | monoclinic |

# Kröhnkite

Named after B. Kröhnke, the first person to analyze it, kröhnkite is a rare blue mineral easily mistaken for others such as chalcanthite. Kröhnkite is abundant in large royal blue crystals in the Chuquicamata mine, which is the largest open-pit copper mine in the world. Twinning in crystals can result in attractive heart-shaped forms. It is formed from sulphate-rich fluids in desert regions and found among copper ores often associated with chalcanthite, antlerite and atacamite. Good localities for finding kröhnkite are Chuquicamata and Quetena mines (Chile), Capo Calamita (Elba, Italy), Wheal Hazard (Cornwall, England), Recsk copper deposit (Matra Mountains, Hungary) and Broken Hill (NSW, Australia).

## Na$_2$Cu(SO$_4$)$_2$.2H$_2$O

| | |
|---|---|
| **Colour:** | blue to light blue |
| **Lustre; opacity:** | vitreous; transparent |
| **Streak:** | white |
| **Hardness:** | 2.5–3 |
| **Specific gravity:** | 2.9 |
| **Cleavage; fracture:** | perfect; conchoidal |
| **Habit:** | prismatic crystals; fibrous and granular crusts and aggregates |
| **Crystal system:** | monoclinic |

# Kainite

Kainite is a double salt formed as a mixture of potassium chloride (sylvite) and magnesium sulphate (epsomite). It is named somewhat obscurely after the Greek *kainos*, meaning 'new' or 'contemporary', alluding to its occurrence in rocks of recent origin. Kainite is a common mineral in evaporites, but difficult to identify. Kainite is used in fertilizers and as a source of potassium compounds. It is found among evaporite deposits associated with halite, sylvite and carnallite; and as a volcanic sublimate. Localities where kainite has been mined are Hallstadt (Austria), Eddy County (New Mexico, USA), Kalus (Ukraine) and Sicily (Italy). It is a major mineral found in the large salt deposits of middle and northern Germany.

## $KMgSO_4Cl.3H_2O$

| | |
|---|---|
| Colour: | white, yellow, greyish |
| Lustre; opacity: | vitreous |
| Streak: | white |
| Hardness: | 3 |
| Specific gravity: | 2.1–2.2 |
| Cleavage; fracture: | good |
| Habit: | rare thick, tabular crystals; usually granular or fibrous aggregates |
| Crystal system: | monoclinic |

# Devilline

Devilline is an attractive blue-green mineral named after the French chemist H. Deville (1818–1881). It is also called devillite or herrengrundite after a locality in Slovakia. A sky-blue zinc-bearing variety is called serpierite or zincian devilline. Devilline is a rare secondary mineral found in copper deposits associated with gypsum, azurite and malachite. It is found in Cornwall (England), Pania Dolina (Slovakia), Tsumeb (Namibia), Montgomery (Pennsylvania, USA) and Vezzani, (Corsica). Serpierite has been found at Kamariza (Laurion, Greece), Ross Island (Ireland) and Broken Hill (NSW, Australia). A light blue manganese–bearing variety campigliaite has been identified at Temerino (Tuscany, Italy).

## $CaCu_4(SO_4)_2(OH)_6$

| | |
|---|---|
| Colour: | blue-green to emerald green |
| Lustre; opacity: | vitreous to pearly; transparent to translucent |
| Streak: | light green |
| Hardness: | 2.5 |
| Specific gravity: | 3.1 |
| Cleavage; fracture: | perfect; brittle |
| Habit: | crystals often lamellar in rosettes or needle-like clusters; crusts, botryoidal aggregates |
| Crystal system: | monoclinic |

# Epsomite

Commonly known when pure as Epsom or bitter salts, epsomite is a white water-soluble hydrate of magnesium sulphate. It is used as a mordant in hide tanning and textile dying, and dried for use as a desiccant. It is precipitated from hot springs, fumaroles and saline waters. The thermal waters at Epsom are well known for encrustations of epsomite. It is found on the walls of mines near weathered pyrite deposits. Crystals up to 2–3m (6½–10ft) come from Kruger Hills (Washington, USA). Epsomite is light and fragile, and loses water in dry air, becoming dull in appearance. It is mined at Carlsbad (New Mexico, USA), Saxony (Germany), Sedlec (Czech Republic) and Valle Antrona (Italy).

## $MgSO_4 \cdot 7H_2O$

| | |
|---|---|
| Colour: | white; can be tinged yellow, green, red |
| Lustre; opacity: | vitreous to silky; transparent to translucent |
| Streak: | white |
| Hardness: | 2–2.5 |
| Specific gravity: | 1.68 |
| Cleavage; fracture: | perfect; conchoidal |
| Habit: | crystals rare; usually crusts, stalactites and earthy masses |
| Crystal system: | orthorhombic |

# Römerite

Römerite is an attractive yellow-brown mineral named after the German geologist Friedrich Römer (1809–1869). Violet-brown aggregates and dark orange crystals are popular, attractive occurrences. It is formed in oxidized zones of iron sulphide deposits, associated with other sulphates, especially halotrichite, copiapite ($Fe_5(SO_4)_6(OH)_2.20H_2O$) and melantesite ($FeSO_4.7H_2O$). It is found in Dresden (Saxony), Rammelsberg (Harz) and Valdsassen (Bavaria, Germany), Rtyne and Pribram (Czech Republic), Madeni Zakh (Iran), Tierra Amarilla and Chuquicamata (Chile), Blyava (Southern Urals) and Kamchatka (Russia).

## $Fe_3(SO_4)_4.14H_2O$

| | |
|---|---|
| Colour: | brown to yellow-brown, occasionally violet-tinged |
| Lustre; opacity: | vitreous, resinous; translucent |
| Streak: | yellow-brown |
| Hardness: | 3–3.5 |
| Specific gravity: | 2.17 |
| Cleavage; fracture: | perfect, good; uneven |
| Habit: | tabular or pseudocubic crystals; crusts, granular layers and stalactites |
| Crystal system: | triclinic |

# Crocoite

Crocoite, also called red lead ore, is named from the Greek *krokos*, meaning 'saffron' or 'crocus', after its bright orange-red colour. It is the mineral from which chromium was first extracted, but is not used as an ore commercially. Crocoite is one of the few naturally occurring chromates, which are always strongly coloured. Pure crocoite forms the pigment chrome yellow. It is formed where chromic-acid rich hydrothermal solutions have attacked lead deposits. It is associated with cerrusite, limonite, anglesite, phoenicochroite and vauquelinite. Crystals up to 15cm (6in) have been found at Dundas (Tasmania); other localities include Minas Gerais (Brazil), Nontron (France) and Mammoth Cave (Arizona, USA).

## $PbCrO_4$

| | |
|---|---|
| Colour: | yellow, orange, red |
| Lustre; opacity: | adamantine; translucent |
| Streak: | orange |
| Hardness: | 2.5–3 |
| Specific gravity: | 6 |
| Cleavage; fracture: | perfect; conchoidal |
| Habit: | prismatic crystals, often striated, often hollow, acicular crystals; massive, granular |
| Crystal system: | monoclinic |

SULPHATES, CHROMATES, MOLYBDATES AND TUNGSTATES

# Scheelite

Scheelite is a major ore of tungsten, used in lightbulb filaments, high-strength steels and tungsten carbide cutting tools. Named after the Swedish chemist K. Scheele (1742–1786), it forms crystals with a high lustre and fire, and was used as an early synthetic diamond. Fluorescing pale blue under UV light, scheelite is used as a scintilator. The fluorescence becomes greener as the content of powellite ($CaMoO_4$) increases. Scheelite is found in pegmatites, hydrothermal veins and medium-grade metamorphic rocks. Crystals of a weight up to 500g (1lb 2oz) are reported from Minas Gerais (Brazil) and of a size up to 7.5cm (3in) in Tong Wha (Korea); other localities are Sardinia, Traversella, Val di Fiemme and Valsugana (Italy).

## $CaWO_4$

| Colour: | grey-white, yellow, brown, reddish, greenish |
|---|---|
| Lustre; opacity: | vitreous to adamantine; transparent to opaque |
| Streak: | white |
| Hardness: | 4.5–5 |
| Specific gravity: | 5.9–6.1 |
| Cleavage; fracture: | imperfect; conchoidal |
| Habit: | crystals as bipyramids, pyramids, plates; massive aggregates, granular, crusts, pseudomorphs |
| Crystal system: | tetragonal |

# Wolframite

Wolframite is a major ore of tungsten, its name coming from *wolfram*, the German word for tungsten. Its composition lies within the ferberite-heubnerite series ($FeWO_4$–$MnWO_4$). The colour darkens as the iron content increases. Tungsten is widely used, but some demand for its use in hardened metals has been taken by depleted uranium. It occurs in pegmatites, hydrothermal veins, pneumatolytic zones and placer deposits. Associated minerals include scheelite, cassiterite, pyrite and sphalerite. Important deposits are in southern China, Queensland (Australia), La Paz (Bolivia), Arizona (USA) and New Mexico (USA); superb crystals at Hualapón (Pasto Bueno, Peru) and Quartz Creek (Idaho, USA).

## $(Fe,Mn)WO_4$

| | |
|---|---|
| Colour: | yellow to reddish-brown to blackish brown |
| Lustre; opacity: | submetallic, resinous; opaque |
| Streak: | brown to black |
| Hardness: | 5–5.5 |
| Specific gravity: | 7.1–7.5 |
| Cleavage; fracture: | perfect; uneven |
| Habit: | vertically striated tabular or lamellar crystals; massive, granular |
| Crystal system: | monoclinic |

# Wulfenite

Wulfenite, or yellow lead ore, a minor ore of molybdenum, is named after the Austrian mineralogist Franz Wülfen (1728–1805). Popular specimens comprise clusters of large square red crystals among smaller ones. As with many lead minerals, wulfenite has a high refractive index (2.3–2.4), which enhances its appearance. Wulfenite occurs in the oxidized zones of lead deposits, associated with cerussite, vanadinite, pyromorphite and mimetite. The best localities include: Red Cloud (Arizona, USA), noted for superb red crystals; Rezbanya (Romania) for reddish crystals; Bleiberg (Austria) for yellow crystals; Tsumeb (Namibia) and Phoenixville (Pennsylvania, USA) for colourless crystals.

## $PbMoO_4$

| | |
|---|---|
| **Colour:** | yellow, orange, red, rarely white |
| **Lustre; opacity:** | resinous; transparent to opaque |
| **Streak:** | yellowish-white |
| **Hardness:** | 2–3 |
| **Specific gravity:** | 6.7–6.9 |
| **Cleavage; fracture:** | imperfect; conchoidal |
| **Habit:** | crystals square tabular or stubby pyramids, often as clusters; massive, granular or earthy aggregates |
| **Crystal system:** | tetragonal |

# Purpurite

**P**urpurite is a very rare mineral, much sought-after by collectors. Its name comes from its characteristic colour when fresh, although it may show surface alteration to a darker brown. It forms through the oxidation and leaching of manganese-iron phosphates, particularly lithiophyllite (LiMnPO$_4$), found in granite pegmatites. It has also been known to form through the reaction of sea water with bat guano, which provides the phosphorus. Associated minerals include lithiophyllite and heterosite. As well as the type locality Faires tin mine (North Carolina, USA), it occurs in the Varuträsk pegmatite (Västerbotten, Sweden), Mangualde (Portugal), La Vilate quarry (Chanteloupe, France) and the Gunong Keriang cave (Malaysia).

## (Mn,Fe)PO$_4$

| | |
|---|---|
| **Colour:** | reddish purple to deep rose red |
| **Lustre; opacity:** | satiny on fresh fractures, or earthy; translucent to opaque |
| **Streak:** | pale purple to pale red |
| **Hardness:** | 4–4.5 |
| **Specific gravity:** | 3.2–3.4 |
| **Cleavage; fracture:** | good, surfaces may be curved or crinkled; uneven, brittle |
| **Habit:** | does not occur as crystals; forms small irregular masses, cleavage fragments may reach 20cm (8in) |
| **Crystal system:** | orthorhombic |

# Monazite

Monazite is a rare earth phosphate, containing up to 12 per cent $ThO_2$, and is feebly radioactive. It is a common accessory in granites, syenites and metamorphic gneisses, and is also found as a placer deposit, being dense and resistant to chemical weathering. Monazite is the main source of rare earths, used as a fuel-cracking catalyst in the petroleum industry, and of thorium. Thorium is important in the computer, electronic and medical industries. It is also the most efficient nuclear reactor fuel, and could potentially be used instead of uranium. Important commercial sources are Australia (with the largest reserve), Florida (USA), Madagascar, Brazil, Travancore (India), Sri Lanka and South Africa.

## $(Ce,La,Nd,Th)PO_4$

| | |
|---|---|
| Colour: | yellow to reddish brown |
| Lustre; opacity: | resinous to waxy, vitreous; transparent to translucent |
| Streak: | white |
| Hardness: | 5–5.5 |
| Specific gravity: | 4.6–5.4 |
| Cleavage; fracture: | good; conchoidal to uneven fracture |
| Habit: | crystals tabular or prismatic; usually as grains |
| Crystal system: | monoclinic |

# Amblygonite

Amblygonite is a fluorophosphate that can luminesce orange in long-wave ultraviolet light. It occurs in coarse-grained granitic rocks and in lithium- and phosphate-rich granitic pegmatites – associated, for example, with apatite, pollucite and spodumene. It is used as a source of lithium, but can also be faceted to make gems when transparent or translucent. Amblygonite being relatively soft, these tend to be of interest only to collectors. Gem-quality material occurs in pegmatites at Minas Gerais (Brazil) and at Newry (Maine, USA), and giant crystals weighing several tons have been found at Custer (Dakota, USA); it also occurs in the pegmatites of Pala (California, USA) and in Yauapa County (Arizona, USA).

## (Li,Na)Al(PO$_4$)F

| | |
|---|---|
| Colour: | milk white, yellow, bluish, greenish, pink or colourless |
| Lustre; opacity: | vitreous to greasy; transparent to translucent |
| Streak: | white |
| Hardness: | 5.5–6 |
| Specific gravity: | 3.1 |
| Cleavage; fracture: | two good cleavages; uneven |
| Habit: | crystals equant, rough, and may be twinned; also as cleavable masses, or compact |
| Crystal system: | triclinic |

# Olivenite

Named after its olive-green colour, olivenite is much in demand by mineral collectors. Although rare, it is the most common secondary copper arsenate found in the oxidized zone of hydrothermal copper deposits. It is associated with other copper minerals such as azurite, malachite, chrysocolla and chalcopyrite, and sometimes with arsenopyrite and spangolite. The type locality is Carharrak Mine in Cornwall, England; elsewhere in Britain it is found on Alston Moor (Cumbria) and Tavistock (Devon). Other localities include Cap Garonne (France), Clara Mine (near Oberwolfach, Germany), and the porphyry copper deposits of Chuquicamata in Chile. Excellent large crystals occur in Tsumeb (Namibia).

## $Cu_2(AsO_4)(OH)$

| | |
|---|---|
| **Colour:** | shades of olive green, dirty white, straw yellow |
| **Lustre; opacity:** | adamantine, vitreous, pearly, silky; transparent to opaque |
| **Streak:** | olive green to brown |
| **Hardness:** | 3 |
| **Specific gravity:** | 4–4.5 |
| **Cleavage; fracture:** | indistinct; forms small conchoidal fragments, very brittle |
| **Habit:** | crystals variable, may be elongated, or of short, prismatic, acicular or fibrous form; also as reniform masses |
| **Crystal system:** | monoclinic; pseudo-orthorhombic |

# Adamite

Adamite forms a series with olivenite $Cu_2(AsO_4)(OH)$. A popular mineral with collectors, adamite is generally shades of yellow, green or brown, although it may be violet to rose-coloured where cobalt has substituted for zinc. Some specimens fluoresce lemon yellow or greenish white, and some phosphoresce. Adamite is a rare secondary mineral found in the oxidized zones of ore deposits containing primary zinc- or arsenic-bearing minerals. It is associated with a variety of minerals, including malachite, reddish limonite, smithsonite or hemimorphite. It occurs at the type locality in the Atacama Desert (Chile), and also at Schwarzwald (Germany), Laurion (Greece), Durango (Mexico) and Tsumeb (Namibia).

## $Zn_2(AsO_4)(OH)$

| | |
|---|---|
| Colour: | yellow, brownish yellow to green, pink or violet |
| Lustre; opacity: | vitreous; transparent to translucent |
| Streak: | white |
| Hardness: | 3.5 |
| Specific gravity: | 4.3–4.5 |
| Cleavage; fracture: | good; uneven to subconchoidal |
| Habit: | crystals elongate tabular, platy or equant; usually forms crusts or spheroidal masses, or roughly radial aggregates |
| Crystal system: | orthorhombic |

# Lazulite

Lazulite derives its name from the Arabic *azul*, meaning 'sky' or 'heaven', and the Greek *lithos*, meaning 'stone'. It has sometimes been confused with lazurite, lapis lazuli or azurite. It is a minor semi-precious stone, and may be polished, carved or tumbled to make beads or attractive ornamental stones. The rare transparent form is pleochroic, changing from blue to colourless. Lazulite occurs in high grade, quartz-rich metamorphic rocks, veins and pegmatites, associated with minerals such as andalusite, kyanite, sillimanite, and garnet. Beautiful crystals up to 5cm (2in) long occur in the Graves Mountains (Georgia, USA). Some of the best specimens occur in veins in iron-rich shales at Rapid Creek (Yukon, Canada).

## $MgAl_2(PO_4)_2(OH)_2$

| | |
|---|---|
| **Colour:** | deep azure blue to light blue or bluish green; mottled |
| **Lustre; opacity:** | vitreous to dull; translucent to opaque |
| **Streak:** | white |
| **Hardness:** | 5.5–6 |
| **Specific gravity:** | 3.1–3.4 (iron rich) |
| **Cleavage; fracture:** | indistinct to good, prismatic; uneven to splintery |
| **Habit:** | crystals show steep pyramidal forms, may be tabular; also massive or granular |
| **Crystal system:** | monoclinic |

# Pseudomalachite

Pseudomalachite differs from malachite because it lacks the characteristic colour banding and does not effervesce in warm hydrochloric acid, whereas malachite does. It is a very rare secondary mineral found in the oxidized zone of copper deposits, associated with azurite, malachite, atacamite, limonite or chalcedony. It is sometimes used as a precious stone. Its use in paint has been recorded in an ancient tomb at the prehistoric Mayan site known as Baking Pot, in Belize. It is found at Virneberg Mine (Rheinbreitbach, Germany), Cornwall (England), Libethen (Slovakia), Harquahala Mine (Arizona, USA), Bogolo (Portugal), Manto Cuba and San Salvador Mines (Atacama, Chile) and in Nizhni Tagil (Russia).

## $Cu_5(PO_4)_2(OH)_4$

| | |
|---|---|
| Colour: | emerald green to blackish green; paler when fibrous |
| Lustre; opacity: | vitreous, greasy; translucent to transparent |
| Streak: | blue-green, paler than colour |
| Hardness: | 4.5–5 |
| Specific gravity: | 4.3 |
| Cleavage; fracture: | perfect; splintery |
| Habit: | crystals rare, rough and rounded; forms radial clusters, coatings, stalactitic, reniform or botryoidal aggregates |
| Crystal system: | monoclinic |

# Brazilianite

Brazilianite is a rare and unusual mineral, named after its discovery at Minas Gerais (Brazil) in 1945. Brazilianite occurs in phosphate-rich pegmatites, and may be associated with clay, lazulite and apatite. A striking yellow or yellowish green, it is sometimes cut for collectors, and is probably the best of the phosphates to be used as a gemstone. Crystals are fragile and easily broken, however, as they have a conchoidal fracture and a very good cleavage parallel to their length. Good crystals occur at Minas Gerais (Brazil) and Palermo Mine (New Hampshire, USA). Other localities include Roĭná (Czech Republic), Hagendorf (Germany), Etiro (Namibia) and the Dawson Mining District (Yukon Territory, Canada).

## $NaAl_3(PO4)_2(OH)_4$

| | |
|---|---|
| Colour: | colourless, light yellow to greenish yellow |
| Lustre; opacity: | vitreous; transparent |
| Streak: | white |
| Hardness: | 5.5 |
| Specific gravity: | 3.0 |
| Cleavage; fracture: | good; conchoidal fracture |
| Habit: | crystals common and well-formed, striated; also as spherical aggregates |
| Crystal system: | monoclinic |

# Clinoclase

Clinoclase forms as a secondary mineral in the oxidation zone of arsenic-rich hydrothermal copper deposits. Associated minerals include liroconite, chalcophyllite, olivenite and cornwallite ($Cu_5(AsO_4)_2(OH)_4$). The type locality is Wheal Gorland (Cornwall, England); now closed, this mine has produced many fine and rare minerals. In common with other unusual secondary copper arsenate minerals, clinoclase occurs at the Majuba Hill Mine (Nevada, USA), also closed. Blue-black crystalline aggregates from this mine have been termed beetle ore. Other localities include Sayda (near Freiberg, Germany), Cap Garonne (France), Novoveská Huta (Slovakia), Stirling Mine (New Jersey, USA) and Tintic (Utah, USA).

## $Cu_3AsO_4(OH)_3$

| | |
|---|---|
| Colour: | greenish black or bluish green |
| Lustre; opacity: | vitreous, pearly on cleavage; subtransparent to translucent |
| Streak: | blue-green |
| Hardness: | 2.5–3 |
| Specific gravity: | 4.2–4.4 |
| Cleavage; fracture: | very good parallel to base; uneven |
| Habit: | crystals small, needle-like, pseudo-orthorhombohedral, or platy; radial, fibrous, spherical aggregates or encrustations |
| Crystal system: | monoclinic |

# Descloizite

Descloizite is the zinc end member of a complete series in which copper substitutes for zinc, mottramite being the copper end member. A secondary mineral, it forms in the oxidized zone of lead, zinc and copper ore deposits, and is often associated with lead minerals such as vanadinite, cerussite, wulfenite and pyromorphite. It also forms in sandstone, having been precipitated from circulating mineralized ground water. It is a rare but important ore of vanadium. Large masses are found at Otavi (Namibia), and particularly fine crystals at Bisbee (Arizona, USA) and Lake Valley (New Mexico, USA). It also occurs at Obir (Corinthia, Austria), Bena de Padru (Sardinia, Italy) and Tsumeb (Namibia).

## PbZn(VO$_4$)(OH)

| | |
|---|---|
| Colour: | orange-red, brown, brownish-red |
| Lustre; opacity: | resinous to greasy; transparent to translucent |
| Streak: | orange to reddish brown |
| Hardness: | 3.5 |
| Specific gravity: | 5.5–6.2 |
| Cleavage; fracture: | poor; uneven to subconchoidal, brittle |
| Habit: | crystals prismatic or platy; fibrous, botryoidal masses or crusts |
| Crystal system: | orthorhombic |

# Apatite

Apatite is the name for a group of minerals including fluorapatite, chlorapatite, and hydroxylapatite, in which fluorine, chlorine and hydroxyl substitute for one another, and carbonate apatite, $Ca_5(PO_4,CO_3,OH)_3(F,OH)$. Apatite is the main inorganic constituent of bones and teeth. It is a common accessory mineral in igneous rocks, and is found in some contact metamorphic calc-silicate rocks. It also occurs in extensive and economically important bedded deposits called phosphorites. Eighty per cent of world production is used in chemical fertilizers and in the production of phosphoric acid. Major mining areas include Florida and North Carolina (USA), Morocco, and the Kola Peninsula (Russia).

## $Ca_5(PO_4)_3(F,Cl,OH)$

| | |
|---|---|
| Colour: | usually green, may be violet, red or brown |
| Lustre; opacity: | vitreous to sub-resinous; transparent to opaque |
| Streak: | white |
| Hardness: | 5 |
| Specific gravity: | 3.1–3.2 |
| Cleavage; fracture: | poor; conchoidal to uneven |
| Habit: | crystals prismatic or needle-like, sometimes tabular; also massive, concretionary, mammillated or oolitic |
| Crystal system: | hexagonal |

# Pyromorphite

Pyromorphite forms one series with mimetite ($Pb_5(AsO_4)_3Cl$) and another with vanadinite ($Pb_5(VO_4)_3Cl$). It is named after the Greek *pyr* ('fire') and *morfe* ('form'), as melted globules will recrystallize. It can luminesce yellow in ultraviolet light. Pyromorphite often occurs in rounded barrel-shaped forms known as campylite. It forms as a secondary mineral in the oxidized zone of lead veins, and rarely as a volcanic sublimate. Associated minerals include galena, wulfenite, cerussite, vanadinite and descloizite. Pyromorphite is a minor ore of lead known as green lead ore. It occurs in Cornwall (England), Cordoba (Spain), Guang Xi (China), Bunker Hill Mine (Idaho, USA), Broken Hill (NSW, Australia) and Zambia.

## $Pb_5(PO_4)_3Cl$

| | |
|---|---|
| Colour: | usually green, can be yellow, orange, brown or colourless |
| Lustre; opacity: | adamantine, vitreous, resinous; transparent to translucent |
| Streak: | white |
| Hardness: | 3.5–4 |
| Specific gravity: | 7.1; unusually dense for a translucent mineral |
| Cleavage; fracture: | poor; uneven to subconchoidal |
| Habit: | crystals sometimes prismatic, occasionally hollow; also reniform or globular |
| Crystal system: | hexagonal |

# Mimetite

**M**imetite was named from the Greek *mimetes*, the 'imitator', alluding to its resemblance to pyromorphite, with which it forms a series. It is a rare secondary mineral formed in the oxidized zone of arsenic-bearing lead deposits. It is commonly associated with pyromorphite and other lead minerals, such as vanadinite, galena and anglesite, and also with hemimorphite and arsenopyrite. It may fluoresce reddish yellow. It is soluble in hydrochloric acid, producing a very strong smell similar to garlic. Mimetite is a minor ore of lead. Well-crystallized material is found at Johanngeorgenstadt (Germany), Pñíbram (Czech Republic) and particularly at Tsumeb (Namibia).

## $Pb_5(AsO_4)_3Cl$

| | |
|---|---|
| **Colour:** | yellow, orange, brown, red, white, or may be colourless |
| **Lustre; opacity:** | vitreous, resinous; subtransparent to translucent |
| **Streak:** | white |
| **Hardness:** | 3.5–4 |
| **Specific gravity:** | 7.0–7.3 |
| **Cleavage; fracture:** | weak; uneven to subconchoidal, brittle |
| **Habit:** | crystals slender, acicular, or may be tabular or barrel-shaped; globular, reniform, stalactitic or granular |
| **Crystal system:** | hexagonal |

# Vanadinite

Vanadinite is a rare mineral that darkens on exposure and loses transparency. It shares the same structure as apatite, and hence similar crystal shapes. It forms as a secondary mineral in the oxidation zone of lead deposits, associated with wulfenite, pyromorphite, mimetite, cerussite or anglesite. Vanadinite obtained as a by-product of other mining operations can be used as an ore of vanadium, used in metal alloys such as steel, in dyes and in ceramics. The best crystals are found at Mibladen (Morocco) and Grootfontein (South Africa). The original material from the type locality of Zimapan (Hildalgo, Mexico) was lost at sea. Vanadinite also occurs in Kabwe (Zambia), Obir (Austria) and Tsumeb (Namibia).

## $Pb_5(VO_4)_3Cl$

| | |
|---|---|
| Colour: | bright reddish-orange to yellow, brown |
| Lustre; opacity: | resinous to adamantine; translucent to opaque |
| Streak: | yellowish-white to brownish-yellow |
| Hardness: | 2.5–3 |
| Specific gravity: | 6.9–7.0 |
| Cleavage; fracture: | none; conchoidal or uneven, brittle |
| Habit: | crystals stubby, hexagonal, may be hollow; as fibrous radiating masses, crusts, granular, or nodular |
| Crystal system: | hexagonal |

# Variscite

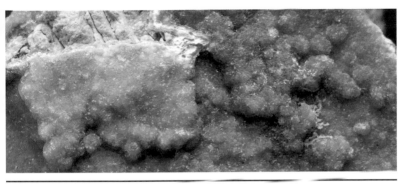

Variscite forms a series with strengite ($FePO_4.2H_2O$). It typically forms where phosphatic meteoric water has circulated through and reacted with aluminium-rich rocks, such as feldspar-rich igneous rocks. It has also been found in caves, the source of the phosphorus being decomposing bat guano. Associated minerals include apatite, wavellite and limonite. The name comes from Variscia, the old name for Vogtland (Germany), the type locality. Nodules up to 30cm (12in) occur at Fairfield (Utah, USA), and greenish encrustations in Montgomery County (Arkansas, USA). Variscite is occasionally smoothed, polished and sold as turquoise, or it can be cut into cabochons.

## $AlPO_4.2H_2O$

| | |
|---|---|
| Colour: | pale green, bluish green, emerald green; may be colourless |
| Lustre; opacity: | waxy to earthy; transparent to translucent |
| Streak: | white |
| Hardness: | 4–5 |
| Specific gravity: | 2.52 (variscite) |
| Cleavage; fracture: | good; conchoidal or uneven to splintery |
| Habit: | crystals very rare; massive, encrusting or reniform |
| Crystal system: | orthorhombic |

# Strengite

Strengite is the iron-bearing end member of the strengite–variscite series. It is a secondary mineral that forms in complex granitic pegmatites, as an alteration product of primary phosphate minerals such as triphylite ($Li(Fe,Mn)PO_4$) – e.g. Bull Moose Mine, South Dakota, USA. It also occurs in limonitic iron ores and gossans, and more rarely in caves where the phosphate from bat guano has been used in the alteration of iron-rich minerals to strengite. It may be associated with dufrenite, cacoxenite, vivianite or apatite. Localities include Hagendorf (Bavaria, Germany), Bomi Hill Caves (Liberia), Indian Mountain (Alabama, USA), Minas Gerais (Brazil) and Iron Monarch Quarry (South Australia).

## $FePO_4.2H_2O$

| | |
|---|---|
| Colour: | shades of violet, pink or red, may be colourless |
| Lustre; opacity: | vitreous; transparent to translucent |
| Streak: | white |
| Hardness: | 3.5 |
| Specific gravity: | 2.87 |
| Cleavage; fracture: | good; conchoidal |
| Habit: | crystals of variable habit; botryoidal, radial, or spherical nodules |
| Crystal system: | orthorhombic |

# Phosphophyllite

Phosphophyllite is found as a primary precipitate in tin-rich hydrothermal veins in Bolivia. Elsewhere, it occurs as a secondary mineral in complex granitic pegmatites, formed by the alteration of sphalerite and iron-manganese phosphates, and in hydrothermal vein deposits. Associated minerals include vivianite, strengite, sphalerite and apatite. It is a highly prized gemstone when a pale bluish green, and may be cut into facets or cabochons. It is brittle and fragile, however, and is rarely cut, as large crystals are too valuable to break up. It is very rare. Crystals up to 10cm (4in) occur at Potosi (Bolivia); other locations include Hagendorf (Germany), North Groton (New Hampshire, USA) and Kabwe (Zambia).

## $Zn_2(Fe,Mn)(PO_4)_2.4H_2O$

| | |
|---|---|
| Colour: | bright blue green, green to colourless |
| Lustre; opacity: | vitreous; transparent |
| Streak: | white |
| Hardness: | 3–3.5 |
| Specific gravity: | 3.1 |
| Cleavage; fracture: | perfect; conchoidal or uneven |
| Habit: | crystals equant to prismatic; drusy, forming in cavities |
| Crystal system: | monoclinic |

# Vivianite

Vivianite was named after J.H. Vivian (1785–1855), the mineralogist who discovered it in St Austell (Cornwall, England). As the pigment blue ochre, it was used in Cologne in the thirteenth and fourteenth centuries, and possibly by the ancient Greeks. It is a common secondary mineral formed by the weathering of metallic ore deposits, and as an alteration product in pegmatites. Associated minerals are siderite, sphalerite and pyrite. It can replace organic matter, forming thin coatings on the damaged surfaces of fossilizing mammoth tusks or skulls (Mexico), whale bones (Richmond, Virginia, USA) or inside bivalves (Kerch iron deposits, Crimea, Russia). It also forms in lake sediments, bog iron ores and peat bogs.

## $Fe_3(PO_4)_2.8H_2O$

| | |
|---|---|
| Colour: | colourless when fresh; darkens on exposure to blue |
| Lustre; opacity: | vitreous, greasy or pearly; transparent to translucent |
| Streak: | colourless to bluish-white |
| Hardness: | 1.5–2 |
| Specific gravity: | 2.7 |
| Cleavage; fracture: | perfect, thin cleavage plates are flexible; fibrous |
| Habit: | crystals prismatic to flattened, may appear bent, acicular (needle-like) or fibrous; concretionary, earthy and encrusting masses |
| Crystal system: | monoclinic |

# Erythrite

Erythrite forms a series with annabergite, in which nickel and cobalt substitute for one another. A rare secondary mineral, it typically forms by weathering in the oxidized zone of ore deposits, as at Cobalt (Ontario, Canada). Associated minerals include silver, cobaltite and skutterudite. Its bright colour is a valuable indicator of the presence of cobalt-bearing ore deposits, hence the alternative name cobalt bloom. When heated, the powdered mineral turns lavender blue and smells of garlic. It was developed in 1803 as a natural pale to medium violet pigment, light cobalt violet, but is rarely used now because of its toxicity. Striking specimens come from Daniel Mine (Saxony, Germany) and Bou Azzer (Morocco).

## $Co_3(AsO_4)_2.8H_2O$

| | |
|---|---|
| **Colour:** | violet red, light pink, purple red; grey surface alteration |
| **Lustre; opacity:** | vitreous, pearly on cleavages; translucent to transparent |
| **Streak:** | pinkish red |
| **Hardness:** | 1.5–2.5 |
| **Specific gravity:** | 3.1–3.2 |
| **Cleavage; fracture:** | perfect, small, flexible plates; uneven |
| **Habit:** | well-formed crystals rare; mostly as crusts or small reniform aggregates |
| **Crystal system:** | monoclinic |

# Annabergite

Annabergite is the nickel end member of the series annabergite–erythrite, in which nickel and cobalt substitute for one another. It was named in 1832 after Annaberg in Saxony. A rare secondary mineral, annabergite is also known as nickel bloom because it forms crusts or films through the surface alteration of other nickel minerals, sometimes completely replacing the original mineral. Like erythrite, it has served as a good indicator of the presence of ore, although rarely being of economic importance itself. It may also be generated during mining as part of the milling process. It occurs in Annaberg (Saxony, Germany), Cobalt (Ontario, Canada), Humboldt County (Nevada, USA) and Allemont (France).

## $Ni_3(AsO_4)_2.8H_2O$

| | |
|---|---|
| **Colour:** | shades of green, white, grey; may be pink |
| **Lustre; opacity:** | vitreous, pearly, dull; translucent to opaque |
| **Streak:** | light green, paler than its colour |
| **Hardness:** | 1.5–2.5 |
| **Specific gravity:** | 3.1 |
| **Cleavage; Fracture:** | perfect; uneven |
| **Habit:** | prismatic, striated crystals, small and rare; more usually as earthy crusts or powdery masses |
| **Crystal system:** | monoclinic |

# Cacoxenite

Cacoxenite is a rare secondary mineral formed through the alteration of other phosphates, and associated with hematite, wavellite, strengite and iron oxides. It is named from the Greek *kakos* ('wrong') and *xenos* ('guest') because the phosphorus content of cacoxenite lessened the quality of smelted iron. It is very attractive, forming golden fibrous and radiating crystals within spherical aggregates. It is also found as inclusions in quartz, particularly amethyst, which detracts from the purple of the amethyst and dulls its appearance. Cacoxenite is found at Diamond Hill Quartz Mine (South Carolina), at Ober-Rosbach (Hesse, Germany), in Indian Mountain (Alabama) and at Avant's Claim (Arkansas, USA).

## $Fe_4(PO_4)_3(OH_3).12H_2O$

| | |
|---|---|
| Colour: | yellow, ochre yellow, golden or brown |
| Lustre; opacity: | vitreous, silky, greasy; translucent to transparent |
| Streak: | straw yellow |
| Hardness: | 3–3.5 |
| Specific gravity: | 2.3 |
| Cleavage; fracture: | poor; fibrous, brittle |
| Habit: | acicular (needle-like) crystals; as spherical aggregates, internally radiating and giving a stellar appearance |
| Crystal system: | hexagonal |

# Wavellite

Wavellite is named after the English physician W. Wavell, who discovered the mineral in 1805. It forms small globular masses that exhibit a characteristic internally radiating structure of acicular crystals. A common secondary mineral, it forms as a low-temperature hydrothermal alteration product in fissures of aluminium-rich rocks, and also in pegmatites with phosphates. At one locality in Arkansas (USA), bluish-green spherulites form the cement of a phosphoritic breccia. Associated minerals are limonite, hematite, pyrolusite. Wavellite is also found in Dünsberg and Waldgermes (Germany), Cerhovice (Czech Republic), in tin veins in St Austell (Cornwall, England) and Llallagua (Bolivia).

## $Al_3(PO_4)_2(OH)_3.5H_2O$

| | |
|---|---|
| **Colour:** | white, yellow, greenish, brown, bluish |
| **Lustre; opacity:** | vitreous, silky, pearly; translucent |
| **Streak:** | white |
| **Hardness:** | 3.5–4 |
| **Specific gravity:** | 2.3–2.4 |
| **Cleavage; fracture:** | three good cleavages; uneven to subconchoidal |
| **Habit:** | very rare as good prismatic crystals; usually flat to spherical, radiating green to yellow-green fibrous clusters |
| **Crystal system:** | orthorhombic |

# Turquoise

Turquoise is a rare and valuable ornamental stone. Its name comes from the French *pierre turquoise*, meaning 'Turkish stone', having been brought from Iran to Europe via Turkey. It has been prized for thousands of years, as evidenced from its use in an Egyptian tomb of c. 3000 BC and in the burial mask of Tutankhamun. A secondary mineral, it forms in the alteration zone of hydrothermal porphyry copper deposits, and in veins and pockets through the alteration of volcanic rocks and phosphate-rich sedimentary rocks. It normally occurs in arid regions. The most important source of turquoise is Iran, where it has been mined for 2000 years, many being worked around Nishapur.

## $CuAl_6(PO_4)_4(OH)_8.4H_2O$

| | |
|---|---|
| Colour: | sky blue to pale blue, greenish blue, green |
| Lustre; opacity: | vitreous, waxy, greasy or dull; transparent to opaque |
| Streak: | white or pale greenish |
| Hardness: | 5-6 |
| Specific gravity: | 2.6–2.8 |
| Cleavage; fracture: | good; conchoidal to even fracture |
| Habit: | crystals rare, small, prismatic; usually massive in veins, concretions or encrustations |
| Crystal system: | triclinic |

# Chalcophyllite

Chalcophyllite is appealing to collectors because of its attractive colour and high lustre, and because it sometimes forms attractive six-sided crystals arranged into a rosette. A rare secondary mineral, it is found in the zone of oxidation of arsenic-bearing hydrothermal copper deposits. Associated minerals include azurite, chrysocolla, malachite, cuprite, spangolite, limonite and clinoclase. It occurs at Wheal Phoenix (Cornwall, England), Clara Mine (Wolfach, Germany), Bisbee (Arizona, USA) and Nizhni Tagil (Russia). It has also been found in vugs within slags derived from ancient to relatively recent copper refining at Val Varenna (Genova, Italy), which were uncovered in 1993 after severe flooding.

## $(Cu,Al)_3(AsO_4,SO_4)(OH)_4.6H_2O$

| | |
|---|---|
| **Colour:** | shades of green to blue |
| **Lustre; opacity:** | adamantine to vitreous, pearly; transparent to translucent |
| **Streak:** | pale green to bluish green |
| **Hardness:** | 2 |
| **Specific gravity:** | 2.68 (light for copper minerals) |
| **Cleavage; fracture:** | perfect, basal; uneven |
| **Habit:** | crystals platy, may be striated, in rosettes; foliated, tabular or massive |
| **Crystal system:** | trigonal |

# Liroconite

Liroconite is named from the Greek *liros* ('pale') and *konia* ('powder'). An extremely rare secondary mineral, it forms in the oxidized zone of copper deposits, associated with other copper minerals such as clinoclase, chalcophyllite, azurite, malachite and limonite. Liroconite was discovered in the 1780s or 1790s in the old copper mines of Cornwall (England), such as Wheal Gorland. The largest known crystal is 35mm (1½in) long, and is in the Rashleigh Collection held at the Royal Cornwall Museum at Truro. Lesser quality specimens occur in Sayda (near Freiburg, Germany), Herrengrund (Slovakia), Cerro Gordo Mine (California, USA), the Khovu-Aksy deposit (Tuva, Russia), N'Kana (Zambia) and Zaire.

## $Cu_2Al(As,P)O_4(OH)_4.4H_2O$

| | |
|---|---|
| Colour: | sky blue, turquoise blue, verdigris green |
| Lustre; opacity: | vitreous to resinous; transparent to translucent |
| Streak: | pale blue, paler than colour |
| Hardness: | 2–2.5 |
| Specific gravity: | 2.9–3.0 |
| Cleavage; fracture: | poor; uneven to subconchoidal, slightly curving surfaces |
| Habit: | well-formed crystals wedge to lens-shaped, frequently appearing bent with rounded edges; also granular |
| Crystal system: | monoclinic |

# Lavendulan

L avendulan, named after its lavender colour, is a rare secondary mineral formed in the oxidized zones of copper deposits. Associated minerals include erythrite, cuprite, malachite, covellite, brochantite and olivenite. World-class specimens of lavendulan were collected from the important former lead-silver-zinc mining district of Mazarron-Aguilas (Murcia, Spain) in 1992. Although copper mining was never significant, the area is renowned for copper arsenates and associated secondary minerals. Specimens include electric blue bladed crystals up to 4mm (⅛in), and radial groups up to 10mm (⅜in). Other localities include Jáchymov (Czech Republic), Bou Azzer (Morrocco) and Wheal Owles (Cornwall, England).

## $CaNaCu_5(AsO_4)_4Cl.5H_2O$

| | |
|---|---|
| **Colour:** | blue, electric blue, greenish blue or lavender |
| **Lustre; opacity:** | vitreous, waxy or satiny in aggregates; translucent |
| **Streak:** | light blue |
| **Hardness:** | 2.5 |
| **Specific gravity:** | 3.54–3.59 |
| **Cleavage; fracture:** | good; uneven |
| **Habit:** | crystals rare, generally less than 3mm, twinning common; radiating fibres or rosettes, botryoidal crusts |
| **Crystal system:** | orthorhombic |

# Autunite

Autunite is a hydrated calcium uranium phosphate, which loses water over time to form meta-autunite. Autunite is strongly radioactive and fluoresces a striking yellowish green. It forms through the alteration of primary uranium minerals such as uraninite, in pegmatites, hydrothermal veins and in the weathering zone of granite. Associated minerals include torbernite ($Cu(UO_2)_2(PO_4)_2.8-12H_2O$), which has similar chemistry and properties, although not forming a series with autunite. It is an important uranium ore, widely used in World War II. Named after Autun in France, it also occurs at Hagendorf (Germany), Shinkolobwe (Zaire), Minas Gerais (Brazil), Mt Spokane (Washington, USA) and Colorado (USA).

## $Ca(UO_2)_2(PO_4)_2.10-12H_2O$

| | |
|---|---|
| Colour: | shades of yellow to greenish yellow |
| Lustre, opacity: | vitreous to pearly; transparent to translucent |
| Streak: | pale yellow |
| Hardness: | 2–2.5 |
| Specific gravity: | 3.1–3.2 |
| Cleavage; fracture: | perfect, thin cleavage sheets are flexible; uneven |
| Habit: | crystals tabular, may be twinned; crusts, scaly aggregates or earthy masses |
| Crystal system: | tetragonal |

# Carnotite

Carnotite is a hydrated potassium uranium vanadate, the water content and hence specific gravity of which varies with temperature and humidity. It is strongly radioactive, but does not fluoresce. It forms through the alteration of minerals such as uraninite, occurring as an impregnation in sands and sandstones, associated with old channels or near playas. It sometimes occurs in small masses associated with vegetable matter, such as petrified trees, or is disseminated throughout, colouring the rock bright yellow. Used as an ore of vanadium and uranium, carnotite occurs in Colorado's desert regions, Utah's San Rafael Swell, Monument Valley (Arizona), New Mexico (USA), the Fergana desert (Russia) and Radium Hill (South Australia).

## $K_2(UO_2)_2(VO_4)_2.3H_2O$

| | |
|---|---|
| **Colour:** | canary yellow to greenish yellow |
| **Lustre; opacity:** | pearly to dull; semi-opaque to transparent |
| **Streak:** | light yellow |
| **Hardness:** | very soft, possibly 2 |
| **Specific gravity:** | 4.7–4.9 |
| **Cleavage; fracture:** | perfect, basal |
| **Habit:** | crystals flat, pseudo-hexagonal, rare; powdered, earthy aggregates |
| **Crystal system:** | monoclinic |

# Willemite

Willemite is a zinc ore that became important after the discovery of huge amounts in marbles at Franklin and Sterling Hill (New Jersey, USA); it was found later in Belgium and named in honour of King Willem I of the Netherlands. Specimens from Franklin show a bright green fluorescence, contrasting beautifully with the red fluorescence of associated calcite. Willemite is a secondary mineral found in zinc-bearing limestones, associated with calcite, franklinite and zincite; specimens displaying all four minerals are popular Other localities include Tiger (Arizona, USA), Tsumeb (Namibia), Altenberg (Belgium), Mont St Hillaire (Quebec, Canada) and Beltana (South Australia).

## $ZnSiO_4$

| | |
|---|---|
| Colour: | greenish-yellow, also dark brown to off-white, bluish |
| Lustre; opacity: | vitreous to resinous; transparent to opaque |
| Streak: | white |
| Hardness: | 5.5 |
| Specific gravity: | 4.0 |
| Cleavage; fracture: | perfect; conchoidal |
| Habit: | rare prismatic crystals; compact, granular or massive aggregates |
| Crystal system: | trigonal |

# Forsterite

Forsterite is a member of the forsterite–fayalite series ($Mg_2SiO_4$–$Fe_2SiO_4$), which comprises an important group of rock-forming minerals called olivines. Olivine is common in basic and in ultrabasic igneous rocks. Forsterite and quartz do not occur together, as they react to form enstatite ($MgSiO_3$). Forsterite is found in metamorphosed siliceous dolomites; fayalite, stable in the presence of quartz, is found in quartz-bearing rocks. Nickel-rich forsterites occur in stony meteorites. Forsterite is found on Bheinn-an-Dubhaich (Skye, Scotland), Vesuvius (Italy), Sapat (Pakistan) and Kovdor massif (Kola Peninsula, Russia). Fayalite occurs in Yellowstone Park (Wyoming, USA) and the Mourne Mountains (Ireland).

## $Mg_2SiO_4$

| | |
|---|---|
| Colour: | white or yellow (forsterite), brown or black (fayalite) |
| Lustre; opacity: | vitreous; transparent to translucent |
| Streak: | white |
| Hardness: | 6.5 (forsterite); 7 (fayalite) |
| Specific gravity: | 3.2 (forsterite); 4.4 (fayalite) |
| Cleavage; fracture: | poor; conchoidal, brittle |
| Habit: | well-formed crystals rare; granular masses, isolated grains in rock |
| Crystal system: | orthorhombic |

# Olivine

Olivine, like mica or serpentine, is not an officially recognized mineral name, but is widely used by petrologists and mineralogists. The gem variety of olivine is called peridot, having a distinctive greasy lustre and an olive- or bottle-green colour. The best peridot stones have about 15 per cent fayalite content to give sufficient green colour, plus possibly a little nickel and/or chromium to provide the best hues. Peridot was used in the Middle Ages to decorate church robes and plates. Gem-quality peridot is found at St John's Island (Zabargad) in the Red Sea, Eiffel (Germany), Mogok (Myanmar), San Carlos (Arizona, USA), Sapat (Pakistan) and Vesuvius (Italy). Olivine can make up half the mass of a stony meteorite.

## $(Mg,Fe)_2SiO_4$

| | |
|---|---|
| Colour: | green, especially olive-coloured |
| Lustre; opacity: | vitreous; transparent to translucent |
| Streak: | white |
| Hardness: | 6.5 –7 |
| Specific gravity: | 3.2–4.4 |
| Cleavage; fracture: | poor; conchoidal, brittle |
| Habit: | well-formed crystals rare; granular masses, isolated grains in igneous rocks |
| Crystal system: | orthorhombic |

# Monticellite

Monticellite is a calcium-rich member of the olivine group, and an end member of the monticellite–kirschsteinite series ($CaMgSiO_4$–$CaFeSiO_4$). It also forms a series with glaucochroite ($CaMnSiO_4$). Consequently, iron and manganese are ubiquitous impurities. It was named after the Italian mineralogist Teodoro Monticelli (1759–1845). Monticellite is formed in contact metamorphic zones between limestones and gabbros, or between granites and dolomites. Associated minerals include gehlenite, spinel, calcite, vesuvianite and apatite. It is found at Vesuvius (Italy), Isle of Muck (Scotland), Magnet Cove (Arkansas, USA), Kovdor (Kola Peninsula, Russia) and Isle Cadieux (Quebec, Canada).

## $CaMgSiO_4$

| | |
|---|---|
| Colour: | colourless, greenish grey, grey |
| Lustre; opacity: | vitreous; transparent |
| Streak: | white |
| Hardness: | 5.5 |
| Specific gravity: | 3.2 |
| Cleavage; fracture: | poor; subconchoidal to uneven |
| Habit: | crystals rare as well-formed prisms; massive, granular |
| Crystal system: | orthorhombic |

# Garnet: Pyrope

Pyrope, alongside almandine and spessartine, belongs to the pyralspite group of garnets. It is one of the less common garnets, widely used as a gem and noted for its clear red crystals. It forms a series with almandine; a member of which is the red-lavender coloured gemstone rhodolite. Unusual for a garnet, pyrope occurs mostly in igneous rocks, such as eclogites and kimberlites. These are formed at high pressures and can contain diamonds. It also occurs in related serpentinites and placer deposits. It is found at Merunice (Czech Republic), Dora-Meira (Piedmont, Italy), Kimberly (South Africa), the Umba River (Tanzania), Cowee Creek (North Carolina, USA), Buell Park (Arizona, USA) and Bingara (NSW, Australia).

## $Mg_3Al_2(SiO_4)_3$

| | |
|---|---|
| Colour: | red-orange to deep red |
| Lustre; opacity: | vitreous; transparent to translucent |
| Streak: | white |
| Hardness: | 7–7.5 |
| Specific gravity: | 3.58 |
| Cleavage; fracture: | absent; conchoidal |
| Habit: | crystals typically rhombic dodecahedra, sometimes trapezohedra; massive, granular |
| Crystal system: | cubic |

# Garnet: Almandine

Almandine, a pyralspite garnet, is darker red than pyrope and sometimes may appear black. Rare transparent specimens are facetted as gemstones, having a high lustre. Specimens having inclusions such as rutile needles are often cut *en cabochon*. Like many garnets in metamorphic rocks, their equant, well-formed crystals often stand out as porphyroblasts against a schistose matrix. It is usually found in medium-grade metamorphic rocks; less often in granites and pegmatites; and also as placer deposits. Fine orange-red crystals are found in sands in Minas Novas and Minas Gerais (Brazil) and in Sri Lanka; other locations include Sticken River (Alaska), Adirondacks (New York, USA) and the Zillertal (Austria).

## $Fe_3Al_2(SiO_4)_3$

| | |
|---|---|
| **Colour:** | red-violet to red-brown |
| **Lustre; opacity:** | vitreous to resinous; transparent to opaque |
| **Streak:** | white |
| **Hardness:** | 7.5 |
| **Specific gravity:** | 4.4 |
| **Cleavage; fracture:** | absent; conchoidal |
| **Habit:** | crystals typically rhombic dodecahedra, sometimes trapezohedra, embedded as separate crystals in metamorphic rocks; massive |
| **Crystal system:** | cubic |

# Garnet: Spessartine

Spessartine, a pyralspite garnet, is rarely found at gem quality. Forming a series with almandine, it usually contains varying amounts of manganese and iron. The crystal shapes of spessartine – i.e. the 12-sided dodecahdron with rhomb-shaped faces or the 24-sided trapezohedron with trapezium-shaped faces – are ubiquitous in the garnet group. These round-looking crystals are characteristic of garnets. Spessartine occurs in rhyolites, granites and pegmatites; in metasomatized manganous rocks; and as placer deposits. It occurs in Seriphos (Greece), the Spessart Mountains (Germany), Minas Gerais (Brazil), Lieper's Quarry (Pennsylvania, USA), Amelia (Virginia, USA) and Tsilaizina and Anjanabonoina (Madagascar).

## $Mn_3Al_2(SiO_4)_3$

| | |
|---|---|
| Colour: | yellow, orange, red, brown, black |
| Lustre; opacity: | vitreous; transparent to translucent |
| Streak: | white |
| Hardness: | 7–7.5 |
| Specific gravity: | 4.2 |
| Cleavage; fracture: | absent; conchoidal |
| Habit: | crystals as the typical rhombic dodecahedra, but more commonly 24-sided trapezohedra; massive, granular |
| Crystal system: | cubic |

# Garnet: Grossular

Grossular, alongside uvarovite and andradite, belongs to the ugrandite group of garnets, giving gem-quality specimens in many colours. Massive green grossular, such as Transvaal jade, is popular, often with black inclusions of magnetite. Some has a distinctive gooseberry colour, hence the name derived from the scientific name *R. grossularia*. Cinnamon orange-red transparent garnets called hessonite were used as gems by the ancient Greeks and Romans. Tsavorite is a transparent green variety. It occurs in metamophosed calcareous rocks and as placer deposits. Fine crystals occur at Chernyshevsk (Russia), Ala Valley (Italy), Asbestos (Canada), Ramona (California, USA), Maharitra (Madagascar) and Telemarken (Norway).

## $Ca_3Al_2(SiO_4)_3$

| | |
|---|---|
| **Colour:** | colourless when pure, green, brown, orange, pink, red, black |
| **Lustre; opacity:** | vitreous; transparent |
| **Streak:** | white |
| **Hardness:** | 6.5–7.5 |
| **Specific gravity:** | 3.59 |
| **Cleavage; fracture:** | none; subconchoidal |
| **Habit:** | crystals as rhombohedra or trapezohedra; granular, compact, massive |
| **Crystal system:** | cubic |

# Garnet: Uvarovite

Uvarovite, a ugrandite garnet, is emerald-green and much sought-after as a gemstone because of its outstanding brilliance and colour. Uvarovite is mostly found as small crystals, so much jewellery uses small druses. The best clear specimens are found in the Urals, lining cavities and fissures. Uvarovite is named after Count Sergei Semenovitch Uvarov (1765–1855), a Russian statesman and amateur mineral collector. It forms a series with grossular and often contains aluminium. It occurs in chromium-rich serpentinites. Fine crystals are found in Yerkaterinberg and the Saranovskii Mine (Urals, Russia), Outokumpu (Finland), Pico do Posets (Pyrenees, Spain), Quebec (Canada) and the Kop Mountains (Turkey).

## $Ca_3Cr_2(SiO_4)_3$

| | |
|---|---|
| Colour: | bright green to dark green |
| Lustre; opacity: | vitreous to adamantine; transparent to translucent |
| Streak: | white |
| Hardness: | 6.5–7 |
| Specific gravity: | 3.4–3.8 |
| Cleavage; fracture: | absent; conchoidal |
| Habit: | crystals as rhombic dodecahedra or trapezohedra; massive, granular |
| Crystal system: | cubic |

# Garnet: Andradite

Andradite, a ugrandite garnet, has many varieties, the most prized being the chromium-rich, emerald-green demantoid. This has a higher dispersion than diamond and is characterized by inclusions of asbestos fibres known as 'horsetails'. A yellow variety is called topazolite and the black variety melanite. It is named after the Brazilian mineralogist J.B. d'Andrada e Silva (1763–1838). Andradite is found in contact-metamorphosed limestones; schists and serpentinites; and in silica-poor igneous rocks. It occurs in Elba and Livorno (Italy), Arendal (Norway) and Franklin (New Jersey, USA); it is found as dementoid in the Urals among gold-bearing sands, and as melanite at Vesuvius and Lazio (Italy).

## $Ca_3Fe_2(SiO_4)_3$

| | |
|---|---|
| **Colour:** | yellow, green, brown, black |
| **Lustre; opacity:** | vitreous; transparent to opaque |
| **Streak:** | white |
| **Hardness:** | 6.5–7 |
| **Specific gravity:** | 3.7–4.1 |
| **Cleavage; fracture:** | absent; conchoidal |
| **Habit:** | crystals as rhombic dodecahedra and trapezahedra; massive, crusts showing many rhombic faces |
| **Crystal system:** | cubic |

# Zircon

Zircon has a similar lustre and fire to that of diamond, with colourless zircons having been used as imitation diamonds. Zircon comes in a variety of colours; the yellow variety alluded to in the name comes from the Arabic *zargun* for 'gold colour'. Heat treatment often changes the colour of zircons. Zircon that is not of gem quality is a major ore for zirconium, as well as hafnium and thorium. It occurs as an accessory mineral in acid igneous rocks, their products of metamorphism, and as placer deposits. Excellent crystals are found in river deposits at Matura (Sri Lanka) and the Ilmen Mountains (Russia). Other localities are Renfrew (Canada), Mt Ampanobe (Madagascar) and Teete (Mozambique).

## $ZrSiO_4$

| | |
|---|---|
| Colour: | colourless, yellow, red, brown, grey, green |
| Lustre; opacity: | vitreous to subadamantine; transparent to opaque |
| Streak: | white |
| Hardness: | 6.5–7.5 |
| Specific gravity: | 3.9–4.8 |
| Cleavage; fracture: | indistinct; conchoidal |
| Habit: | crystals dipyramidal or prismatic; irregular granules |
| Crystal system: | tetragonal |

# Sillimanite

Sillimanite is a polymorph of aluminium silicate, alongside kyanite and andalusite. The appearance of one of these minerals in metamorphic rocks is a key indicator of the temperatures and pressures undergone by the rock. The presence of sillimanite indicates a high temperature of formation (at least 650°C/1202°F). The slim, prismatic crystals of sillimanite distinguish it, and may be raised on weathered rocks. It is found in metamorphosed pelitic rocks and in pegmatites associated with corundum, tourmaline and topaz. Blue and violet transparent sillimanite is found in Mogok (Myanmar); grey-green varieties are found in Sri Lanka; and other locations are Minas Gerais (Brazil), Maldan (Czech Republic) and Freiberg (Germany).

## $Al_2SiO_5$

| | |
|---|---|
| Colour: | grey, brown, pale green |
| Lustre; opacity: | vitreous to subadamantine; translucent to transparent |
| Streak: | white |
| Hardness: | 6.5–7.5 |
| Specific gravity: | 3.2 |
| Cleavage; fracture: | perfect; uneven |
| Habit: | crystals long, slender prisms, occasionally acicular, poorly terminated; often silky, fibrous aggregates (fibrolite) |
| Crystal system: | orthorhombic |

# Andalusite

Andalusite is a polymorph of aluminium silicate, alongside kyanite and sillimanite. Its presence in a rock indicates that the rock has undergone low pressures during metamorphism (i.e. has been formed within a few kilometres of the Earth's surface). Greenish-red transparent crystals are used as gems. Twinned crystals called chiastolite form cross shapes (+ shapes) with x-shaped dark lines at the centre. Chiastolite has been used in amulets as a religious symbol. Andalusite occurs in metamophosed pelites, especially contact-metamorphosed slates, and in pegmatites. Large crystals are found at Lisenz (Austria); chiastolite is found in schists at Santiago de Compostela (Spain) and Keiva (Kola Peninsula, Russia).

## $Al_2SiO_5$

| | |
|---|---|
| Colour: | white, pink, pearl-grey, green, brown |
| Lustre; opacity: | vitreous, greasy; transparent to opaque |
| Streak: | white |
| Hardness: | 7.5 |
| Specific gravity: | 3.1–3.2 |
| Cleavage; fracture: | good; uneven |
| Habit: | crystals as square, stubby prisms, often twinned; granular, rod-like aggregates |
| Crystal system: | orthorhombic |

# Kyanite

Kyanite is a polymorph alongside andalusite and sillimanite. The presence of kyanite in rocks indicates that they have undergone moderate temperatures and medium to high pressures during metamorphism. Kyanite is named after the Greek *kyanos* for blue; it is also known as disthene, meaning 'double strength', after the hardness, which is greater across the crystal than lengthwise. Kyanite occurs in pelitic schists and gneisses, associated with garnet, staurolite and micas; and in eclogites. Large blue crystals come from Minas Gerais (Brazil) and Pizzo Forno (Switzerland); green crystals up to 30cm (12in) from Machakos (Kenya); and grey radiating crystals from Bolzano (Italy), the Tyrol (Austria) and Morbihan (France).

## $Al_2SiO_5$

| | |
|---|---|
| **Colour:** | often blue, lighter towards the margins; colourless, grey, green |
| **Lustre; opacity:** | vitreous, pearly; transparent to translucent |
| **Streak:** | white |
| **Hardness:** | 4–4.5 along cleavage planes, 6–7 across cleavage planes |
| **Specific gravity:** | 3.6–3.7 |
| **Cleavage; fracture:** | perfect |
| **Habit:** | flat, bladed crystals in schists and gneisses, rosettes in quartz; massive aggregates |
| **Crystal system:** | triclinic |

# Topaz

Topaz has been a highly prized gemstone for millenia. It is found in a variety of colours and is often heat-treated and/or irradiated to give different hues; blue topaz resembling aquamarine is produced thus from colourless stones. Yellow topaz from Brazil turns pink on heating to 300°–450°C (572°–842°F). Crystals in pegmatites can be huge (up to 300kg/661lb). The Brazilian Princess, a pale blue topaz from Teofilo Otoni, is the largest cut topaz, weighing 4266g (9¼lb). Topaz is found in pneumatolytic veins in granites and pegmatites, and as a placer deposit. The largest crystals are found at Minas Gerais (Brazil) and Albaslika (Siberia, Russia); it is also found in Mino Province (Japan), at Pikes Peak (Colorado, USA) and on Elba (Italy).

## $Al_2SiO_4(F,OH)_2$

| | |
|---|---|
| **Colour:** | colourless, yellow, pink, blue, green |
| **Lustre; opacity:** | vitreous; transparent to translucent |
| **Streak:** | opacity |
| **Hardness:** | 8 |
| **Specific gravity:** | 3.5–3.6 |
| **Cleavage; fracture:** | perfect; conchoidal, uneven |
| **Habit:** | vertically striated prismatic crystals; columnar, granular |
| **Crystal system:** | orthorhombic |

# Staurolite

Staurolite is a common mineral in pelitic schists and gneisses, occurring often as large porphyroblasts. Its presence is useful when assessing the degree of metamorphism, indicating that the rock has undergone medium temperature conditions. As a gem mineral, the opaque cross-shaped twins characteristic of staurolite are used in jewellery, often as amulets or religious items. The crosses occur at angles of both 90° and 60°. Fine crystals up to about 12cm (5in) are found in Pizzo Forno and Alpe Piona (Switzerland), Finistère and Morbihan (France), Mt Greiner (Austria), Keivy massif (Kola Peninsula, Russia), Franconia (New Hampshire), Blue Ridge (Georgia) and Taos County (New Mexico, USA).

## $(Fe,Mg)_2(Al,Fe)_9(Si_4O_{20})(O,OH)_2$

| | |
|---|---|
| Colour: | reddish-brown, brown, black |
| Lustre; opacity: | vitreous, resinous, dull; translucent to opaque |
| Streak: | white |
| Hardness: | 7–7.5 |
| Specific gravity: | 3.65–3.83 |
| Cleavage; fracture: | poor; uneven to conchoidal |
| Habit: | crystals prismatic or tabular, pseudohexagonal truncated diamond shapes, often twinned giving cross shapes |
| Crystal system: | monoclinic |

# Titanite

Titanite is now the more common name for sphene. Titanite displays interesting colours and strong fire, and is often faceted for display. Impurities such as iron and aluminium are always present, and rare earths such as cerium and yttrium are commonly present. Titanite is a common accessory mineral in intermediate and felsic plutonic rocks, pegmatites and veins, and is also found in gneisses and schists. Large crystals occur at St Gotthard (Switzerland), Bridgewater (Pennsylvania, USA), the Urals (Russia), Kola Peninsula (Russia), Minas Gerais (Brazil), Renfrew (Canada). Gem-quality crystals can be found at Pino Solo and La Huerta (Baja California Norte, Mexico).

## $CaTiSiO_5$

| | |
|---|---|
| Colour: | yellow, green, red, reddish brown, brown, black |
| Lustre; opacity: | vitreous to subadamantine; transparent to opaque |
| Streak: | white |
| Hardness: | 5–5.5 |
| Specific gravity: | 3.4–3.6 |
| Cleavage; fracture: | distinct; conchoidal, brittle |
| Habit: | crystals usually flattened, prismatic, wedge-shaped; compact or lamellar masses, disseminated grains |
| Crystal system: | monoclinic |

# Chloritoid

Chloritoid is found as small, platy crystals or occasionally as porphyroblasts in metamorphic rocks. Two related minerals are the magnesium-rich sismondine and the manganese-rich otrellite. Chloritoid indicates that the rock formed under low to medium pressures and temperatures. It shows a strong pleochrism, dark green to light green or yellow in varying orientations. Chloritoid occurs in metamorphic pelites, especially schists and marbles, associated with muscovite, staurolite, garnet, chlorite, kyanite and quartz. It is found at Kosoi Brod (Urals, Russia), Svalbard (Norway) and Natick (Rhode Island, USA). Sismondine is found at Zermatt (Switzerland) and Pregatten (Austria); otrellite at Ottré (Belgium).

## $(Fe,Mn)_2Al_4Si_2O_{10}(OH)_4$

| | |
|---|---|
| Colour: | dark grey, greenish-grey |
| Lustre; opacity: | vitreous, pearly |
| Streak: | white, pale grey, pale green |
| Hardness: | 6.5 |
| Specific gravity: | 3.56–3.61 |
| Cleavage; fracture: | perfect; brittle |
| Habit: | pseudohexagonal tabular crystals; commonly compact, foliated aggregates, massive |
| Crystal system: | monoclinic or triclinic (but always pseudohexagonal) |

# Datolite

Datolite is an ore of boron when available in sufficient quantities. It forms complex crystals that can superficially look like cubic forms such as dodecahedra or trapazohedra, but on closer inspection are revealed as lacking in symmetry. Datolite occurs as a secondary mineral in basalts, serpentinites and in hydrothermal deposits. It is often found in vesicles, associated with zeolites, prehnite and calcite. Datolite can be found in Kratzenberg (Austria), Serra dei Zanchetti and Alpe de Siusi (Italy), St Andreasberg (Harz, Germany), Arendal (Norway), Lane (Massachusetts, USA) and Prospect Park (New Jersey, USA).

## $CaBSiO_4(OH)$

| | |
|---|---|
| Colour: | colourless, white, sometimes light green or yellow |
| Lustre; opacity: | vitreous, greasy; transparent to translucent |
| Streak: | white |
| Hardness: | 5–5.5 |
| Specific gravity: | 2.9–3 |
| Cleavage; fracture: | imperfect; irregular, subconchoidal |
| Habit: | crystals as plates or prisms, sometimes large and complex; granular to compact, crusty aggregates with radiating fibres called botryolites |
| Crystal system: | monoclinic |

# Gadolinite

Gadolinite has varying amounts of other rare-earth elements such as cerium, lanthanum and neodymium substituting for yttrium; it also contains varying amounts of thorium and uranium, making it radioactive, and the crystals often metamict. Gadolinite is an ore of thorium and the rare-earth elements, which are finding an increasing variety of uses. It is named after the Finnish chemist Johan Gadolin (1760–1852), who discovered yttrium. Gadolinite occurs in granite and syenite pegmatites, and in veins in metamorphic rocks. Crystals (up to 500kg/ 1100lb) occur in Hitterö, Iveland and Hundholmen (Norway). Other localities include Finbo and Ytterby (Sweden), Llano County (Texas, USA) and Novara (Italy).

## $Be_2FeY_2Si_2O_{10}$

| | |
|---|---|
| Colour: | green, greenish-brown, black |
| Lustre; opacity: | vitreous; transparent to opaque |
| Streak: | grey–green |
| Hardness: | 6.5–7 |
| Specific gravity: | 4.0–4.5 |
| Cleavage; fracture: | none; conchoidal, splintery |
| Habit: | rare prismatic crystals of diamond-shape cross-section; microgranular, earthy masses |
| Crystal system: | monoclinic |

# Euclase

Euclase forms extremely attractive hard crystals; blue and green varieties are popular. The name is derived from the Greek *eu* for 'well' and *klasis* for 'break', alluding to its facile cleavage. The distinctive crystal shapes can be confused only with barite or celestite, minerals which do not occur in the same environment as euclase. Euclase is formed as an alteration product of beryl in pegmatites and veins, and may be found as a placer deposit. The best crystals are found at Ouro Prêto (Minas Gerais, Brazil) as colourless, blue and green gem-quality stones. Other locations include the Sanarka River (Russia), Park County (Colorado, USA) and Las Cruces (Chivor, Colombia).

## $AlBeOHSiO_4$

| | |
|---|---|
| Colour: | colourless, white, green, blue |
| Lustre; opacity: | vitreous to adamantine; transparent to translucent |
| Streak: | white |
| Hardness: | 7.5 |
| Specific gravity: | 3.1 |
| Cleavage; fracture: | perfect, conchoidal |
| Habit: | stubby prismatic crystals with non-symmetrical slanted terminations; reniform, stalactitic, mammilliary masses |
| Crystal system: | monoclinic |

# Humite

H umite is part of a rare related group of minerals (called the humite group), which also includes norbergite, chondrodite, clinohumite and titanclinohumite. The structure of humites comprises alternating layers of brucite ($Mg(OH)_2$) and olivine ($Mg_2SiO_4$). It was named after Sir Abraham Hume (1749–1838), English collector of art, gems and minerals. Humite occurs in hydrothermal veins and contact-metamorphosed limestones and dolomites. Associated minerals include magnetite, diopside, spinel, biotite, serpentine, olivine and calcite. It is found at Vesuvius (Italy), Los Llanos de Januar (Spain), Pargas (Finland), Varmland (Sweden), Franklin (New Jersey, USA) and the Tilly Foster mine (New York, USA).

## $Mg_7(OH,F)_2(SiO_4)_3$

| | |
|---|---|
| Colour: | often yellow or yellow-green; white, brown, orange |
| Lustre; opacity: | vitreous; transparent to translucent |
| Streak: | white |
| Hardness: | 6 |
| Specific gravity: | 3.2–3.3 |
| Cleavage; fracture: | poor; conchoidal |
| Habit: | small prismatic crystals; granular, grains embedded in matrix |
| Crystal system: | orthorhombic |

# Braunite

Braunite, named after K. Braun (1790–1872), Adviser of the Chambers, of Gotha (Germany), is sometimes referred to as braunite-I to differentiate it from the calcium-bearing variant braunite-II $(Ca(Mn,Fe)14Si_2O_{24})$. Crystals are usually small and rarely well formed, but they can have an attractive metallic grey sheen. Braunite is formed by metamorphism of manganese-rich silicates and by weathering. Associated minerals are calcite, quartz, pyrolusite, hausmannite, rhodonite and spessartine. It is found at Friedrichroda (Thuringia, Germany), Långban and Jacobsberg (Sweden), Sitapar (India), Postmasburg (South Africa), Val d'Aosta (Italy), Batesville (Arkansas, USA) and Mason County (Texas, USA).

## $Mn^{2+}Mn^{3+}_6SiO_{12}$

| | |
|---|---|
| Colour: | black, brownish-black, greyish-black |
| Lustre; opacity: | metallic, greasy; opaque |
| Streak: | brownish-black |
| Hardness: | 6–6.5 |
| Specific gravity: | 4.7–4.8 |
| Cleavage; fracture: | perfect; uneven; subconchoidal |
| Habit: | crystals pseudooctahedral and bipyramidal up to 5cm (2in), rare; granular or massive aggregates |
| Crystal system: | tetragonal |

223

# Dumortierite

Dumortierite is a borosilicate second only in abundance to tourmaline. It forms attractive violet to blue masses used for items such as cabochons, beads and sculptures. It was named after Eugène Dumortier (1802–1873), a French palaeontologist. Dumortierite can be mistaken for sodalite, the latter being less dense and usually including more white minerals. Dumortierite is found in aluminium-rich metamorphic rocks, pegmatites and contact metamorphosed rocks. Large deposits are found in Oreana and Rochester (Nevada, USA), Dehesa (California, USA), Arizona (USA); it is also found at the type locality Chaponost (Rhône-Alps, France) and at Minas Gerais (Brazil), Sondria (Italy), Mogra (India) and Madagascar.

## $Al_7(BO_3)(SiO_4)_3O_3$

| | |
|---|---|
| Colour: | blue or violet crystals, sometimes reddish-brown |
| Lustre; opacity: | silky, vitreous; translucent |
| Streak: | white |
| Hardness: | 7–8.5 |
| Specific gravity: | 3.2–3.4 |
| Cleavage; fracture: | good; uneven |
| Habit: | rare prismatic or acicular needles; columnar or fibrous, radiating aggregates |
| Crystal system: | orthorhombic |

# Gehlenite-Åkermanite

The gehlenite–åkermanite group is a solid solution series where magnesium and silicon replace aluminium; melilite is a term applied to intermediate minerals. Specimens can be attractive, varying from transparent white or reddish to opaque grey-green, especially as micromounts. Gehlenite and åkermanite are found in contact-metamorphosed limestones and dolomites, respectively. Melilite occurs in silica-deficient lavas, associated with nepheline or leucite. Åkermanite is found on Vesuvius (Italy) and often in blast furnace slag; gehlenite in Trento (Italy) and Oravita (Banat, Romania); melilite at Mount Monzoni and Canzocoli (Italy), Isle of Muck and Ardnamurchan (Scotland), and Relerberg (Eifel, Germany).

## $Ca_2Al_2SiO_7 – Ca_2MgSi_2O_7$

| | |
|---|---|
| Colour: | white, grey, yellow, grey-green, brownish-red |
| Lustre; opacity: | vitreous, greasy; transparent to opaque |
| Streak: | white |
| Hardness: | 5 |
| Specific gravity: | 2.95–3.05 |
| Cleavage; fracture: | good; conchoidal, uneven |
| Habit: | crystals as small, stubby, square prisms or plates; granular and massive aggregates |
| Crystal system: | tetragonal |

225

# Ilvaite

Ilvaite, named from Ilva, the old Latin name for Elba, is a blackish, almost opaque mineral. It forms attractive large black crystals and fibrous radiating aggregates, often with calcite, hedenbergite, magnetite, andradite and pyrite. It melts readily in a flame, leaving a magnetic residue. Ilvaite appears translucent on freshly exposed surfaces, but almost opaque on old specimens. It forms in contact metasomatic rocks and metamorphosed iron-rich limestones, and less commonly in syenites. It is found at Livorno and Elba (Italy), Seriphos (Greece), Julianahaab (Greenland), Dal'negorsk (Primorskiy Kray, Russia), Laxey (Idaho, USA), Dragoon Mountains (Arizona, USA), Kamioka (Oita, Japan) and Thyrill (Iceland).

## $CaFe_3(SiO_4)_2(OH)$

| | |
|---|---|
| Colour: | brownish-black, black |
| Lustre; opacity: | submetallic, vitreous, greasy; semi-opaque |
| Streak: | black, greeny-black |
| Hardness: | 5.5–6 |
| Specific gravity: | 3.8–4.1 |
| Cleavage; fracture: | good; conchoidal |
| Habit: | crystals as striated prisms; radiating fibrous, massive, granular |
| Crystal system: | orthorhombic |

# Hemimorphite

Hemimorphite is a common mineral in all lead, zinc and silver deposits. It forms part of the altered top of sphalerite deposits called 'gossan', or 'iron cap'. It is named from the hemimorphism displayed by its crystals; the prisms usually have different terminations (ends), one being rather blunt and the other being pyramidal. It has long been mined alongside smithsonite as a zinc ore. It forms in the oxidized zones of zinc-bearing veins below 240°C (464°F), above which willemite is formed. It is found at Chihuahua (Mexico), Moresnet (Belgium), Cumberland and Derbyshire (England), Carinthia (Austria), Nerchinsk (Siberia, Russia), Franklin (New Jersey) and Granby (Missouri, USA) and Balta (Romania).

## $Zn_4Si_2O_7(OH)_2.H_2O$

| | |
|---|---|
| Colour: | colourless, white, tinged yellow, blue or green, grey, brown |
| Lustre; opacity: | vitreous, pearly, silky; transparent to translucent |
| Streak: | white |
| Hardness: | 5 |
| Specific gravity: | 4.0 |
| Cleavage; fracture: | perfect; conchoidal, splintery |
| Habit: | crystals hemimorphic prismatic or plates; stalactitic, encrustations, massive granular, fan-shaped aggregates |
| Crystal system: | orthorhombic |

# Clinozoisite

Clinozoisite forms a series with the iron-bearing mineral epidote, but tends to be paler. Attractive specimens are transparent rodlike crystals, clusters of randomly orientated prisms and pinkish radiating fibrous aggregates. Clinozoisite occurs in low- to medium-grade metamorphic rocks, in contact-metamorphosed calcium-rich sediments and as altered calcium-rich plagioclase. Associated minerals include amphiboles, plagioclase and quartz. It is found at Goslarwand (Tirol, Austria), Camaderry Mountain (Wicklow, Ireland), Amborompotsy (Madagascar), Chiampernotto (Turin, Italy), Belvidere Mountain (Vermont, USA), Spade Spring Canyon (California, USA), Nightingale (Nevada, USA) and Baja California (Mexico).

## $Ca_2Al_3Si_3O_{12}(OH)$

| | |
|---|---|
| **Colour:** | grey, yellow, greenish, light rose |
| **Lustre; opacity:** | vitreous; transparent to opaque |
| **Streak:** | white |
| **Hardness:** | 6.5 |
| **Specific gravity:** | 3.2 |
| **Cleavage; fracture:** | perfect; uneven |
| **Habit:** | prismatic crystals; granular, massive, fibrous aggregates |
| **Crystal system:** | monoclinic |

# Epidote

Epidote is noted for its characteristic green colour, sometimes described as 'pistachio'. It is a common secondary mineral in a number of rocks. Epidote is pleochroic, displaying greens, yellows and browns. Rock composed mostly of epidote may be polished or tumbled as unakite. Epidote occurs in low- to medium-grade metamorphic rocks of mafic composition. Associated minerals depend on the degree of metamorphism and the bulk composition of the rock. It is found at Bourg d'Oisans (France), Arendal (Norway), Traversella (Piedmont, Italy), Knappenwand (Austria), Sulzer (Prince of Wales Island, Alaska, USA), Seven Devils (Idaho, USA) and San Quentin (Baja California, Mexico).

## $Ca_2(Al,Fe)_3Si_3O_{12}(OH)$

| | |
|---|---|
| **Colour:** | dark green to yellow-green |
| **Lustre; opacity:** | vitreous; translucent |
| **Streak:** | grey |
| **Hardness:** | 6.7 |
| **Specific gravity:** | 3.3–3.5 |
| **Cleavage; fracture:** | perfect; uneven |
| **Habit:** | crystals as columnar prisms, finely striated lengthwise; granular, massive, fibrous aggregates |
| **Crystal system:** | monoclinic |

# Piemontite

Piemontite or piedmontite is a member of the epidote group. Named after the Piedmont area in northwest Italy, it is also referred to as manganiferous epidote. The manganese content gives piemontite a red coloration, which can be difficult to distinguish from red varieties of clinozoisite. Piemontite is widespread and found in low- to medium-grade metamorphic rocks, metasomatized manganese deposits and hydrothermal veins. It is associated with epidote, glaucophane, quartz, orthoclase and calcite. It is found at Saint Marcel (Piedmont, Italy), Ceres (Turin, Italy), Groix (France), Shikoku (Japan), Old Bookoomata (South Australia), Garnet Lake (California, USA), Tucson Mountains (Arizona, USA) and Tachgagalt (Morocco).

## $Ca_2(Al,Mn,Fe)_3Si_3O_{12}(OH)$

| | |
|---|---|
| **Colour:** | red, purple, reddish brown, reddish black |
| **Lustre; opacity:** | vitreous; translucent to nearly opaque |
| **Streak:** | red |
| **Hardness:** | 6 |
| **Specific gravity:** | 3.4–3.5 |
| **Cleavage; fracture:** | perfect; splintery |
| **Habit:** | blocky, equant, prismatic bladed or acicular crystals; massive, granular |
| **Crystal system:** | monoclinic |

# Allanite

Allanite is a member of the epidote group, calcium being replaced by rare earth elements and thorium. When thorium-rich, allanite can be sufficiently radioactive to be metamict. Allanite–(Ce), (La) and –(Y) are minerals particularly rich in cerium, lanthanum or yttrium. It is named after the Scottish mineralogist Thomas Allan (1777–1833), its discoverer. It occurs as an accessory in granites and in pegmatites; and rarely in schists, gneisses and contact-metamorphic limestones. Associated minerals are epidote, muscovite and fluorite. Allanite is found at Qáqassuatsiaq (Aluk Island, Greenland), Ytterby and Finbo (Sweden), Miask (Urals, Russia), Franklin (New Jersey, USA) and Barringer Hill (Texas, USA).

## $(Ce,Ca,Y)_2(Al,Fe)_3Si_3O_{12}(OH)$

| | |
|---|---|
| Colour: | brown to black |
| Lustre; opacity: | vitreous, resinous, submetallic; translucent to opaque |
| Streak: | grey |
| Hardness: | 5.5–6 |
| Specific gravity: | 3.5–4.2 |
| Cleavage; fracture: | imperfect; conchoidal, uneven |
| Habit: | tabular, prismatic or acicular crystals; massive, granular |
| Crystal system: | monoclinic |

# Zoisite

Zoisite is an epidote noted for its gem and ornamental use. The violet-blue variety tanzanite is very popular, having more fire than tourmaline or peridot. It shows a distinct purple to blue to slate-grey pleochroism and can appear more violet in incandescent light. Massive green zoisite containing rubies is a popular rock among collectors and can be polished or carved. A massive manganous pink variety called thulite is also polished and carved. Zoisite occurs in high-grade metamorphic rocks, in hydrothermal veins and as altered calcic plagioclase. Excellent tanzanite is found at Merelani Hills (Letatina Mountains, Tanzania); thulite is found at Telemark (Norway) and in Tennessee and South Carolina (USA).

## $Ca_2Al_3Si_3O_{12}(OH)$

| | |
|---|---|
| **Colour:** | white, blue, pale green, pink, violet-blue |
| **Lustre; opacity:** | vitreous, pearly; transparent to translucent |
| **Streak:** | white |
| **Hardness:** | 6–6.5 |
| **Specific gravity:** | 3.15–3.36 |
| **Cleavage; fracture:** | perfect; uneven |
| **Habit:** | finely striated, elongated, prismatic crystals, usually poorly terminated; grains, granular masses, aggregates |
| **Crystal system:** | orthorhombic |

# Vesuvianite

Also known as idocrase, vesuvianite is a popular mineral that forms fine transparent crystals and is often confused with other gemstones. It is commonly cut for collections, but not for wearing. Varieties include green californite or california jade, blue cyprine, yellow-green xanthite and pale-green or whitish wiluite. Vesuvianite is formed by metamorphism of limestones and metasomatism of serpentinized ultrabasic rocks. Associated minerals are grossular, andradite, wollastonite and diopside. Vesuvianite is found at Vesuvius (Italy), California (USA), Morelos and Chiapas (Mexico), Zermatt (Switzerland), Arendal (Norway), the Akhmatovsk mine (Urals, Russia) and Chernyshevsk (Yakutia, Russia).

## $Ca_{10}Mg_2Al_4(SiO_4)_5(Si_2O_7)_2(OH)_4$

| | |
|---|---|
| Colour: | yellow, green, brown, colourless, white, blue, violet, red , black |
| Lustre; opacity: | vitreous to resinous; transparent to translucent |
| Streak: | white |
| Hardness: | 6.5 |
| Specific gravity: | 3.27–3.45 |
| Cleavage; fracture: | poor; subconchoidal to irregular |
| Habit: | stubby, prismatic crystals, rare pyramidal terminations; compact granular masses |
| Crystal system: | tetragonal |

# Benitoite

Benitoite is a rare mineral, until recently known only from Diablo Range (San Benito, California). Discovered in 1906, it was mistaken for sapphire. Benitoite shows a high dispersion, similar to diamond, and is strongly pleochroic (i.e. it displays different colours in different orientations), changing from blue to colourless. It gives a pale blue fluorescence under ultraviolet light. Clusters of blue benitoite and black-red neptunite on a matrix of white natrolite are appealing and rare specimens. Benitoite is formed in hydrothermal veins cutting serpentinites associated with natrolite, albite, neptunite and joaquinite. Other localities include Magnet Cove (Arkansas, USA), Ohmi (Niigata, Japan) and Broken Hill (NSW, Australia).

## $BaTiSi_3O_9$

| | |
|---|---|
| Colour: | sapphire-blue, white, colourless |
| Lustre; opacity: | vitreous; transparent to translucent |
| Streak: | white |
| Hardness: | 6–6.5 |
| Specific gravity: | 3.65 |
| Cleavage; fracture: | poor; conchoidal |
| Habit: | crystals stubby, prismatic, dipyramidal |
| Crystal system: | hexagonal |

# Axinite

Axinite is a complex mineral in the ferroaxinite-manganaxinite series. Iron-rich axinite is brown to black whereas manganese-rich specimens are yellow-orange. Magnesioaxinite is a blue-grey magnesium-rich analogue and tinzenite is a low-calcium variety. Axinite is named after the sharp axe- or spearhead-shaped crystals. Axinite occurs in cavities in granites and adjacent zones, associated with diopside, andradite, quartz, calcite, scheelite and prehnite. It is found at Bourg d'Oisans (France), St Just (Cornwall, England), Obira (Japan) and Luning and Pala (California, USA); manganaxinite is found at Franklin (New Jersey, USA), Tinzon (Switzerland) and Liguria (Italy); and ferroaxinite at Baveno (Italy).

## $Ca_2(Fe,Mn)Al_2BO_3(OH)Si_4O_{12}$

| | |
|---|---|
| Colour: | yellow to brown, violet, grey |
| Lustre; opacity: | vitreous; transparent to translucent |
| Streak: | white |
| Hardness: | 6.5–7 |
| Specific gravity: | 3.25 |
| Cleavage; fracture: | perfect; conchoidal |
| Habit: | sharp-edged crystals, varying shape; granular and platy masses |
| Crystal system: | triclinic |

# Beryl

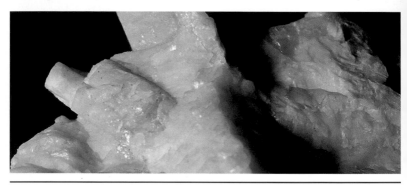

Beryl is famous for forming a wide variety of gemstones. It has been known since ancient times, the Greeks naming it after the colour of the sea, and druids believing it to aid psychic powers. Beryl is also of great importance as the main ore of beryllium, one of the lightest metals known. Beryl is formed in granites and pegmatites, where crystals can grow to enormous sizes (6m, 18 tonnes). It is also found in metamorphic rocks, hydrothermal veins and placer deposits. The availability varies enormously; non-precious varieties are easily obtained whereas emerald is so expensive that even small crystals are much sought-after. It is mined in Brazil, USA, Madagascar, Germany, Czech Republic, Russia and India.

## $Be_3Al_2Si_6O_{18}$

| | |
|---|---|
| Colour: | colourless, white, blue, green to yellows, rose, peach, red |
| Lustre; opacity: | vitreous, resinous; transparent to translucent |
| Streak: | white |
| Hardness: | 7.5–8 |
| Specific gravity: | 2.63–2.97 |
| Cleavage; fracture: | imperfect; conchoidal |
| Habit: | hexagonal prismatic crystals, often without clear terminations; rarely in druses or compact masses |
| Crystal system: | hexagonal |

# Beryl: Gem varieties

Emerald is the most famous and long-prized variety of beryl, having a beautiful green colour, derived from the presence of chromium and vanadium. It is rarely faultless, making good specimens very expensive, and stones are often oiled to disguise faults. The best emeralds come from Muso and Chivor (Colombia). Aquamarine is usually sky-blue to dark-blue, but in the nineteenth century a sea-green variety was favoured (the name meaning 'sea water'). A dark blue variety comes from Madagascar, often enhanced by heat treatment. The best-quality yellow to golden yellow heliodor comes from the Urals (Russia). Often associated with the Sun, heliodor is found only rarely as gem-quality material.

## $Be_3Al_2Si_6O_{18}$

| | |
|---|---|
| Colour: | colourless, white, blue, green to yellows, rose, peach, red |
| Lustre; opacity: | vitreous, resinous; transparent to translucent |
| Streak: | white |
| Hardness: | 7.5–8 |
| Specific gravity : | 2.63–2.97 |
| Cleavage; fracture: | imperfect; conchoidal |
| Habit: | hexagonal prismatic crystals, often without clear terminations; rarely in druses or compact masses |
| Crystal system: | hexagonal |

# Cordierite

Cordierite is a common mineral in metamorphic rocks, frequently occurring as porphyroblasts. The most interesting variety is the transparent violet-blue stone often known as iolite or water-sapphire. A black iron-rich variety called sekaninaite occurs only in Dolni Bory (Moravia, Czech Republic). Cordierite is named after the French geologist Pierre Cordier (1777–1861), who first described it, although it had been used as a gem long before this. Associated minerals include sillimanite, potassium feldspar, muscovite, biotite and andalusite. It is found at Bodenmais (Germany), Orijärvi (Finland), Kragerö (Norway), Bity (Madagascar), Tamil Nadu (India) and Thompson (Manitoba, Canada).

## $Mg_2Al_4Si_5O_{18}$

| | |
|---|---|
| Colour: | grey, rarely blue |
| Lustre; opacity: | vitreous; transparent to translucent |
| Streak: | white |
| Hardness: | 7 |
| Specific gravity: | 2.6–2.66 |
| Cleavage; fracture: | fair; subconchoidal |
| Habit: | stubby, pseudohexagonal, twinned crystals; granular, compact, massive |
| Crystal system: | orthorhombic |

# Dioptase

Dioptase is a beautiful deep green mineral, mistaken for emerald when first discovered in the eighteenth century. The strong green colour can hide the fire and transparency of some crystals. The crystal faces are usually very reflective and sparkling in clusters. The name comes from the Greek for 'see through', after clearly visible cleavages in crystals. Dioptase is found in the oxidized zones of copper deposits, associated with chrysocolla, malachite, wulfenite, cerrusite and quartz. It was first found at Altin-Tyube (Kirghiz Steppe, Kazakhstan); other locations include Tsumeb (Namibia), Copiapo and Atacama (Chile), Mindouli (Congo), Mammoth Mine (Tiger, Arizona, USA) and Baita (Romania).

## $CuSiO_2(OH)_2$

| | |
|---|---|
| Colour: | emerald-green, blue-green |
| Lustre; opacity: | vitreous; transparent to translucent |
| Streak: | green |
| Hardness: | 5 |
| Specific gravity: | 3.3 |
| Cleavage; fracture: | perfect; conchoidal to uneven |
| Habit: | crystals short, six-sided prisms with rhombohedral ends; granular, massive |
| Crystal system: | hexagonal |

# Tourmaline

Tourmalines are a group of aluminoborosilicates, notably elbaite (lithium-rich), dravite (magnesium-rich), schorl (iron- and manganese-rich) and uvite (iron- and magnesium-rich). Tourmalines crystallize as characteristic long prisms of triangular cross-section. All are strongly piezoelectric and pyroelectric, finding use in high-pressure gauges. Tourmalines are found in granites, pegmatites and quartz veins, and as an accessory in schists and gneisses. Elbaite occurs in Elba (Italy), the Urals (Russia), Sri Lanka, at Pala and Ramona (California, USA), and Newry (Maine, USA); uvite is found at Franklin (New Jersey, USA) and Gouverneur (New York, USA); and dravite at Yinniethara (Australia) and New York (USA).

## $NaAl_9(BO_3)_3Si_6O_{18}(OH)_4$

| | |
|---|---|
| Colour: | colourless, yellow, blue, olive-green, brown, black |
| Lustre; opacity: | vitreous; transparent to translucent |
| Streak: | white |
| Hardness: | 7–7.5 |
| Specific gravity: | 3.01–3.26 |
| Cleavage; fracture: | poor; uneven to conchoida |
| Habit: | prismatic crystals, often striated and elongated |
| Crystal system: | trigonal |

# Tourmaline: Gem Varieties

O f the tourmaline gem varieties, dravite is usually brown, with strong dichroism. Rubellite is a pink or red variety. Fibrous rubellite is cut *en cabochon*, for a cat's-eye effect. Watermelon tourmaline is coloured pink and green, resembling contrasting flesh and rind of the watermelon. Tourmaline may vary throughout the crystal, with up to 10 or more colours or shades. Achroite is a rare colourless variety of elbaite; it is easier to cut than other tourmalines, the strong dichroism of which dictates the direction of cuts. Indicolite is a rare deep blue variety; paraiba tourmaline is deep blue to bluish green. The black opaque iron-rich variety schorl can be found as crystals up to several metres long. Verdelith is a yellow-green.

## $NaAl_9(BO_3)_3Si_6O_{18}(OH)_4$

| | |
|---|---|
| Colour: | colourless, yellow, blue, olive-green, brown, black |
| Lustre; opacity: | vitreous; transparent to translucent |
| Streak: | white |
| Hardness: | 7–7.5 |
| Specific gravity: | 3.01–3.26 |
| Cleavage; fracture: | poor; uneven to conchoida |
| Habit: | prismatic crystals, often striated and elongated |
| Crystal system: | trigonal |

# Milarite

Milarite is a rare mineral and the end member of the milarite–osumilite group of minerals. Osumilite contains magnesium and iron, but no beryllium. Crystals of milarite are rarely transparent and usually small, but are excellent as micromounts. Crystals are often well-shaped hexagonal prisms in muted shades of green to yellow. It has been called giufite, but milarite is now the preferred name. Milarite is found in hydrothermal veins, classically in Val Giuf and Val Striem (Grissons, Switzerland), as crystals up to 3cm (1¼in); it is also found on the Kola Peninsula (Russia) and in Valencia Guanajuato (Mexico) and Jaguaraçú (Minas Gerais, Brazil). Osumilite is found on the volcano Sakurajima near Osumi (Japan).

## $K_2Ca_4Be_4Al_2Si_{24}O_{60}.H_2O$

| | |
|---|---|
| Colour: | colourless, green to yellow |
| Lustre; opacity: | vitreous; transparent to translucent |
| Streak: | white |
| Hardness: | 5.5–6 |
| Specific gravity: | 2.4–2.6 |
| Cleavage; fracture: | absent; conchoidal, uneven |
| Habit: | hexagonal prismatic crystals; radial-fibrous aggregates and intergrowths |
| Crystal system: | hexagonal |

# Eudialite

Eudialite is a rare mineral popular for the attractive colours of some specimens. Crystals are commonly red and usually found embedded in a matrix of host rock. The site on the Kola peninsula is well known for pegmatites rich in sodium and some rarer elements giving rise to unusual minerals such as eudialite. The name comes from the Greek, alluding to its ready solubility in acids. Eudialite occurs in nepheline syenites, granites and associated pegmatites, associated with quartz, albite, nepheline, aegerine and natrolite. Notable localties are the Kangerdluarssuk Plateau (Greenland), Magnet Cove (Arkansas, USA), Pajarito Mountain (New Mexico, USA) and the Lovozero and Khibiny massifs (Kola Peninsula, Russia).

## $(Na,Ca,Fe)_6Zr(OH,Cl)(Si_3O_9)_2$

| | |
|---|---|
| Colour: | pink, red, yellow-brown, violet |
| Lustre; opacity: | vitreous; translucent |
| Streak: | white |
| Hardness: | 5–5.5 |
| Specific gravity: | 2.8–3.0 |
| Cleavage; fracture: | imperfect; conchoidal, uneven, splintery |
| Habit: | crystals as plates, rarely well formed; granular, massive aggregates |
| Crystal system: | hexagonal |

# Hedenbergite

The pyroxenes are an important group of rock-forming minerals. Their structure is characterized by straight chains of linked silicon oxide ($SiO_4$) tetrahedra. They can be distinguished from the amphiboles by the angle between their two good cleavages (about 90° rather than 120°). Hedenbergite and diopside ($CaMgSi_2O_6$) are monoclinic clinopyroxenes, forming a calcium-bearing series in which magnesium and iron substitute for one another. Hedenburgite is common in iron-magnesium skarns at the contact of granitic rocks with limestones, and in contact-metamorphosed iron-rich sediments. Good hedenburgite crystals have been found in the Skardu area (Pakistan), Broken Hill (NSW, Australia) and the Harstig Mine (Varmland, Sweden).

## $CaFeSi_2O_6$

| | |
|---|---|
| **Colour:** | brownish-green, black; almost opaque |
| **Lustre; opacity:** | vitreous or dull; translucent to opaque |
| **Streak:** | white, grey |
| **Hardness:** | 5.5–6.5 |
| **Specific gravity:** | 3.6 |
| **Cleavage; fracture:** | good in two directions at about 90°; uneven to subconchoidal |
| **Habit:** | crystals short, prismatic; radiating aggregates, granular, massive |
| **Crystal system:** | monoclinic |

# Diopside

Diopside is a calcium-bearing clinopyroxene that forms a solid solution series with hedenbergite ($CaFeSi_2O_6$). Pure diopside is common in contact-metamorphic siliceous magnesian limestones, associated with calcite, dolomite and sometimes forsterite, as on Skye (Scotland). There are several varieties of diopside: chrome diopside is a chromium-rich gem variety found in Burma, Siberia (Russia), Pakistan and South Africa. Some specimens have inclusions (probably of rutile) that may form a 'cat's eye' effect when polished. Violane is a rare blue manganese-bearing variety from Italy. One dark green to black variety from southern India, known as star diopside, shows a four-rayed star when cut *en cabochon*.

## $CaMgSi_2O_6$

| | |
|---|---|
| **Colour:** | pale to dark green or black, may be colourless |
| **Lustre; opacity:** | vitreous or dull; transparent to opaque |
| **Streak:** | white, grey, grey-green |
| **Hardness:** | 5.5–6.5 |
| **Specific gravity:** | 3.29 |
| **Cleavage; fracture:** | good in two directions at about 90°; uneven to subconchoidal |
| **Habit:** | prismatic crystals; granular, columnar, massive |
| **Crystal system:** | monoclinic |

# Jadeite

Jadeite is the characteristic pyroxene of high-pressure metamorphic rocks, in which it may be associated with glaucophane, aragonite and quartz, and also of eclogites, along with garnet. It occurs in the high-pressure metamorphic belt in California (USA) and at Shibukawa (Japan). Jadeite is used as an ornamental stone for carving, and as a precious stone in jewellery. Of the two minerals known as jade, (the other being nephrite, an amphibole), it is less common. The emerald green chromium-bearing variety is most prized, and known as imperial jade. For more than two centuries, China has been supplied with such jade from Burma, whereas the Central American Indians used jadeite from Guatemala.

## $Na(Al,Fe)Si_2O_6$

| | |
|---|---|
| **Colour:** | shades of light and dark green; rarely white or violet |
| **Lustre; opacity:** | subvitreous, pearly on cleavages; translucent |
| **Streak:** | white |
| **Hardness:** | 6–7 |
| **Specific gravity:** | 3.2–3.4 |
| **Cleavage; fracture:** | good in two directions at about 90°; splintery |
| **Habit:** | crystals rare, prismatic; commonly massive, granular, compact felty masses |
| **Crystal system:** | monoclinic |

# Spodumene

The pyroxene spodumene was named from the Greek for 'ash', in reference to its colour. Spodumene comes in other colours: gem varieties include the lilac pink kunzite, coloured by manganese, and bright emerald green hiddenite, coloured by chromium. Well-cut stones display strong pleochroism from colourless to two shades of body colour. Crystals can weigh up to 65 tonnes (72 tons). Spodumene is mined as a raw material for lithium compounds and ceramics. It is commonly found in lithium-rich granitic pegmatites and also occurs in gneisses. Associated minerals include quartz, albite, petalite, lepidolite and beryl. Notable localities include the Black Hills (South Dakota, USA) and Sterling and Chesterfield (Massachussetts, USA).

## $LiAlSi_2O_6$

| | |
|---|---|
| Colour: | commonly yellowish-grey, but shows a range of colours |
| Lustre; opacity: | vitreous, dull; transparent to translucent |
| Streak: | white |
| Hardness: | 6.5–7 |
| Specific gravity: | 3.1–3.2 |
| Cleavage; fracture: | good in two directions at about 90°; uneven to subconchoidal |
| Habit: | crystals prismatic, may be striated; commonly massive |
| Crystal system: | monoclinic |

# Aegirine

First described from Norway, aegirine is named after Aegir, a Scandinavian god of the sea. It is also known as acmite, from the Greek for 'point', in reference to its unusually sharply pointed crystals. This helps to distinguish it from augite, which is very similar. Aegerine occurs in alkaline rocks such as sodium-rich nepheline syenites, carbonatites and pegmatites, and rarely in regionally metamorphosed schists, gneisses and iron formations. Associated minerals include analcime, nepheline, clinochlore, eudialyte and rhodochrosite. Good crystals occur at Malosa (Zomba District, Malawi), Mont Saint-Hilaire (Quebec, Canada), Khibiny Massif (Kola Peninsula, Russia) and Magnet Cove, Arkansas (USA).

## $NaFeSi_2O_6$

| | |
|---|---|
| **Colour:** | dark green, greenish-black, reddish-brown |
| **Lustre; opacity:** | vitreous to resinous; translucent to opaque |
| **Streak:** | yellowish-grey |
| **Hardness:** | 6 |
| **Specific gravity:** | 3.5 |
| **Cleavage; fracture:** | good in two directions at about 90°; uneven, brittle |
| **Habit:** | acicular crystals terminated by a steep pyramid, striated; disseminated grains, fibrous, in radiating aggregates |
| **Crystal system:** | monoclinic |

# Augite

Augite is a calcium-bearing clinopyroxene, similar to the diopside-hedenbergite series, but with aluminium, titanium and sodium incorporated into the structure. The commonest pyroxene, it can be distinguished from hornblende by the angle between the cleavages. It is an important rock-forming mineral in basic igneous rocks (basalt and gabbro) and some syenite, and in ultrabasic rocks (pyroxenites and peridotites). It also forms in high-temperature metamorphic rocks such as pyroxene gneisses and pyroxene granulites. It is commonly associated with plagioclase feldspars, amphiboles, olivine and orthopyroxenes. Rare well-formed crystals occur at Vesuvius and Stromboli (Italy), and at Eifel (Germany).

## $(Ca,Na)(Mg,Fe,Al,Ti)(Si,Al)_2O_6$

| | |
|---|---|
| Colour: | dark green, brown, black, rarely cream |
| Lustre; opacity: | vitreous, resinous to dull; transparent to opaque |
| Streak: | greyish-green |
| Hardness: | 5.5–6 |
| Specific gravity: | 3.2–3.6 |
| Cleavage; fracture: | good in two directions at about 90°; uneven to subconchoidal |
| Habit: | short prismatic crystals of four- or eight-sided cross-section, often twinned; compact, granular |
| Crystal system: | monoclinic |

# Enstatite

$E$nstatite and ferrosilite ($Fe_2Si_2O_6$) form a series in which iron and magnesium substitute for each other. The intermediate composition, $MgFeSi_2O_6$, is called hypersthene. Minerals of this series are calcium-poor and are mostly orthorhombic. These orthopyroxenes are important rock-forming minerals, and occur worldwide in basic and ultrabasic igneous rocks, and high-temperature metamorphic rocks such as pyroxene gneisses. Enstatite is also found in meteorites. Crystals are quite rare, but rolled pebbles are sometimes faceted as gems. The variety chrome-enstatite is emerald green; a dark brown six-rayed star enstatite occurs in Mysore (India); and unique gem-quality colourless crystals are found at Embilipitiya (Sri Lanka).

## $Mg_2Si_2O_6$

| | |
|---|---|
| **Colour:** | pale to dark brownish-green, white, greyish, yellowish |
| **Lustre; opacity:** | vitreous; transparent to opaque |
| **Streak:** | white to greyish |
| **Hardness:** | 5–6 |
| **Specific gravity:** | 3.2–3.4 |
| **Cleavage; fracture:** | good in two directions at about 90°; uneven |
| **Habit:** | crystals stumpy, may be twinned; as grains, lamellar or massive |
| **Crystal system:** | orthorhombic |

# Bronzite

The orthopyroxene bronzite is characterized by a bronze sheen on its cleavage surface; however, it is now regarded as an iron-bearing enstatite, and is no longer recognized as a separate species. It is affected by partial alteration of a type called 'schillerization', which gives rise to the bronzelike submetallic lustre. Bronzite is sometimes cut and polished for ornaments, and may have a fibrous structure. It occurs in the basic igneous rock norite in the Fichtelgebirge (Germany) and in the serpentine of Kraubat (Styria, Austria). Relict crystals of more highly altered bronzite or enstatite occurring in serpentinite are known as bastite, after the locality Baste (Harz, Germany); it also occurs in the Lizard (Cornwall, England).

## $(Mg,Fe)_2Si_2O_6$

| | |
|---|---|
| Colour: | grey-green or bronze-brown |
| Lustre; opacity: | vitreous, pearly, bronze sheen on cleavage; translucent to opaque |
| Streak: | white to greyish |
| Hardness: | 5–6 |
| Specific gravity: | 3.2–3.3 |
| Cleavage; fracture: | good in two directions at about 90°; scaly; uneven |
| Habit: | coarse prismatic crystals; massive, granular |
| Crystal system: | orthorhombic |

# Cummingtonite

Cummingtonite belongs to the amphibole group, whose structure is characterized by double chains of silicon oxide ($SiO_4$) tetrahedra. It is in the middle compositional range of a magnesium–iron series, the end members of which are magnesiocummingtonite and grunerite. Cummingtonite cannot be distinguished from anthophyllite, its polymorph, with the naked eye. It forms in medium-grade regionally metamorphosed rocks. The only commercial source of brown asbestiform amosite was the Precambrian ironstone formations of Transvaal (South Africa). Grunerite is found in the iron deposits of Lake Superior (USA); cummingtonite is found at Cummington (Massachusetts, USA) and Val d'Ossola (Italy).

## $(Mg, Fe)_7Si_8O_{22}(OH)_2$

| | |
|---|---|
| **Colour:** | dark green, pale to dark brown depending on iron content |
| **Lustre; opacity:** | vitreous to silky; translucent to transparent |
| **Streak:** | white |
| **Hardness:** | 5–6 |
| **Specific gravity:** | 3.1–3.6 (increasing with iron content) |
| **Cleavage; fracture:** | two good cleavages at about 120°; splintery |
| **Habit:** | individual crystals rare; aggregates of rodlike or fibrous crystals, often radiating |
| **Crystal system:** | monoclinic |

# Glaucophane

G laucophane is named after the Greek *glaucos* ('blue') and *fanos* ('appearing'). It is an alkali-bearing amphibole which, like riebeckite, has a characteristic blue-grey colour, and typical 120° prismatic amphibole cleavage. It characteristically forms in subduction zones under high-pressure, low-temperature conditions, and may eventually be exposed at the surface. Glaucophane-rich schists are known as blueschists. Glaucophane may be associated with the high-pressure minerals lawsonite, jadeite and aragonite, and also with garnet, epidote or pumpellyite. Glaucophane occurs in the Franciscan belt of California (USA), in Shikoku (Japan), Anglesey (Wales), Zermatt (Switzerland) and Euboea Island (Greece).

## $Na_2(Mg,Fe)_3Al_2Si_8O_{22}(OH)_2$

| | |
|---|---|
| Colour: | grey-blue to lavender blue |
| Lustre; opacity: | vitreous, silky in fibrous varieties; translucent |
| Streak: | blue–grey |
| Hardness: | 6 |
| Specific gravity: | 3.08–3.22 |
| Cleavage; fracture: | good in two directions at about 120°; uneven to subconchoidal |
| Habit: | good crystals rare, slender prismatic to acicular; sometimes massive, fibrous, columnar or granular |
| Crystal system: | monoclinic |

# Riebeckite

Named after the German traveller E. Riebeck, riebeckite is a blue-grey alkali-amphibole formed in alkali granites, syenites, more rarely in granite pegmatites and in some volcanic rocks. The asbestiform variety crocidolite is found in iron formations and was formerly mined in South Africa and Australia. The associated health risk means that specimens should be professionally sealed in boxes or bags. Associated minerals include nepheline, albite, aegerine, tremolite, magnetite, hematite or siderite. Crocidolite inclusions in quartz, and their pseudomorphing by quartz, have given rise to the gems tiger's eye and hawk's eye. The type locality for riebeckite is Socotra Island (Indian Ocean, Yemen).

## $Na_2(Mg,Fe)_5Si_8O_{22}(OH)_2$

| | |
|---|---|
| **Colour:** | dark blue to black |
| **Lustre; opacity:** | vitreous or silky; translucent |
| **Streak:** | none determined |
| **Hardness:** | 5 |
| **Specific gravity:** | 3.32–3.38 |
| **Cleavage; fracture:** | two good cleavages at about 120°; conchoidal to uneven |
| **Habit:** | long, prismatic and striated crystals; massive, fibrous or asbestiform |
| **Crystal system:** | monoclinic |

# Tremolite

Tremolite is a calcic amphibole that forms a series with the iron-bearing ferroactinolite. Pure tremolite is creamy white, but grades to green with increasing iron content. It may fluoresce yellow or pink. It forms through the contact metamorphism of calcium- and magnesium-bearing siliceous sediments, impure dolomitic limestones, or ultramafic rocks. It can be associated with calcite, dolomite, garnet, wollastonite, talc, diopside or forsterite. A fibrous variety of tremolite has been mined for use as asbestos. It is named after Tremola (Italy). Other notable localities include St Marcel (Piedmont, Italy), Franklin (New Jersey, USA), Wilberforce (Ontario, Canda) and Brumada Mine (Bahia, Brazil).

## $Ca_2Mg_5Si_8O_{22}(OH)_2$

| | |
|---|---|
| **Colour:** | colourless, white, grey, can be green, pink or brown |
| **Lustre; opacity:** | vitreous or silky to dull; transparent to translucent |
| **Streak:** | white |
| **Hardness:** | 5–6 |
| **Specific gravity:** | 2.9–3.2 |
| **Cleavage; fracture:** | two good cleavages at about 120°; uneven to subconchoidal |
| **Habit:** | crystals long, bladed, often twinned; columnar, fibrous, plumose aggregates, radiating or granular |
| **Crystal system:** | monoclinic |

# Actinolite

A ctinolite is a fairly common calcic amphibole within the series tremolite–ferroactinolite. It occurs in relatively low-grade metamorphosed mafic, ultramafic or magnesian carbonate rocks, and also in glaucophane-bearing blue schists. It is a common alteration product of primary pyroxenes in gabbro or dolerite, and used to be called uralite. Byssolite is an asbestiform type. The variety nephrite is the more common of the two types of green gemstone known as jade; it is tough, and takes a good polish. Beautiful nephrites from New Zealand are known as Maori stone because of their widespread use in traditional Maori art. Actinolite is found in the Zillertal (Austria), Val Malenco (Italy) and the Urals (Russia).

## $Ca_2(Mg,Fe)_5Si_8O_{22}(OH)_2$

| | |
|---|---|
| **Colour:** | bright to greyish green |
| **Lustre; opacity:** | vitreous, silky when fibrous; transparent to translucent |
| **Streak:** | white |
| **Hardness:** | 5–6 |
| **Specific gravity:** | 3.0–3.24 |
| **Cleavage; fracture:** | two good cleavages at about 120°; uneven or splintery |
| **Habit:** | long bladed or prismatic crystals, may be bent; columnar, radiating fibrous to asbestiform, granular, massive |
| **Crystal system:** | monoclinic |

# Hornblende

Hornblende is a calcic amphibole and a very important rock-forming mineral. It is widespread in igneous rocks (granodiorites, diorites, syenites and some gabbros) and in medium-temperature metamorphosed basalts (amphibolites) accompanied by plagioclase feldspar and sometimes garnet. It is occasionally found in metamorphosed impure dolomitic limestones and ironstones. It forms complex solid-solution series with several other amphiboles. The variety edenite is pale green, iron-poor and found at Edenville (New York, USA); pargasite is dark green, iron-rich and found in Pargas (Finland); hastingsite is richer in sodium and aluminium, and occurs in gabbros in Ontario (Canada).

## $(Ca,Na)_{2-3}(Mg,Fe,Al)_5(Al,Si)_8O_{22}(OH)_2$

| | |
|---|---|
| Colour: | black to dark green |
| Lustre; opacity: | vitreous to dull; opaque |
| Streak: | brown to grey |
| Hardness: | 5–6 |
| Specific gravity: | 3.28–3.41 |
| Cleavage; fracture: | two good cleavages at about 120°; uneven |
| Habit: | crystals long and thin, or short and stumpy, generally six-sided; granular, may form radiating aggregates |
| Crystal system: | monoclinic |

# Anthophyllite

Anthophyllite is the orthorhombic polymorph of monoclinic cummingtonite, from which it can be distinguished only through optical, density or x-ray study. It occurs in medium-grade metamorphic rocks, derived from mafic or ultramafic igneous rocks, or dolomitic sedimentary rocks. It can form through the hydration of olivine. It is associated with talc, cordierite, chlorite, mica, hornblende or olivine. Anthophyllite has been commercially used in asbestos, with the associated health hazards. It is named from the Latin *anthophyllum*, meaning 'clove', in reference to its distinctive colour. Good crystals occur at Köngsberg (Norway); it is also found at Fahlan (Sweden), Orijarvi (Finland) and the Isle of Elba (Italy).

## $(Mg,Fe)_7Si_8O_{22}(OH)_2$

| | |
|---|---|
| Colour: | grey-brown, cinnamon or clove brown, green |
| Lustre; opacity: | vitreous, silky when fibrous; translucent to translucent |
| Streak: | white |
| Hardness: | 5.5–6 |
| Specific gravity: | 2.85–3.57 |
| Cleavage; fracture: | two good cleavages at about 120°; uneven, brittle |
| Habit: | individual crystals rare; usually aggregates of prismatic crystals, fibrous, asbestiform |
| Crystal system: | orthorhombic |

# Wollastonite

Wollastonite, formerly known as table spar, is found in thermally metamorphosed siliceous limestones at igneous contacts, or in regionally metamorphosed rocks, associated with calcium-rich garnets, diopside, epidote and tremolite. It also occurs in xenoliths in igneous rocks. There are many different polymorphs, generally called wollastonite. Although common, commercially viable deposits are unusual, occurring in New York (USA), Finland, Mexico, China, India and Africa. Wollastonite has many applications, e.g. in refractory ceramics, plastics, and sealants. It was named after the British mineralogist and chemist William H. Wollaston (1766–1828), who also discovered palladium and rhodium.

## $CaSiO_3$

| | |
|---|---|
| Colour: | white or greyish |
| Lustre; opacity: | vitreous, may be silky; subtransparent to translucent |
| Streak: | white |
| Hardness: | 4.5–5 |
| Specific gravity: | 2.87–3.09 |
| Cleavage; fracture: | perfect; splintery, uneven |
| Habit: | crystals tabular to short prismatic, twinning common; fibrous masses, radial, granular, compact |
| Crystal system: | triclinic (or monoclinic) |

# Pectolite

Pectolite must be handled carefully, as the fine white needles are sharp and easily puncture the skin and can become embedded. Some specimens are triboluminescent. A variety called larimar is a fine pale blue and green, and comes from the Dominican Republic. Pectolite occurs as a primary mineral in nepheline syenites, but is also formed by hydrothermal processes, filling cavities in basalts, associated with zeolites, datolite, prehnite and calcite. It is also found filling fractures in serpentinites and peridotites, and in contact-metamorphosed limestones. Notable occurrences include Lake County (California, USA), Franklin (New Jersey, USA), Bahamas, Mt Baldo (Trento Province, Italy) and England.

## $NaCa_2Si_3O_8(OH)$

| | |
|---|---|
| Colour: | colourless, white or grey, larimar is pale blue |
| Lustre; opacity: | vitreous to silky; translucent to opaque |
| Streak: | white |
| Hardness: | 4.5–5 |
| Specific gravity: | 2.84–2.90 |
| Cleavage; fracture: | perfect in two directions close to 90°; uneven, splintery |
| Habit: | crystals tabular or acicular; fibrous tufts or fibrous-radiating spherical aggregates or compact masses |
| Crystal system: | triclinic |

# Rhodonite

Rhodonite has a similar structure to wollastonite and pectolite, built of chains of silicon oxide ($SiO_4$) tetrahedra with bases that do not lie in a plane. It has a distinctive pink colour and can be distinguished from rhodochrosite (which is also pink) because it is harder and does not dissolve in dilute hydrochloric acid. It often occurs in association with manganese ore deposits in hydrothermal veins, or in contact and regional metamorphosed manganese-bearing sedimentary rocks. Rhodonite from Sverdlovsk in the Urals (Russia) has been used as an ornamental stone. It also occurs at Långban (Sweden) in iron ore, at Broken Hill (NSW, Australia) and at Franklin and Sterling Hill (New Jersey, USA).

## $(Mn,Fe,Mg)SiO_3$

| | |
|---|---|
| **Colour:** | deep pink, with brown or black surface oxidation |
| **Lustre; opacity:** | vitreous, pearly on cleavages; transparent to translucent |
| **Streak:** | white |
| **Hardness:** | 5.5–6.5 |
| **Specific gravity:** | 3.57–3.76 |
| **Cleavage; fracture:** | perfect in two directions close to 90°, with a third good cleavage; conchoidal to uneven |
| **Habit:** | crystals rare, tabular or prismatic; massive or granular |
| **Crystal system:** | triclinic |

# Babingtonite

Babingtonite is a rare mineral named after the Irish physicist and mineralogist W. Babington (1757–1833). Relatively recently discovered, it contains both ferrous iron ($Fe^{2+}$) and ferric iron ($Fe^{3+}$) (which takes the place of aluminium typical of many silicates), and is weakly magnetic. It tends to grow in cavities in mafic volcanic rocks and gneisses, which enables crystals to grow freely; it is also found in veins cross-cutting granite and diorite, and in skarns. It is commonly associated with prehnite, epidote, pyrite and quartz, and with zeolites. Notable occurrences include Poona (India), Devon (England), Herbornseelbach (Germany), Baveno (Italy), Yakubi Mine (Japan) and Massachusetts (USA), where it is the official mineral emblem.

## $Ca_2(Fe,Mn)FeSi_5O_{14}(OH)$

| | |
|---|---|
| **Colour:** | dark greenish-black to brownish-black |
| **Lustre; opacity:** | brilliantly vitreous; opaque to translucent |
| **Streak:** | green-grey |
| **Hardness:** | 5–6 |
| **Specific gravity:** | 3.0–3.2 |
| **Cleavage; fracture:** | good in two directions at about 90°; uneven to subconchoidal |
| **Habit:** | crystals short, columnar, often striated; as platey, radial or fan-shaped aggregates |
| **Crystal system:** | triclinic |

# Neptunite

Neptunite is a rare mineral that forms as an accessory in intermediate plutonic igneous rocks such as nepheline syenite, and its pegmatites. It is also found in serpentinites associated with benitoite and natrolite. Its name is derived from Roman mythology, Neptune being the god of the sea, and alludes to its close association at its type locality with aegerine, named after Aegir, the Scandinavian sea god. Excellent crystals occur at San Benito (California, USA), where it is found in natrolite veins in a serpentinite body, along with blue benitoite; other localities include Barnavave (Ireland), Kola Peninsula (Russia), Igaliko (Greenland) and Mont St Hilaire (Quebec, Canada).

## $Na_2KLi(Fe,Mn)_2Ti_2Si_8O_{24}$

| | |
|---|---|
| **Colour:** | black with deep reddish-brown internal reflections |
| **Lustre; opacity:** | vitreous to submetallic; opaque to translucent |
| **Streak:** | dark reddish-brown |
| **Hardness:** | 5–6 |
| **Specific gravity:** | 3.19–3.23 |
| **Cleavage; fracture:** | perfect; conchoidal |
| **Habit:** | elongate prismatic crystals of square cross-section and pointed terminations |
| **Crystal system:** | monoclinic |

# Bavenite

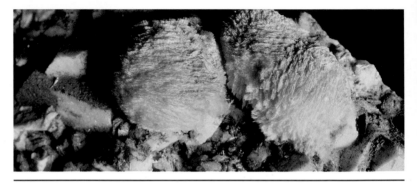

Bavenite is an extremely rare mineral, named in 1901 after Baveno (Italy) where it was discovered. It is formed by the alteration of beryl and other beryllium-bearing minerals, and occurs as druses in cavities in granite and associated pegmatites. It is also found in hydrothermal veins and skarns. Associated minerals include orthoclase, fluorite, albite and beryl. It has a distinctive habit, with very thin tabular crystals forming diverging groups like the pages of a book. It can also form fibrous crystals, as in the granitic pegmatite bodies of Bustarviejo (Madrid, Spain). Other localities include Shap Pink Quarry (Cumbria, England), Mont St Hilaire (Quebec, Canada), Strzegom (Poland) and Londonderry (Australia).

## $Ca_4Al_2Be_2(OH)_2Si_9O_{26}$

| | |
|---|---|
| Colour: | colourless, white, green, pink, brown |
| Lustre; opacity: | silky, vitreous, pearly; transparent to translucent |
| Streak: | white |
| Hardness: | 5.5–6 |
| Specific gravity: | 2.7 |
| Cleavage; fracture: | perfect; uneven |
| Habit: | very thin tabular crystals, may be twinned; lamellar, rose-shaped aggregates, radiating tufts of needle-like crystals |
| Crystal system: | orthorhombic |

# Prehnite

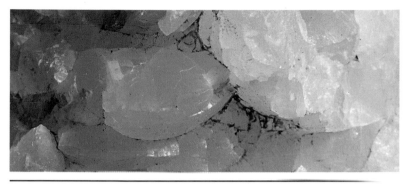

Prehnite is found in hollows in basaltic lavas, often associated with zeolites; it also occurs in very low grade metamorphic rocks, and through the decomposition of plagioclase feldspar. Associated minerals include datolite, epidote or calcite. It was the first mineral to be named after a person, the Dutchman Colonel Hendrick von Prehn (1733–1785), who discovered it at the Cape of Good Hope. It occasionally forms epimorphs (crystal growth over another mineral surface) on laumontite, which may subsequently dissolve, leaving the prehnite as a crust. Yellowish brown prehnite is occasionally cut *en cabochon*. Pale green masses are found in Scotland, and dark green or greenish-brown prehnite in Australia.

## $Ca_2Al_2Si_3O_{10}(OH)_2$

| | |
|---|---|
| Colour: | pale watery or oily green, sometimes white or yellowish |
| Lustre; opacity: | vitreous, pearly; transparent to translucent |
| Streak: | white |
| Hardness: | 6–6.5 |
| Specific gravity: | 2.8–2.9 |
| Cleavage; fracture: | distinct; uneven, rather brittle |
| Habit: | crystals rare, prismatic, tabular or pyramidal; usually botryoidal or globular masses with a radiating structure |
| Crystal system: | orthorhombic |

# Apophyllite

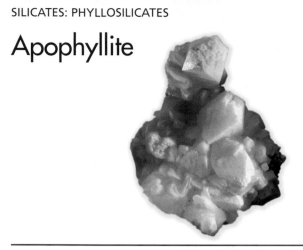

Apophyllite is the name given to a group of minerals including fluoroapophyllite and hydroxyapophyllite. Its name, from the Greek, roughly means 'to flake off' because it peels apart in leafs on heating as water is driven off. Apophyllite is quite abundant and popular, forming some attactive clear, colourless crystals and some of pale pastel shades; the most famous is an emerald-green variety from India. Apophyllite occurs in cavities in basalts, associated with stilbite, scolecite, calcite, prehnite and analcime. Excellent crystals occur at Bolzano (Italy), Poona (India), Mont St Hilaire (Canada), St Andreasburg (Harz, Germany), Paterson (New Jersey, USA) and Rio Grande do Sul (Brazil).

## $KCa_4Si_8O_{20}(F,OH).8H_2O$

| | |
|---|---|
| Colour: | colourless, white, pale pink, green or yellow |
| Lustre; opacity: | vitreous, pearly; transparent to translucent |
| Streak: | white |
| Hardness: | 4.5–5 |
| Specific gravity: | 2.33–2.37 |
| Cleavage; fracture: | perfect; irregular |
| Habit: | tabular pseudocubic or pseudooctahedral crystals, sometimes dipyramidal or platy; aggregates |
| Crystal system: | tetragonal |

# Pyrophyllite

**P**yrophyllite is named after the Greek for 'fire' and 'leaf', after its behaviour on heating, when water is driven off and the mineral peels into flakes. Breaking into thin flakes like this is typical of phyllosilicates and reflects a sheetlike structure. Pyrophyllite has a greasy feel and is used as a dry lubricant like talc, from which it is almost indistinguishable. The variety agalmatolite has been used for carved ornaments in China. Pyrophyllite occurs in hydrothermal veins and schists, associated with kyanite, andalusite, topaz, mica and quartz. It is found in Orange County (North Carolina), Graves Mountain (Georgia) and La Paz County (Arkanas, USA), Ibitiara (Bahia, Brazil), Zermatt (Switzerland) and Krassik (Urals, Russia).

## $Al_2Si_4O_{10}(OH)_2$

| | |
|---|---|
| **Colour:** | yellowish-white, grey, green |
| **Lustre; opacity:** | pearly, dull; translucent to opaque |
| **Streak:** | white |
| **Hardness:** | 1–1.5 |
| **Specific gravity:** | 2.8 |
| **Cleavage; fracture:** | perfect; uneven or splintery |
| **Habit:** | lamellar or radiating foliated aggregates, granular, massive |
| **Crystal system:** | monoclinic |

# Talc

Talc, a member of the mica group, is noted for being soft, by definition 1 on Moh's scale. It is used in many industries, including paper, paints, personal care and roofing. Massive steatite, or soapstone (after its greasy feel), is easily carved or turned on a lathe. Talc is a good electrical and heat insulator, and repels water. The name comes from the Persian or Arabic *talq*. Talc occurs in schists and hydrothermally altered mafic rocks, associated with serpentine, actinolite, chlorite, vermiculite, dolomite and calcite. It is found at Mt Greiner (Austria), Zermatt (Switzerland), Pfitschal (Italy), Trimouns (Ariège, France), Onotosk (Siberia, Russia), Yellowstone mine (Montana, USA) and Delta (Pennsylvania, USA).

## $Mg_3Si_4O_{10}(OH)_2$

| | |
|---|---|
| **Colour:** | white, brown, green |
| **Lustre; opacity:** | greasy when massive, pearly on cleavage; translucent |
| **Streak:** | white |
| **Hardness:** | 1 |
| **Specific gravity:** | 2.58–2.83 |
| **Cleavage; fracture:** | perfect; uneven, lamellar |
| **Habit:** | very rare crystals as pseudohexagonal plates; usually scaly, foliated aggregates |
| **Crystal system:** | monoclinic |

# Muscovite

M uscovite is the most common mica, well known for its cleavage into thin, flexible lamellae – a manifestation of its underlying two-dimensional sheetlike structure. The name comes from muscovy glass, after its former use in windows. Muscovite is used for electrical and heat insulation, as a dry lubricant and in paper, rubber, paints and plastics. The variety fuchsite is emerald green and popular among collectors. Muscovite is a very common rock-forming mineral in granites, pegmatites, phyllites, schists and gneisses. Crystals up to 30–50 m$^2$ (323–538 sq ft) are found in pegamatites in Methuen and Calvin (Ontario, Canada), Nellore (Andhra Pradesh, India), Custer (South Dakota, USA) and Minas Gerais (Brazil).

## $KAl_2(AlSi_3)O_{10}(OH)_2$

| | |
|---|---|
| **Colour:** | white, grey, yellow, brown, greenish; bright green |
| **Lustre; opacity:** | vitreous, pearly, silky; transparent to translucent |
| **Streak:** | white |
| **Hardness:** | 2.5 |
| **Specific gravity:** | 2.76–2.88 |
| **Cleavage; fracture:** | perfect; uneven, lamellar |
| **Habit:** | pseudo-hexagonal tabular crystals, deep striations on prism faces; foliated, scaly, lamellar masses |
| **Crystal system:** | monoclinic |

# Phlogopite

**P**hlogopite forms a series with the more common mica biotite, which is iron-rich and generally of darker colour. It is used in electronics for its excellent heat- and electrical-insulating properties. Phlogopite forms tabular crystals up to 2m (6½ft) across, some strikingly transparent. It decomposes in concentrated sulphuric acid, distinguishing it from muscovite. The name comes from the Greek *flogopos*, meaning 'to resemble fire'. It occurs in metamorphosed dolomites and in ultramafic rocks, associated with dolomite, calcite, diopside and epidote. It is found at Campolungo (Switzerland), Frontenac (Ontario, Canada), Ødegården (Norway), Franklin (New Jersey, USA), Saharakara (Madagascar) and Anxiety Point (New Zealand).

## $KMg_3(Al,Fe)Si_3O_{10}(F,OH)_2$

| | |
|---|---|
| **Colour:** | brown, reddish-brown, yellow, green |
| **Lustre; opacity:** | pearly; transparent to translucent |
| **Streak:** | white |
| **Hardness:** | 2–3 |
| **Specific gravity:** | 2.86 |
| **Cleavage; fracture:** | perfect; uneven, lamellar |
| **Habit:** | crystals as six-sided plates; foliated, granular aggregates |
| **Crystal system:** | monoclinic |

# Biotite

Biotite, named after the French mineralogist J.-B. Biot (1774–1862), is also called black mica, as opposed to white mica (muscovite). It can form enormous crystals in pegmatites, but is most common as small dark plates in granites, contrasting with larger, paler quartz and feldspar. Biotite in exposed surfaces of rocks can sparkle in sunlight, occasionally with a golden sheen. It is an important mineral in schists, gneisses, granites, nepheline syenites and contact-metamorphosed rocks. Associated minerals include muscovite, pyroxenes, amphiboles, andalusite and cordierite. Good crystals occur at Vesuvius (Italy), Miass (Ilmen Mountains, Russia), Arendal (Norway), Franklin (New Jersey, USA) and Bancroft (Ontario, Canada).

## $K(Mg,Fe)_3(AlSi_3)O_{10}(F,OH)_2$

| | |
|---|---|
| Colour: | brown, black, dark green, greyish-yellow |
| Lustre; opacity: | vitreous, pearly on cleavage; transparent to translucent |
| Streak: | grey-white |
| Hardness: | 2.5–3 |
| Specific gravity: | 2.8–3.2 |
| Cleavage; fracture: | perfect; irregular, lamellar |
| Habit: | rare tabular or short prismatic pseudohexagonal crystals; foliated masses or aggregates, disseminated grains |
| Crystal system: | monoclinic |

# Lepidolite

Lepidolite, or lithium mica, named after the Greek for 'scale', is an ore of lithium and a source of rubidium and caesium. The pink colour is fairly characteristic, but may be confused with pink muscovite. Like other micas, lepidolite can be found as 'books' of crystal sheets. Large forms are carved, shaped or used as polished stones. Attractive specimens from Brazil comprise lepidolite with red tourmaline and colourless quartz. Lepidolite occurs in lithium-rich pegmatites and altered granites, associated with quartz, feldspars, spodumene and tourmaline. It is found at Pala (California, USA), Mount Mica (Maine, USA), Rozna (Czech Republic), Alabashka (Urals, Russia) and Virgem de Lape (Minas Gerais, Brazil).

## $K(Li,Al)_3(Si,Al)_4O_{10}(F,OH)_2$

| | |
|---|---|
| Colour: | pink to lilac |
| Lustre; opacity: | pearly; transparent to translucent |
| Streak: | white |
| Hardness: | 2.5–4 |
| Specific gravity: | 2.8–2.9 |
| Cleavage; fracture: | perfect; uneven, lamellar giving flexible sheets |
| Habit: | six-sided tabular crystals; fine, platy aggregates, massive |
| Crystal system: | monoclinic |

# Zinnwaldite

Zinnwaldite is a widespread but rare mica, difficult to distinguish from other micas but for the environment in which it occurs. Its colour is usually darker than muscovite, but lighter than biotite. Zinnwaldite forms six-sided crystals up to 20cm (8in). As with other micas, zinnwaldite occurs as 'books' of pseudohexagonal crystals. Zinnwaldite occurs in tin-bearing pneumatolytic deposits in greisens and rarely in pegmatites and quartz veins, associated with topaz, cassitrerite, lepidolite, wolframite and spodumene. It is found at Cínovec (Zinnwald, Czech Republic), Altenberg and Waldstein (Germany), St Just (Cornwall, England), Amelia (Virginia, USA), Pala (California, USA) and Antaboaka (Madagascar).

## $KLiFeAl(Al_2Si_2)O_{10}(F,OH)_2$

| | |
|---|---|
| Colour: | grey-brown, yellow-brown, pale violet, dark green |
| Lustre; opacity: | vitreous, pearly; transparent to translucent |
| Streak: | white |
| Hardness: | 2.5–4 |
| Specific gravity: | 2.9–3.2 |
| Cleavage; fracture: | perfect; uneven, lamellar giving flexible, elastic scales |
| Habit: | short prismatic or tabular crystals; rosettes, lamellar or scaly aggregates, disseminated |
| Crystal system: | monoclinic |

# Margarite

Margarite is a brittle mica named from the Greek for 'pearl', after its lustre. Brittle micas differ from common micas in that the thin platy crystals are inflexible and readily broken. Beryllian margarite is a related brittle mica, rich in beryllium. Brittle micas have doubly charged ions positioned between the aluminosilicate sheets, whereas common micas have singly charged ions. It occurs in low- to medium-grade metamorphic rocks; commonly in emery deposits, associated with corundum, diaspore, tourmaline, chlorite, andalusite, calcite and quartz. It is found at Mt Greiner (Austria), Naxos (Greece), Smyrna (Turkey), Chester (Massachusetts, USA), Glen Esk (Scotland) and Sverdlovsk (Russia).

## $CaAl_2(Al_2Si_2)O_{10}(OH)_2$

| | |
|---|---|
| **Colour:** | pale pink, white, grey, green |
| **Lustre; opacity:** | pearly |
| **Streak:** | white |
| **Hardness:** | 3.5–4.5 |
| **Specific gravity:** | 2.99–3.1 |
| **Cleavage; fracture:** | perfect; uneven, giving brittle lamellae |
| **Habit:** | rare, tabular, pseudohexagonal crystals; usually foliated aggregates |
| **Crystal system:** | monoclinic |

# Vermiculite

Vermiculite, when heated to 300°C (572°F), quickly loses water and expands 18 to 25 times its original volume, giving long, twisted forms of a golden yellow colour; hence the name, from the Greek for breeding worms. The expanded material is used extensively as packing and insulating material, in soil conditioners, hydroponics, fireproof fillings, and many others. It is formed by hydrothermal alteration of biotite or phlogopite, especially at the contact between felsic intrusions in ultramafic rocks. Associated minerals include corundum, serpentine and talc. Large masses are found at Bulong (Western Australia), Palabora (South Africa), Libby (Montana, USA), Macon (North Carolina, USA) and Ajmer (Rajasthan, India).

## $(Mg,Fe,Al)_3(Al,Si)_4O_{10}(OH)_2.4H_2O$

| | |
|---|---|
| Colour: | white, yellow, green, brown |
| Lustre; opacity: | vitreous, pearly; transparent to opaque |
| Streak: | white |
| Hardness: | 1.5 |
| Specific gravity: | 2.2–2.6 |
| Cleavage; fracture: | perfect; uneven |
| Habit: | large crystalline plates, possibly pseudohexagonal; scaly aggregates |
| Crystal system: | monoclinic |

# Pennine

Pennine, or penninite, is a pseudotrigonal variety of clinochore. It is a silica-rich member of the chlorite group and occurs as complex admixtures with chromium-rich kammererite. Pennine forms hexagonal platy crystals and it flakes on heating. It is named after the Pennine Alps in Switzerland, where it was first found. Massive pennine is easily carved and is used for ornaments. Pennine occurs in low-grade metamorphic and hydrothermally altered rocks, associated with actinolite, epidote and garnet. It is an essential component of some massive chlorite schists. Pennine is found at Rimpfischwäge and Zermatt (Switzerland), Zillertal (Austria), Val d'Ala (Turin, Italy) and Harstigen (Värmland, Sweden).

## $(Mg,Fe)_5Al(Si,Al)_4O_{10}(OH)_8$

| | |
|---|---|
| Colour: | white, yellow, green |
| Lustre; opacity: | vitreous, pearly; translucent |
| Streak: | white |
| Hardness: | 2–2.5 |
| Specific gravity: | 2.5–2.6 |
| Cleavage; fracture: | perfect; uneven |
| Habit: | crystals as plates or rhombohedra; scaly, massive, granular aggregates |
| Crystal system: | monoclinic |

# Kämmererite

Kämmererite is a rare chromium-rich variety of clinochlore, displaying a variety of shades of red. The red colours contrast with the green colours produced by iron substitution in clinochlore. It is usually a mixture with pennine, which is regarded by some as a green variety of kämmererite. Particularly good clusters of deep magenta crystals come from Kop Daglari (Erzerum Province, Turkey), many of the crystals being clear, well-formed rhombohedra. Kämmererite occurs in metamorphic rocks, especially serpentinized rocks containing chromium-rich olivines. It is associated with serpentine, chromite and uravorite. It is found at Miass (Ilmen Mountains, Russia), Texas (USA) and the Shetland Islands (UK).

## $(Mg,Cr)_3(OH)_2AlSi_3O_{10}Mg_3(OH)_6$

| | |
|---|---|
| Colour: | red to purple |
| Lustre; opacity: | vitreous; transparent to translucent |
| Streak: | reddish |
| Hardness: | 2–2.5 |
| Specific gravity: | 2.64 |
| Cleavage; fracture: | perfect; uneven |
| Habit: | pseudohexagonal crystals; scaly aggregates |
| Crystal system: | monoclinic |

# Sepiolite

Sepiolite, also called meerschaum or sea foam, is a light and porous clay mineral named after the Greek for 'cuttle-fish'. It has been traditionally used in tobacco pipes, and is now used to absorb oil on workshop floors or as a filler, binder or free-flow agent in formulations. Thousands of tons per year are imported to the United Kingdom from Spain. Possible asbestos contamination requires monitoring of its use. It is a sedimentary clay mineral formed by surface alteration of magnesite or serpentine. It is associated with opal and dolomite. Sepiolite is found at Eskiflhahir (Turkey), Vallecas and Cabañas (Spain), Middletown (Pennsylvania, USA), Amarillo (Texas, USA), Hobbs (New Mexico, USA) and Cerro Mercado (Mexico).

## $Mg_4(OH)_2Si_6O_{15}.2-4H_2O$

| | |
|---|---|
| Colour: | white, greyish-, yellowish- or reddish-white |
| Lustre; opacity: | dull; opaque |
| Streak: | white |
| Hardness: | 2–2.5 |
| Specific gravity: | 1–2 |
| Cleavage; fracture: | unknown; conchoidal |
| Habit: | compact, nodular, earthy, massive |
| Crystal system: | orthorhombic |

# Clinochlore

Clinochlore is a common mineral of the chlorite group, the members being difficult to distinguish and usually referred to simply as chlorite by petrologists. Clinochlore is magnesium-rich and forms a series with the iron-rich chamosite. Massive green clinochlore, often banded with a silvery iridescence, is used for carving and polishing as seraphinite. It is an essential mineral in chlorite and talc schists and is found in serpentinites and marbles, associated with serpentine, biotite, actinolite, plagioclase, calcite and dolomite. It is found at Val d'Ala (Turin, Italy), Val Malenco (Sondrio, Italy), Chester (Massachusetts, USA,) Chester County (Pennsylvania, USA), the Zillertal (Austria) and Akhmatovsk (Urals, Russia).

## $(Mg,Fe)_5Al(Si,Al)_4O_{10}(OH)_8$

| | |
|---|---|
| Colour: | grass-green, olive-green, white, pink, yellowish |
| Lustre; opacity: | pearly, greasy, dull; transparent to translucent |
| Streak: | greenish-white to white |
| Hardness: | 2–2.5 |
| Specific gravity: | 2.6–2.8 |
| Cleavage; fracture: | perfect; uneven, giving inelastic lamellae |
| Habit: | pseudohexagonal crystals with tapering prismatic faces; foliated, granular, earthy, massive |
| Crystal system: | monoclinic |

# Chrysotile

Chrysotile is a fibrous variety of serpentine and the main type of asbestos. Formerly widely used for thermal and electrical insulation, it is now being removed because of the carcinogenic properties of some fibrous forms. The fibres are flexible enough to form woven products, such as fire blankets. It is produced by low-grade metamorphism of ultrabasic rocks in water-rich environments (especially the ocean floor). It is associated with antigorite and lizardite in serpentinites, often filling veins, with the fibres aligned in the direction of the vein. Large masses are found in Asbestos (Quebec, Canada), Eden Mills (Vermont, USA), Brewster (New York, USA), the Urals (Russia), the Alps and Cyprus.

## $Mg_3Si_2O_5(OH)_4$

| | |
|---|---|
| Colour: | greyish-white, green, yellow, brown |
| Lustre; opacity: | silky; translucent to opaque |
| Streak: | white |
| Hardness: | 2.5–4 |
| Specific gravity: | 2.55 |
| Cleavage; fracture: | none; splintery |
| Habit: | microcrystalline; aggregates of flexible fibres |
| Crystal system: | monoclinic (clinochrysotile) and orthorhombic (orthochrysotile) |

# Chrysocolla

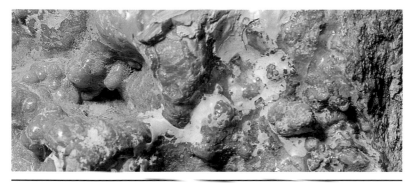

Chrysocolla is an attractive blue-green copper silicate used as an ornamental stone. It is softer than tourquoise or chalcedony, with which it can be confused. Specimens of chrysocolla with quartz not only go well together but also tend to be harder ('agatized') and are more suitable for use in jewellery. It is named from the Greek for 'gold' and 'glue', after its use in soldering gold in ancient times. It occurs in the oxidized zones of copper deposits, associated with malachite, tenorite, quartz and cuprite. Chrysocolla is found at Chuquicamata (Chile), Nizhni Tagil (Urals, Russia), Lubumbashi (Katanga, Congo), Timna (King Solomon's) mine (Israel), Santa Rita (New Mexico, USA) and Clifton (Arizona, USA).

## $CuSiO_3.nH_2O$

| Colour: | green, blue-green |
|---|---|
| Lustre; opacity: | vitreous, greasy, earthy; translucent to opaque |
| Streak: | light green |
| Hardness: | 2–4 |
| Specific gravity: | 2.0–2.4 |
| Cleavage; fracture: | none; conchoidal |
| Habit: | rare acicular crystals in radiating clusters; concretions, porcellanous masses, earthy |
| Crystal system: | monoclinic |

# Serpentine

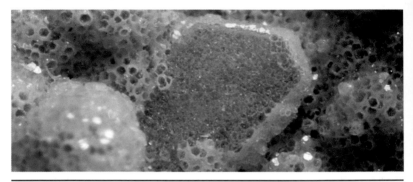

Serpentine is a group of closely related minerals: antigorite, lizardite and chrysotile, the latter most likely to be fibrous and form asbestos. Fibrous serpentine is now regarded as a health hazard. Antigorite and lizardite are the main components of the rock serpentinite, which is formed under oceans by low-grade metamorphism of ultrabasic rocks. Such rocks may be cut by veins of fibrous chrysotile. Attractive, multi-hued and easily worked, serpentine is popular for ornaments; some varieties (bowenite and williamsite) are used for jewellery. The name refers to the snakelike appearance of massive forms. It is found widely, including at Stillwater (Montana, USA), Val Malenco (Italy), Lizard Peninsula (England) and Troodos Mountains (Cyprus).

## $(Mg,Fe)_3Si_2O_5(OH)_4$

| | |
|---|---|
| **Colour:** | mostly green, also yellow, brown, black, red |
| **Lustre; opacity:** | greasy, dull; translucent to opaque |
| **Streak:** | white, grey |
| **Hardness:** | 2.5–4 |
| **Specific gravity:** | 2.5–2.6 |
| **Cleavage; fracture:** | none; conchoidal, splintery |
| **Habit:** | microcrystalline; lamellar (antigorite), fibrous (chrysotile), scaly (lizardite) |
| **Crystal system:** | monoclinic/orthorhombic/hexagonal |

# Nepheline

Nepheline is a major rock-forming mineral found in igneous rocks that are low in silica and contain no quartz, such as nepheline syenites. It is a feldspathoid, a group of minerals like alkali feldspars, but poorer in silica. Although abundant, nepheline rarely forms attractive specimens. Nepheline is especially liable to alteration; it becomes cloudy when treated with acids, hence the name from the Greek for 'cloud'. Nepheline is often altered to zeolites, often natrolite. It occurs in alkaline rocks and pegmatites associated with feldspar, leucite, augite and olivine. Some of the many locations include Vesuvius (Italy), Kola Peninsula and Urals (Russia), Bancroft (Canada) and Litchfield (Maine, USA).

## (Na,K)AlSiO$_4$

| | |
|---|---|
| Colour: | off-white, grey, brown, other tints |
| Lustre; opacity: | greasy; translucent |
| Streak: | white |
| Hardness: | 5.5–6 |
| Specific gravity: | 2.56–2.66 |
| Cleavage; fracture: | poor; conchoidal |
| Habit: | prismatic crystals; compact, granular aggregates |
| Crystal system: | hexagonal |

# Petalite

Petalite is one of the less common feldspathoids and an ore of lithium. It is too fragile and too rarely of high quality to be commonly used in jewellery, but is sometimes cut for collectors. When heated, petalite slowly gives a blue phosphorescence; it is easily melted and colours a flame crimson (due to lithium). Petalite is named from the Greek for 'leaf', after its perfect cleavage. Petalite occurs in lithium-rich granite pegmatites associated with spodumene, lepidolite, tourmaline, topaz, albite, microcline and quartz. Good localities for petalite include Varaträsk (Sweden), Bikita (Zimbabwe), Norwich (Massachusetts, USA), Oxford County (Maine, USA) and Minas Gerais (Brazil).

## $LiAlSi_4O_{10}$

| | |
|---|---|
| Colour: | colourless or white, grey to reddish-grey |
| Lustre; opacity: | vitreous to pearly; transparent to translucent |
| Streak: | white |
| Hardness: | 6–6.5 |
| Specific gravity: | 2.4 |
| Cleavage; fracture: | perfect; conchoidal |
| Habit: | tabular or columnar crystals; usually massive |
| Crystal system: | monoclinic |

# Leucite

Leucite is a feldspathoid found abundantly in potassium-rich, silica-poor volcanic rocks. The usual trapezohedral crystal form of leucite is pseudomorphic after the cubic ,-leucite, which forms above 605°C (1121°F). Leucite usually occurs as single crystal grains embedded in host rock. The garnets and analcime are the only other common minerals to crystallize in the form of a trapezohedron. The name is derived from the Greek for 'white', and leucite has been known as white garnet. Good crystals occur in many localities, including Alban Hills and Vesuvius (Italy), Leucite Hills (Wyoming, USA), Bear Paw Mountains (Montana, USA), Mount Nyiragongo (Congo) and Kaiserstuhl (Germany).

## $KAlSi_2O_6$

| | |
|---|---|
| Colour: | white |
| Lustre; opacity: | vitreous; transparent to translucent |
| Streak: | white |
| Hardness: | 5–5.5 |
| Specific gravity: | 2.24–2.29 |
| Cleavage; fracture: | absent; conchoidal, brittle |
| Habit: | trapezohedral crystals; round grains |
| Crystal system: | tetragonal |

# Sanidine

Sanidine is a potassium-feldspar formed at high temperatures, above 900°C (1652°F) (orthoclase and microcline are polymorphs formed at medium/high and low temperatures, respectively). It forms a partial series with albite, $NaAlSi_3O_8$, which can form up to 20 per cent of its composition. Sanidine is found in felsic igneous rocks, potassium-rich contact metamorphic rocks and hydrothermal veins. Associated minerals include quartz, sodic plagioclase, biotite, muscovite, hornblende and magnetite. Locations include Vesuvius and Monte Cimine (Italy), Drachenfels and Hohenfels (Germany), Daichi (Japan), Tooele (Utah), Cottonwood Canyon (Arizona) and Rabb Canyon (New Mexico, USA), and Kanchin-do (Korea).

## $KAlSi_3O_8$

| | |
|---|---|
| Colour: | colourless, white, greyish, yellowish |
| Lustre; opacity: | vitreous, pearly; transparent to translucent |
| Streak: | white |
| Hardness: | 6 |
| Specific gravity: | 2.5 |
| Cleavage; fracture: | perfect; uneven,conchoidal |
| Habit: | tabular, prismatic crystals, often twinned |
| Crystal system: | monoclinic |

# Orthoclase

Orthoclase is abundant as an essential mineral in granitic rocks, forming between about 500° and 900°C (932° and 1652°F). It also occurs in pegmatites and syenites; cavities in basalts; high-grade metamorphic rocks; and hydrothermal veins. Adularia is a transparent colourless gem variety with a bluish sheen. Yellow orthoclase is often faceted when transparent or cut *en cabochon* when displaying a cat's-eye effect. Moonstone is opalescent with a blue or white sheen resembling moonlight. Locations include Madagascar, Sri Lanka and Burma for gem varieties; fine crystals are found at Baveno and Elba (Italy), Carlsbad (Czech Republic), Kirkpatrick (Scotland) and Sverdlovsk (Urals, Russia).

## $KAlSi_3O_8$

| | |
|---|---|
| Colour: | colourless or white, pale yellow, pink, blue or grey |
| Lustre; opacity: | vitreous, pearly; transparent to translucent |
| Streak: | white |
| Hardness: | 6 |
| Specific gravity: | 2.55–2.63 |
| Cleavage; fracture: | perfect; conchoidal |
| Habit: | prismatic, columnar or tabular crystals; compact, granular masses |
| Crystal system: | monoclinic |

# Microcline

Microcline is a potassium feldspar that forms at low temperatures (usually less than 400°C/752°F), abundant in granites and related rocks. Amazonite is a blue-green semi-opaque stone resembling jade or turquoise. Perthite is microcline or orthoclase containing undulating layers or intergrowths of plagioclase feldspar, which have separated out on cooling. Microcline is found in felsic plutonic igneous rocks, metamorphic rocks and hydrothermal veins; it is associated with quartz, sodic plagioclase, biotite, muscovite and hornblende. Localities include Arendal (Norway), Ilmen Mountains (Russia), Cala Francese (Sardinia, Italy); amazonite is found at Pikes Peak (Colorado, USA), Bancroft (Canada) and Minas Gerais (Brazil).

## $KAlSi_3O_8$

| | |
|---|---|
| **Colour:** | white, pink, red, yellowish, blue-green |
| **Lustre; opacity:** | vitreous; transparent to translucent |
| **Streak:** | white |
| **Hardness:** | 6–6.5 |
| **Specific gravity:** | 2.55–2.63 |
| **Cleavage; fracture:** | perfect; conchoidal, uneven |
| **Habit:** | prismatic crystals, often twinned; compact aggregates |
| **Crystal system:** | triclinic |

# Hyalophane

Hyalophane is an unusual barium-rich feldspar forming a series with orthoclase and celsian ($BaAl_2Si_2O_8$). The clarity of the crystals, which may be found up to 20cm (8in) long, inspires the name from the Greek for 'glassy'. Hyalophane often shows a weak violet fluorescence under ultraviolet light. Found in metamorphosed manganese-rich rocks and manganiferous deposits, it is associated with epidote, rhodonite, plagioclase and analcime. Some excellent crystals have come from the Zagradski Potok region of Bosnia. Other locations include Lengenbach (Switzerland), Långban and Värmland (Sweden), Slyudyanka (Baikal, Russia), Broken Hill (NSW, Australia) and Kaso (Japan).

## $(K,Ba)Al(Al,Si)Si_2O_6$

| | |
|---|---|
| **Colour:** | colourless, white, yellow |
| **Lustre; opacity:** | vitreous; transparent to translucent |
| **Streak:** | white |
| **Hardness:** | 6–6.5 |
| **Specific gravity:** | 2.6–2.8 |
| **Cleavage; fracture:** | perfect; uneven, conchoidal |
| **Habit:** | crystals as prisms or rhombohedra; compact, massive |
| **Crystal system:** | monoclinic |

# Albite

Albite is a plagioclase feldspar in the series albite–anorthite ($NaAlSi_3O_8$–$CaAl_2Si_2O_8$) containing less than 10 per cent anorthite. It forms a high-temperature series with sanidine, but separates at lower temperatures to give intergrowths (perthites). A thin, platy and often transparent variety often associated with tourmaline is called cleavelandite. Albite is abundant in many acid igneous rocks; it is also found in mica schists and gneisses, and in rocks altered ('albitized') by sodium-rich fluids (sea-floor metamorphism). It is associated with orthoclase, quartz, muscovite and biotite. Good crystals are found at St Gotthard (Switzerland), Baveno (Italy), Cazadero (California, USA) and Rio Grande do Sul (Brazil).

## $NaAlSi_3O_8$

| | |
|---|---|
| Colour: | colourless or white |
| Lustre; opacity: | vitreous; transparent to translucent |
| Streak: | white |
| Hardness: | 6–6.5 |
| Specific gravity: | 2.62 |
| Cleavage; fracture: | perfect; conchoidal |
| Habit: | crystals as prisms or plates, often twinned; granular and massive aggregates |
| Crystal system: | triclinic |

# Anorthite

Plagioclase feldspars range from sodium-rich albite, through oligoclase, andesine, labradorite and bytownite, to calcium-rich anorthite (contains up to 10 per cent albite). Sunstone is a variety of oligoclase containing reflective platy inclusions, red, orange or green in colour, which give a metallic glitter. Labradorite (50–70 per cent anorthite) is used as a gem or ornamental stone, displaying a play of colours produced by internal interference of light. Plagioclase occurs in igneous and metamorphic rocks, becoming more calcium-rich as the rocks become more mafic. Labradorite occurs in Larvik-Tvedalen (Norway) and Labrador (Canada). Anorthite is found at Vesuvius (Italy), Hokkaido (Japan) and Tunaberg (Sweden).

### $CaAl_2Si_2O_8$

| | |
|---|---|
| Colour: | white to grey, yellowish, greenish, reddish |
| Lustre; opacity: | vitreous, pearly; transparent to translucent |
| Streak: | white |
| Hardness: | 6 |
| Specific gravity: | 2.62–2.76 |
| Cleavage; fracture: | good; uneven |
| Habit: | crystals as prisms or plates, often twinned; granular or massive aggregates |
| Crystal system: | triclinic |

# Hauyne

H auyne, or hauynite, is a feldspathoid and a member of the sodalite group, where calcium partially substitutes for sodium, and sulphate groups replace chlorine atoms. It is popularly collected as bright blue grains in a matrix and occasionally faceted, but is difficult to cut because of its perfect cleavage. Hauyne is found in phonolites and related silica-poor rocks, associated with nepheline, leucite, augite, sanidine, biotite and apatite. It is named after the French crystallographer Abbé René Haüy (1743–1822), who discovered it on Vesuvius (Italy); other localities are Laacher See and Niedermendig (Germany), Winnett (Montana, USA), Edwards Mine (New York, USA), Tasmania (Australia) and Nanjing (Jiangsu, China).

## $(Na,Ca)_{4-8}(Al_6Si_6)O_{24}(SO_4,Cl)_{1-2}$

| | |
|---|---|
| Colour: | bright blue to greenish-blue, white, grey, brown |
| Lustre; opacity: | vitreous, greasy; transparent to translucent |
| Streak: | white |
| Hardness: | 5.5 |
| Specific gravity: | 2.44–2.5 |
| Cleavage; fracture: | perfect; conchoidal |
| Habit: | rare octahedral or dodecahedral crystals; usually rounded grains |
| Crystal system: | cubic |

# Sodalite

S odalite is a feldspathoid mostly notable for its occurrence in a bright blue, massive form, used as a semi-precious stone for carvings and jewellery. It is a component of lapis lazuli, but, unlike it, sodalite rarely contains contrasting golden yellow pyrite and has a lower density. Crystals of sodalite are rare and usually small. Sodalite is found in nepheline syenites, phonolites and related rocks, and in metasomatic calcareous rocks. Associated minerals include nepheline, microcline and sanidine. Excellent massive sodalite is found at Bancroft (Canada), Litchfield (Maine, USA), Magnet Cove (Arkansas, USA), Ilimaussaq (Greenland) and Cerro Sapo (Bolivia); clear crystals are found in the calcium-rich lavas of Vesuvius (Italy).

## $Na_8Cl_2(AlSiO_4)_6$

| | |
|---|---|
| Colour: | bright blue, white, grey, green |
| Lustre; opacity: | vitreous, greasy; transparent to opaque |
| Streak: | white |
| Hardness: | 5–6 |
| Specific gravity: | 2.3 |
| Cleavage; fracture: | perfect; conchoidal, uneven |
| Habit: | very rare dodecahedral crystals; compact masses |
| Crystal system: | cubic |

# Lazurite

Lazurite is most commonly found as a component of lapis lazuli, the semi-precious massive stone used for jewellery and carved ornaments. Lapis lazuli is mostly lazurite, but contains blue sodalite and hauyne, white calcite and brassy pyrite. The deposits in Afghanistan were worked 6000 years ago for high-quality lapis lazuli used, for example, for the mask of Tutunkhamun. Lazurite is found in contact metamorphosed limestones. Exceptional crystals and fine lapis lazuli are found at Sar-e-Sang (Kokscha Valley, Afghanistan); other locations include Vesuvius and the Alban Hills (Italy), Sayan Mountains (Russia), Baffin Island (Canada) and California and Colorado (USA).

## $(Na,Ca)_8(Al,Si)_{12}O_{24}(S,SO_4)$

| | |
|---|---|
| **Colour:** | deep blue, blue-green |
| **Lustre; opacity:** | vitreous; translucent to opaque |
| **Streak:** | light blue |
| **Hardness:** | 5–5.5 |
| **Specific gravity:** | 2.38–2.42 |
| **Cleavage; fracture:** | imperfect; uneven |
| **Habit:** | very rare octahedral crystals; compact masses |
| **Crystal system:** | cubic |

# Scapolite

Scapolite is a member of the complex scapolite series, between meionite $(Ca_4(Si,Al)_{12}O_{24}(CO_3,SO_4))$ and marialite $(Na_4(Si,Al)_{12}O_{24}Cl)$. It is formed by alteration of plagioclase feldspars, its composition generally reflecting the sodium/calcium ratio of the parent mineral. Clear crystals may be faceted; those containing inclusions are cut *en cabochon*. Scapolite is named from the Greek for 'rod', alluding to the crystal shape. Scapolite is found in metamorphosed limestones and hydrothermally altered basic rocks. Crystals up to 50cm (20in) are found at Rossie and Pierrepoint (New York, USA); other localities are Renfrew (Ontario) and Grenville (Quebec, Canada), Lake Tremorgio (Switzerland) and Minas Gerais (Brazil).

## $(Na,Ca)_8(Cl_2,SO_4,CO_3)(AlSi_3O_8)_6$

| | |
|---|---|
| Colour: | white, bluish, grey, pink |
| Lustre; opacity: | vitreous; transparent to translucent |
| Streak: | white |
| Hardness: | 5–6.5 |
| Specific gravity: | 2.54–2.77 |
| Cleavage; fracture: | poor; conchoidal |
| Habit: | columnar prismatic crystals; fibrous or massive aggregates |
| Crystal system: | tetragonal |

# Natrolite

Natrolite is a zeolite forming attractive sprays of radiating needles. It is named from the Greek *natron* for 'soda', alluding to its sodium content. Being a typical molecular sieve, it holds water in voids in its structure. On heating to 300°C (572°F), it loses water without changing crystal structure, which it will reabsorb from the atmosphere when cooled. Natrolite may also exhibit orange fluorescence under ultraviolet light. It is found in hydrothermal veins in basalts, associated with nepheline, sodalite, quartz and other zeolites. Good crystals come from Nova Scotia and British Columbia, and specimens up to 1m (3¼ft) long from Asbestos (Canada); other localities are Puy-de-Dôme (France) and White Head (Antrim, Northern Ireland).

## $Na_2(Al_2Si_3)O_{10}.2H_2O$

| | |
|---|---|
| **Colour:** | colourless, white, pink, yellowish |
| **Lustre; opacity:** | vitreous; transparent to translucent |
| **Streak:** | white |
| **Hardness:** | 5.5–6 |
| **Specific gravity:** | 2.2–2.4 |
| **Cleavage; fracture:** | good; conchoidal |
| **Habit:** | acicular needles; globular aggregates of radiating needles, rarely compact |
| **Crystal system:** | orthorhombic |

# Mesolite

**M**esolite forms characteristic sprays of transparent acicular crystals. A typical zeolite, it forms only as a secondary mineral from the breakdown of feldspars and fills voids in altered igneous rocks. It is a molecular sieve and easily loses and absorbs water. It is named from the Greek for 'middle', having a composition between natrolite and scolecite. Mesolite is found in cavities in volcanic rocks, especially basalt, and hydrothermal veins. It is associated with natrolite and scolecite (from which it is difficult to distinguish), and other zeolites and calcite. Locations include Nova Scotia (Canada), Grant County (Oregon, USA), Faeroe Islands (Norway), Puy-de-Dôme (France) and Poona (Maharashtra, India).

## $Na_2Ca_2(Al_2Si_3O_{10})_3.8H_2O$

| | |
|---|---|
| **Colour:** | white, grey, yellow |
| **Lustre; opacity:** | vitreous, silky; transparent to translucent |
| **Streak:** | white |
| **Hardness:** | 5–5.5 |
| **Specific gravity:** | 2.2–2.4 |
| **Cleavage; fracture:** | perfect; conchoidal, uneven |
| **Habit:** | acicular needles; massive, spherulitic aggregates, earthy |
| **Crystal system:** | monoclinic |

# Thomsonite

Thomsonite is a rare zeolite, difficult to distinguish from natrolite. The name, after the Scottish chemist Thomas Thomson, is applied to the series thomsonite-Ca to thomsonite-Sr. The strontium-rich minerals are visually indistinguishable and rarer. Thomsonite is found filling voids in mafic igneous rocks, especially basalts, and in hydrothermal veins in other igneous rocks. Associated minerals are calcite, prehnite, quartz and other zeolites. Localities include Mount Monzoni (Italy), Faeroe Islands (Norway), Old Kilpatrick and Bishopton (Scotland), Disko Island (Greenland) and Springfield (Oregon, USA). Attractively banded specimens of massive nodules are found on the southern shore of Lake Superior.

## $NaCa_2(Al_5Si_5)O_{20}.6H_2O$

| | |
|---|---|
| Colour: | white, brown |
| Lustre; opacity: | vitreous, pearly; transparent to translucent |
| Streak: | white |
| Hardness: | 5–5.5 |
| Specific gravity: | 2.2–2.4 |
| Cleavage; fracture: | perfect; uneven |
| Habit: | individual crystals rare; radiating globular clusters |
| Crystal system: | monoclinic |

# Scolecite

Scolecite is a rare zeolite occurring as sprays of white needles. It is closely related to natrolite and mesolite, and difficult to distinguish from these. The name, from the Greek *skolec* for 'worm', is an allusion to its behaviour in a blowpipe flame, when it curls into wormlike forms before melting. Scolecite is found lining cavities in lavas, especially basalts; and also in veins in contact-metamorphosed pelites and limestones. Associated minerals are calcite, prehnite and other zeolites. Excellent crystals are found at Teigarhorn (Iceland), Ben More, Isle of Mull and Talisker Bay, Isle of Skye (Scotland) and the Faeroe Islands (Norway); other locations include the Deccan Traps (Poona, India) and Vesuvius (Italy).

## $Ca(Al_2Si_3)O_{10}.3H_2O$

| | |
|---|---|
| Colour: | colourless or white |
| Lustre; opacity: | vitreous, silky; transparent |
| Streak: | white |
| Hardness: | 5–5.5 |
| Specific gravity: | 2.2–2.4 |
| Cleavage; fracture: | perfect; fragile |
| Habit: | prismatic crystals; fibrous, radiating masses |
| Crystal system: | orthorhombic |

# Mordenite

Mordenite is a rare but widespread zeolite, found often as clusters of white or pinkish needles. It is used in catalysis, petrochemicals and fine chemicals, and is synthetically produced for such applications. Mordenite, like other zeolites, has holes in its molecular framework of exact sizes, making it specific in interactions for absorption and catalysis. It is a secondary mineral, found in veins and cavities in igneous rocks, associated with calcite, kaolinite, glauconite and other zeolites; it is also deposited among some sediments. Locations include Morden (Nova Scotia, Canada), Berufjord (Iceland), Elba (Italy), Isle of Mull (Scotland), Custer County (Colorado, USA) and Hoodoo Mountains (Wyoming, USA).

## $(Ca,K_2,Na_2)(AlSi_5O_{12})_2.6H_2O$

| | |
|---|---|
| **Colour:** | colourless, white, yellowish, pinkish |
| **Lustre; opacity:** | vitreous, pearly; transparent to translucent |
| **Streak:** | white |
| **Hardness:** | 4.5 |
| **Specific gravity:** | 2.1 |
| **Cleavage; fracture:** | perfect; uneven |
| **Habit:** | crystals as striated needles; fibrous, reniform aggregates |
| **Crystal system:** | orthorhombic |

# Laumontite

Laumontite crystals can be impressive when large, almost acicular prisms. It is a zeolite named after the Frenchman François de Laumont (1747–1834), who found the mineral. Specimens exposed to dry air become opaque and powdery due to partial dehydration; this can be avoided by using a sealant or airtight containment. Laumontite is found in veins and cavities in most rock types and as a cement in sandstones. Associated minerals include datolite, calcite, chlorite and other zeolites. Crystals up to 30cm (12in) are found at Bishop (California, USA); good crystals are also found in the eastern Pyrenees (France), St Gotthard (Switzerland), the Tirol (Austria), Baveno (Italy) and Poona and Khandivali (Maharashtra, India).

## $Ca(Al_2Si_4)O_{12}.4H_2O$

| | |
|---|---|
| Colour: | white to grey, yellowish, brownish, pink |
| Lustre; opacity: | vitreous, pearly; transparent to translucent |
| Streak: | white |
| Hardness: | 3–4 |
| Specific gravity: | 2.2–2.3 |
| Cleavage; fracture: | perfect; uneven |
| Habit: | square, prismatic crystals often elongated; columnar, fibrous and radiating aggregates |
| Crystal system: | monoclinic |

# Heulandite

Heulandite is a common zeolite forming attractive aggregates of tabular crystals in a range of different hues. Distinguished from stilbite in 1818, it was first named euzeolite, meaning 'beautiful zeolite', but eventually named after the English mineral collector John Heuland (1778–1856). Heulandite is now a term referring to a series of calcium-, sodium-, potassium- or strontium-rich rocks. It is found in cavities in volcanic rocks, in veins in schists and gneisses, and disseminated in sedimentary rocks; it is usually associated with stilbite and chabazite. Good crystals are found at Paterson (New Jersey, USA), Poona (Maharashtra, India), Berufjord (Iceland), Stirlingshire (Scotland), Nova Scotia (Canada) and Hawaii (USA).

## $(Na,Ca)_{4-6}Al_6(Al,Si)_4Si_{26}O_{72}.24H_2O$

| | |
|---|---|
| Colour: | colourless, yellow, green, reddish-orange |
| Lustre; opacity: | vitreous, pearly; transparent, usually translucent |
| Streak: | white |
| Hardness: | 3.5–4 |
| Specific gravity: | 2.2 |
| Cleavage; fracture: | perfect; uneven |
| Habit: | tabular crystals; aggregates |
| Crystal system: | monoclinic |

# Stilbite

Stilbite is a common mineral and one of the most popularly collected zeolites. It is named from the Greek for 'shine', after the pearly effect on the cleavage plane. The structure of stilbite contains channels that hold certain sizes of molecules and ions. This is put to use in the separation of hydrocarbons in petroleum refining and in ion-exchange processes. Stilbite is soluble in acids and melts easily, giving a white glass. It is found in hydrothermal veins in basalts, associated with calcite and other zeolites, especially heulandite. Fine crystals are found at Paterson (New Jersey, USA), Kilpatrick and Isle of Skye (Scotland), Nova Scotia (Canada), Rio Grande do Sul (Brazil), Teigarhorn (Iceland) and Poona (India).

## $NaCa_2(Al_5Si_{13})O_{36}.14H_2O$

| | |
|---|---|
| **Colour:** | white, grey, reddish-brown |
| **Lustre; opacity:** | vitreous, pearly; transparent to translucent |
| **Streak:** | white |
| **Hardness:** | 3.5–4 |
| **Specific gravity:** | 2.1 |
| **Cleavage; fracture:** | perfect; conchoidal, fragile |
| **Habit:** | prismatic crystals, usually in sheaflike aggregates, cruciform twins; radiating fibrous masses |
| **Crystal system:** | monoclinic |

# Harmotome

Harmotome is a rare zeolite, but popular for its twinned crystals. Single twinning gives crosses of interpenetrating prisms, with the ends resembling blunt Phillips head screwdrivers; more uncommonly, double twinning can result in three prisms interpenetrating at 90° to each other. Harmotome is named from the Greek for 'joint' and 'cut', after the easily separated twinned crystals. Harmotome occurs in hydrothermal veins in basalts and other volcanic rocks, in gneisses and in some ore veins; it is associated with calcite, barite and quartz. Good crystals are found in St Andreasburg (Germany), Argyll (Scotland), Pribram (Czech Republic), Thunder Bay (Ontario, Canada) and Manhattan (New York City, USA).

## $BaAl_2Si_6O_{16}.6H_2O$

| | |
|---|---|
| **Colour:** | white, grey, yellow, red, brown |
| **Lustre; opacity:** | vitreous, pearly; transparent to translucent |
| **Streak:** | white |
| **Hardness:** | 4.5 |
| **Specific gravity:** | 2.44–2.5 |
| **Cleavage; fracture:** | distinct; uneven, subconchoidal |
| **Habit:** | prisms, plates, often twins; aggregates |
| **Crystal system:** | monoclinic |

# Gismondine

Gismondine is a rare zeolite, often forming clear colourless pseudotetragonal crystals. It was named after Professor Carlo Gismondi (1762–1824), the Italian mineralogist who first examined it. A similar mineral gismondine-Ba has been found on lead-rich slags. Gismondine is easily melted in a flame and soluble in hydrochloric acid. It occurs in hydrothermal veins in nepheline and olivine basalts, associated with calcite, quartz, chlorite and other zeolites. It is found at Capo di Bove (Lazio, Italy), Bühne (Westphalia), Fulde (Hesse) and Arensberg (Eiffel, Germany), Round Top (Oahu) and Alexander Dam (Kauai, Hawaii), Antrim (Northern Ireland) and Reydarfjord and Fáskrúdsfjord (Iceland).

## $CaAl_2Si_2O_8 \cdot 4H_2O$

| | |
|---|---|
| Colour: | white, grey, bluish, reddish |
| Lustre; opacity: | vitreous; transparent to translucent |
| Streak: | white |
| Hardness: | 4.5 |
| Specific gravity: | 2.26 |
| Cleavage; fracture: | imperfect; conchoidal |
| Habit: | bipyramidal crystals; stellate or radiating spherulitic aggregates |
| Crystal system: | monoclinic |

# Chabazite

Chabazite is a lesser known zeolite forming rhombohedral crystals that appear almost like cubes, with angles close to 90°. Chabazite-Na, -K and -Sr are varieties rich in sodium, potassium or strontium. It is used as an acid-resistant absorbant in natural gas production and to remove heavy metals from waste streams. Chabazite occurs in hydrothermal veins in basalts and andesites; and rarely in limestones, schists and ore veins. Associated minerals include nepheline, olivine, pyroxenes, tridymite, calcite and dolomite. Chabazite is found at Idar-Oberstein (Germany), Repcice (Czech Republic), Kilmalcolm (Scotland), Breidhdalsheidhi (Iceland), Bowie (Arizona, USA) and Paterson (New Jersey, USA).

## $Ca(Al_2Si_4)O_{12}.6H_2O$

| | |
|---|---|
| **Colour:** | colourless, white, yellow, pink, red |
| **Lustre; opacity:** | vitreous; transparent to translucent |
| **Streak:** | white |
| **Hardness:** | 4.5 |
| **Specific gravity:** | 2.08 |
| **Cleavage; fracture:** | distinct; uneven |
| **Habit:** | crystals as rhombohedra, twins; druses, granular, massive |
| **Crystal system:** | trigonal |

# Gmelinite

Gmelinite is a rare zeolite that forms characteristic crystals in the form of shallow six-sided double pyramids, which have been described as 'flying saucers'. It can also occur as thin plates and attractive rosettes of such crystals. Varieties are rich in calcium, sodium or potassium. It is named after Christian Gmelin (1792–1860), a German chemist. Gmelinite occurs in basalts, related rocks and pegmatites, associated with calcite, aragonite, quartz and other zeolites, especially chabazite and analcime. Locations include Montecchio Maggiore (Vicenza, Italy), Glenarm (Antrim, Northern Ireland), Pyrgos (Cyprus), Paterson (New Jersey, USA), Sarbay-Sokolov (Kazakhstan) and Bekiady (Madagascar).

## $(Na,Ca)Al_2Si_4O_{12}.6H_2O$

| | |
|---|---|
| Colour: | white, yellow, pink, reddish |
| Lustre; opacity: | vitreous; transparent to opaque |
| Streak: | white |
| Hardness: | 4.5 |
| Specific gravity: | 2.03 |
| Cleavage; fracture: | imperfect; uneven |
| Habit: | crystals as plates, bipyramids, rhombohedra, twins; druses, rarely radiating aggregates or granular |
| Crystal system: | hexagonal |

# Analcime

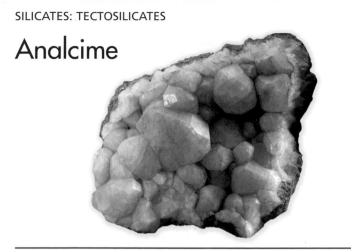

Analcime, or analcite, is a popular zeolite forming distinctive trapezohedral crystals, a shape commonly found only in garnets (harder and strongly coloured) and leucite (lower specific gravity). It has been classified as a feldspathoid, but has an open structure, typical of zeolites. It is named from the Greek for 'weak', after the weak static charge produced on heating or rubbing. Analcime occurs in basalts and phonolites, associated with prehnite, glauconite, quartz and other zeolites. It is found at Kotchechovmo (Krasnoyarski, Russia), St Keverne (Cornwall, England), Breidhdalsheidhi (Iceland), Lake Superior (Michigan, USA), Bergen Hill (New Jersey, USA) and Mt Saint Hilaire (Quebec, Canada).

## $NaAlSi_2O_6.2H_2O$

| | |
|---|---|
| **Colour:** | white, colourless, grey, pink, greenish |
| **Lustre; opacity:** | vitreous, dull; transparent to translucent |
| **Streak:** | white |
| **Hardness:** | 5.5 |
| **Specific gravity:** | 2.2–2.3 |
| **Cleavage; fracture:** | perfect; uneven, conchoidal |
| **Habit:** | trapezohedral crystals; granular, compact, massive, showing concentric structure |
| **Crystal system:** | cubic |

# Pollucite

Pollucite is a zeolite and the major ore of caesium. Typically pollucite contains about 28 per cent caesium, and it may also be a source of rubidium, which is present at about 1–2 per cent. Caesium compounds are used in catalyst promoters, special glasses and radiation monitoring equipment. The name comes from its association with petalite (castorite) from classical mythology, Pollux being the brother of Castor. Pollucite occurs in kilotonne quantities in lithium-rich granite pegmatites, associated with spodumene, lepidolite, potassium feldspar, microcline and quartz. Pollucite is found at Varutrask (Sweden), Elba (Italy), Bikita (Zimbabwe), Bernic Lake (Manitoba, Canada) and Shengus, Skardu and Gilgit (Pakistan).

## $(Cs,Na)AlSi_2O_6.H_2O$

| | |
|---|---|
| Colour: | colourless, white, grey, pale pink, pale blue |
| Lustre; opacity: | vitreous; transparent to translucent |
| Streak: | white |
| Hardness: | 6.5 |
| Specific gravity: | 2.44–2.5 |
| Cleavage; fracture: | absent; brittle, uneven |
| Habit: | cubic crystals; grains, granular and massive aggregates |
| Crystal system: | cubic |

# Amber

A mber is a fossil tree resin that, although not mineralized, is widely used in jewellery. It often has small insects preserved inside, but it can also contain plant remains, moss, pine needles, spiders or even frogs and lizards. Amber will become electrically charged when rubbed. Unlike most minerals, amber will melt and burn on heating, being chiefly of polymerized hydrocarbons called 'terpenes'. Most amber is *c.* 30–90 million years old; semi-fossilized resin is called copal. The best known amber deposits, known as succinite, are in the Baltic region, along the coasts of Poland and Russia, especially the Sambia Peninsula near Kaliningrad. Burmese amber is called burmite and amber from Sicily is known as simetite.

## Formula

| | |
|---|---|
| **Colour:** | golden yellow/orange, brown, reddish, green, violet, black |
| **Lustre; opacity:** | resinous; transparent to translucent |
| **Streak:** | white |
| **Hardness:** | 1.5–3 |
| **Specific gravity :** | 1.05–1.1 |
| **Cleavage; fracture:** | absent; conchoidal |
| **Habit:** | irregular nodules in marine sands and clays; often a placer deposit washed up on shore |
| **Crystal system:** | amorphous |

# Petrified wood

Petrified wood is really a fossil, but is included here, as it is very popular as ornaments and polished articles. Like opal, it is usually composed of hydrated silica, which has slowly replaced the lignin and cellulose of the wood as they have decomposed. The original structure of the wood is often preserved in great detail, down to microscopic levels. Various colours can be produced by small amounts of impurities such as iron, manganese and copper, which can help to pick out the original structure. The most famous petrified forests are those of Santa Cruz (Patagonia, Argentina), Nává Paka (Czech Republic), Lesbos (Greece) and the Petrified Forest National Park (Arizona, USA).

## $SiO_2.nH_2O$

| | |
|---|---|
| Colour: | various |
| Lustre; opacity: | translucent to opaque |
| Streak: | white |
| Hardness: | 5–7 |
| Specific gravity : | 1.9–2.5 |
| Cleavage; fracture: | absent; conchoidal |
| Habit: | best examples are intact tracts of forest, with trees up to 3m (10ft) diameter and 30m (98ft) long and complete root systems |
| Crystal system: | amorphous |

# Jet

Jet is a hard gem variety of lignite (a type of coal), which is often carved or faceted, and takes a good polish. Occasionally it has pyrite inclusions displaying a brassy, metallic lustre. Used in jewellery since ancient times, jet has been traditionally made into rosaries for monks. As part of her mourning attire, Queen Victoria wore jet from Whitby (England), famous at the time for the mining and crafting of jet. Unlike higher grade coals, jet retains a microscopic, woody structure. Jet is found at Pictou (Nova Scotia, Canada), Cabo Mondego (Coimbra, Portugal), Wet Mountain Valley (Colorado, USA), Acoma (New Mexico, USA), Anne Arundel County (Maryland, USA) and Henry Mountains and Coaly Basin (Utah, USA).

## Formula

| | |
|---|---|
| Colour: | dark brown, black |
| Lustre; opacity: | velvety, waxy; opaque |
| Streak: | brown |
| Hardness: | 2.5 |
| Specific gravity : | 1.33 |
| Cleavage; fracture: | none; conchoidal |
| Habit: | masses in bituminous shales |
| Crystal system: | amorphous |

# Pearl

Once thought to be the tears of the gods, pearls are used widely in jewellery and decorations. They form in modern shellfish, such as mussels, as protection against a natural or emplaced irritant (e.g. a piece of sand) within the soft parts. Layers of nacre are secreted around the foreign body at a rate of up to 0.6mm per year. The nacre consists of aragonite crystals held together by conchiolin, a hornlike substance, and water. Light reflecting from overlapping layers produces the characteristic iridescent lustre. The most important source of creamy white pearls is the Persian Gulf, attracting the highest prices; they have also been collected from the Gulf of Manaar (Sri Lanka) and the Red Sea for thousands of years.

## Formula

| | |
|---|---|
| Colour: | pale yellow, white, salmon pink to grey, brown or black |
| Lustre; opacity: | pearly, iridescent; translucent to opaque |
| Streak: | generally white |
| Hardness: | 3 |
| Specific gravity : | 2.71 |
| Cleavage; fracture: | pearls are soft and easily damaged |
| Habit: | roughly spherical, but a variety of shapes depending on original irritant and whether the pearl has moved |
| Crystal system: | orthorhombic (aragonite) |

# Glossary

| | |
|---|---|
| **accessory mineral** | minor component of a rock; not necessary to define the rock type |
| **acid** | (of igneous rock) containing at least 10% quartz and chemically, more than 65% $SiO_2$ |
| **amorphous** | non-crystalline, having no regular microscopic structure |
| **aqua regia** | a mixture of 3:1 nitric and hydrochloric acids |
| **basic** | (of igneous rock) containing 45–55% $SiO_2$ |
| **cation** | a positively charged ion such as $Na+$ or $Fe_2+$ |
| **columnar** | elongated prismatic form of a crystal |
| **druse** | fine crystalline coating on a matrix or filling a cavity |
| *en cabochon* | a rounded, convex cut of a stone |
| **essential mineral** | one that is necessary for the definition of a rock |
| **euhedral** | (of a mineral) having well-formed crystal faces |
| **evaporite** | sedimentary rock formed by evaporation of an igneous rock |
| **felsic** | (of rocks) composed mostly of light-coloured minerals, especially feldspar and quartz or feldspathoid |
| **fluorescence** | the emission of visible light on absorption of invisible ultraviolet (uv) light, giving an apparent 'glow-in-the-dark' effect |
| **foliated** | made up of thin aligned plates that flake easily |
| **fumarole** | a vent for volcanic gasses |
| **gangue** | the waste component of a mineral deposit |
| **grade, metamorphic** | degree of metamorphism, mostly related to temperatures and pressures experienced by a rock |
| **hydrothermal vein** | a vein produced by hot, mineral-rich waters of igneous origin |
| **igneous rock** | a rock produced from magma or lava |
| **iridescence** | a play of colours on a surface produced by light interference |
| **lamellar** | made of crystals mostly developed in parallel to each other |
| **mafic** | (of rocks) composed mostly of dark, ferromagnesian minerals, especially olivine, pyroxene and amphibole |

| | |
|---|---|
| magma | hot, molten rock material, called lava on reaching the surface |
| matrix | fine-grained background mass of a rock |
| metamict | pertaining to a mineral whose structure has been broken down by radiation damage, typically powdery |
| metamorphic rock | rock produced by increased temperature and/or pressure when minerals are altered without substantial melting |
| metasomatism | the alteration of a mineral or rock by hot fluids, either removing or adding chemical elements |
| oxidation | chemical process involving addition of oxygen |
| pelitic | (of a rock or sediment) of high aluminium and low calcium content, especially of mudstones and clays |
| phosphorescence | the emission of light after illumination (by visible or ultaviolet light) has ceased |
| placer deposit | concentration of residual resistant, heavy minerals found in river gravels after removal of other components of a weathered and eroded rock |
| pneumatolysis | the reaction of magma-derived hot gasses with the surrounding rock |
| porphyroblast | large, well-developed crystal found in a metamorphic rocks |
| schist | metamorphic rock containing platy minerals, usually mica, in a roughly parallel arrangement |
| secondary | (of minerals) one produced by alteration of pre-existing minerals |
| sedimentary rock | rock formed by sedimentary processes such as weathering, erosion, transport, deposition, compaction and cementation |
| solid solution | (of minerals) a product of two or more minerals mixing at a molecular level while retaining the same structure to give intermediate compositions |
| sublimate | a material condensing as a solid from a gas |
| thermoluminescence | luminescence produced by heating |
| triboluminescence | luminescence produced by rubbing |
| ultrabasic | (of rocks) containing <45% $SiO_2$ |
| ultramafic | (of rocks) containing >90% mafic minerals |
| vein | an irregular but essentially tabular intrusion, of a width between a millimetre and tens of centimetres |

# Index

# INDEX